AF394219

PRAISE FOR JEREMY HUNT'S PREVIOUS BOOKS

CAN WE BE GREAT AGAIN?
Why a dangerous world needs Britain

'Crisp, optimistic and easy to read'

ANDREW MARR

'Jeremy Hunt points the way to how we British can recover our confidence – at a crucial time in world affairs when we are going to need it. It is a timely and positive reminder of our vast potential'

WILLIAM HAGUE

'The message in this book is urgent and Jeremy delivers it with force and style: in politics and technology Britain has unique strengths at one of history's turning points'

TONY BLAIR

'A compelling book about what really happens in the labyrinth of politics when someone actually tries to make the world better, as Jeremy did – not least for people like me who were languishing in prison'

NAZANIN ZAGHARI-RATCLIFFE

'A masterly analysis of why Britain has much more global influence than it thinks'

ERIC SCHMIDT, FORMER CEO, GOOGLE

ZERO
Eliminating Unnecessary Deaths
in a Post-Pandemic NHS

'A real understanding of the NHS's many problems … essential reading for everybody involved in healthcare'

HENRY MARSH, AUTHOR OF DO NO HARM

'Humane and often persuasive … I expect that, if his suggestions were generally followed, thousands fewer would die unnecessarily'

CHARLES MOORE, DAILY TELEGRAPH

'A deeply moving personal account about what needs to change in the NHS – I wish I had read it when I started out as a doctor'

DAME CLARE GERADA

'A timely, salutary and occasionally contrarian intervention with an honesty and humanity that will rightly shape the NHS for years to come'

LORD SIMON STEVENS,
FORMER CHIEF EXECUTIVE NHS ENGLAND

'Readable, honest and sometimes unsettling … a powerful case for transparency and supporting a frontline workforce under huge pressure'

DAME CLARE MARX, FORMER PRESIDENT OF
THE ROYAL COLLEGE OF SURGEONS

JEREMY HUNT

CAN WE BE RICH AGAIN?

*The Surprising Potential of
Britain's Economy*

Swift

SWIFT PRESS

First published in Great Britain by Swift Press 2026

1 3 5 7 9 8 6 4 2

Copyright © Jeremy Hunt 2026

All rights reserved

The right of Jeremy Hunt to be identified as the Author of this Work has been asserted in accordance with the Copyright, Designs and Patents Act 1988

Text design and typesetting by Tetragon, London
Printed and bound in Great Britain by CPI Group (UK) Ltd, Croydon, CRO 4YY

All URLs are correct at time of writing

A CIP catalogue record for this book is available from the British Library.

We make every effort to make sure our products are safe for the purpose for which they are intended. Our authorised representative in the EU for product safety is Easy Access System Europe, Mustamäe tee 50, 10621 Tallinn, Estonia gpsr.requests@easproject.com

ISBN: 9781800756878
eISBN: 9781800756885

CONTENTS

'Once one starts to think about economic growth,
it is hard to think about anything else.'

ROBERT E. LUCAS, JR

INTRODUCTION

'Bloody hell, how did that happen?'

After scraping home with the tiniest of majorities in the 2024 general election, I was gobsmacked. The exit polls were dire for the Conservatives – and even worse for me personally. One election website gave me a 2% chance of holding my seat. After the polls closed, I went to bed to snatch a couple of hours' sleep. As I shut my eyes, I was certain I was toast. More than that, I was about to become the first sitting Chancellor in history to be unseated. It would be what political junkies call a 'Portillo moment', a high-profile decapitation that becomes the defining moment of election night.

At 2.30 a.m., I woke up to go to the count. When I arrived, my team told me to my surprise that we were still in the game. Peter Martin, my oldest political ally in the constituency, had an ability to detach himself from emotion when looking at numbers. He had counted samples from the ballot papers being tipped out onto tables. He told me, hardly believing his own words, that I could win by as much as a thousand votes. It felt too good to be true. Sixty journalists from the national press pack had trekked down to Surrey to make sure they didn't miss a public execution. They should have gone to Liz Truss's seat in South West Norfolk, because Peter was right. I won by 891 votes.

Of course it was no consolation for my party's worst ever defeat. But at least it wasn't a surprise. The mini-budget of 2022 – whose collapse led to my becoming Chancellor – destroyed trust in the government, just as Black Wednesday had done for John Major three decades earlier. Personally, I felt a certain grim relief. After a gruelling campaign and over a decade in government, I needed a break. But I worried about my children, who had been living happily in Downing Street for nearly two years. A few days earlier, my twelve-year-old daughter had told me, 'Daddy, I'm embarrassed that you're Chancellor, but I'll be embarrassed if you're not Chancellor.' Now we would have to up sticks in an undignified hurry. With no handover period, the transfer of power from one government to another is perhaps the only area where the British state is more clinically efficient than anywhere else.

Departing chancellors typically disappear quietly through the back door of Downing Street. But in order to stop the children feeling as if it was a moment of shame for the family, I negotiated with No 10 to depart through the front door. I got permission for the kids to miss school. Then my wife, Lucia, and I raced back to London after the count. We showered and changed into fresh clothes. The Downing Street flat was mayhem, with packing boxes everywhere.

Minutes before our scheduled departure at 9.30 a.m., my fourteen-year-old son asked to have a final look around Downing Street. In a rather dazed state, I took him and his sisters around the State Rooms for the last time. We walked through the understated but beautiful rooms that are not open to the public but had been part of our extended home. Normally they have a calm, almost serene feel to them, but that morning they were a hive of activity as officials scurried around preparing for the incoming prime minister. I was still Chancellor and technically we were still residents of Downing Street, so everyone was respectful. But they and I both knew I would soon be history. I was politely told not to go into the Thatcher Room, where Rishi Sunak was preparing his resignation speech. But we popped our heads around the door and Rishi gave a generous goodbye hug to the kids from next door.

Then it was the moment of departure. We emerged from the front door of the Chancellor's flat for a final descent of the No 11 staircase. Just like the more famous No 10 staircase, it is hung with portraits of former holders of the office, although the No 11 tradition is for caricatures rather than photographs. Mine was already up, a front cover from *The Week* showing me arriving as Chancellor under a Mary Poppins umbrella.

Finally it was time to say goodbye to my Treasury team. We had been through many battles together and I thought the world of them. They were loyal, hard-working and, most importantly, fun. You need a sense of humour (ideally a black one) to get through a budget and they did. But whatever personal loyalty they felt, I never knew how they voted and never asked. Not that I didn't speculate endlessly with my special advisers about which way they leaned.

After brief and slightly awkward goodbyes – we all knew that their loyalty would soon shift to our political opponents – I was ready to leave. 'Sunday best, heads high, big smiles,' I said to the family. We walked out of the No 11 front door into bright July sunshine. I held our yellow Labrador, Poppy, on a lead. Someone posted on social media, 'He's got a Labrador, can I change how I voted?' Then followed a lengthy online discussion about how difficult Poppy would find adjusting to a new home. No one cared remotely about the humans having to relocate – very British.

On that bright July morning, the turbulent period when I became Chancellor seemed an age ago. In fact, it had been only a couple of years earlier. And it nearly didn't at all happen, because, as I have recounted earlier, I thought the text message I got from Liz Truss asking me to call her was a hoax. But throughout my time in office, the chaos of the markets in those early days was never far from my mind. I now realise that in some ways it shaped everything I did. It also shaped the way many people – at home and abroad – viewed Britain and the British economy.

Previously, the UK had always been considered a bastion of stability. But the events of that period seemed to confirm to many that post-Brexit Britain had lost its way. When I met fellow finance ministers on the international circuit, there was pity. How the mighty have fallen, their eyes seemed to say, with barely disguised schadenfreude. At home there was an insidious defeatism. Left-leaning commentators blamed Brexit. Right-leaning newspapers thought we had blown our prospects with too much tax. Many, from all sides, pointed out that despite taxes being high, we had poorer public services than elsewhere. A few commentators (the smarter ones) identified an even knottier challenge, namely unsustainable levels of debt. There was truth to many – but not all – of the criticisms.

A combination of the financial crisis, the pandemic and an energy shock has stalled the high levels of growth we have become used to. The measure economists look at most closely is productivity, because it links to living standards – wages can only go up if we are producing more. Since 2008, productivity has grown at a measly 0.5% a year. Since the pandemic it has been just 0.1% a year.[1] To get it rising again, we need businesses to invest more. Instead, as a nation, we have continued to put our savings into every Briton's favourite investment – bricks and mortar. As a result, house prices have risen by 80% since the financial crisis while lending to small businesses has flatlined.[2] Many hoped things might be better under a new government, but their hopes have been dashed: taxes have risen to their highest ever level, business confidence has fallen and it has become riskier and more expensive to employ people. Growth remains anaemic and a Middle East energy shock could wipe it out altogether. Many entrepreneurs and investors have concluded they are better off moving abroad.

Yet this bleak picture is not the whole story. Despite volatility in energy prices and general negativity about the economy, I am optimistic about Britain's prospects. I have written this book to try to persuade you that the sceptics are wrong – and there is all to play for.

The biggest mistake critics make about the UK involves downplaying its strengths relative to other countries. Living standards have indeed been growing more slowly since the global financial crisis, but when I left office, the economy overall had been growing faster than those of France, Germany, Italy and Japan for over a decade. Some of that is because of population growth, but, even with declining migration levels, the IMF says we will continue to grow faster than many other large economies.[3] Indeed, the Centre for Economics and Business Research says that, by the end of the decade, we will narrow the gap with Germany, pull further ahead of France and even overtake Japan, making us the fifth largest economy in the world. The overall size of an economy matters when it comes to global influence, trade wars and the ability to fund our defence. But even when it comes to GDP per head, the measure I focus on in this book because it links directly to living standards, we are not projected to move significantly from our current position.

We clearly need to do better. But any fair assessment of our prospects would say that we still have a lot going for us. Britain is known for the integrity of its institutions, strong property rights and a good legal system. A recent poll of young people across the G20 economies shows that our institutions are the second most trusted overall after Japan.[4] We are also the most open large economy, more willing to absorb new ideas from around the world than many. That is greatly helped by English being the language of business. English common law remains the basis for 40% of commercial and financial contracts worldwide, making our legal sector a major services exporter.[5]

The UK also has particularly strong advantages when it comes to the new industries that will shape this century. We have the third largest technology ecosystem after the US and China.[6] Despite a lack of tech giants, we have a commanding position in AI, far ahead of anywhere else in Europe. Strengths in tech and life sciences are powered by universities that include three of the world's top 10 – and remain the most respected globally outside the US. That strength in academic research is down to our higher education institutions continuing their long tradition of attracting the brightest and best brains from all over the world, furnishing us with more Nobel Prizes than anywhere apart from the US. With a huge financial services sector, thriving professional services and Europe's largest film and TV industry, we have become the world's second largest services exporter. We also have an established and competitive defence industry, something sadly becoming increasingly important. And foreigners have voted with their wallets: for the last fifteen years, the UK has attracted more greenfield foreign direct investment than anywhere else in Europe.

Such foundations matter. But when it comes to addressing the many challenges we face, I have a bigger reason for optimism. In nearly every case, the solutions are in plain sight. Need to encourage more risk-taking? Learn from America. Get more people into work? Try Denmark. Pension reform? Australia is an excellent model. Reduce regional disparities? Try Switzerland. Want good public services and lower taxes? Switzerland again, or Japan and Taiwan. Make it easier to build things? Look at France. Just because something has been done elsewhere, it doesn't mean it will work in the same way here or be easy to deliver. But it does show solutions are possible in democracies not dissimilar to our own.

The book starts by looking at the two most important foundations for economic growth: lower tax and lower debt. Without clarity on both, they become elephants in the room. Not everyone agrees that tax and debt do need to be lower, so I look carefully at the evidence that connects them to growth. Because taxes fund public services and most people (including me) want decent ones, I then explore whether it is possible to pay for them while keeping taxes low. I also look at pragmatic ways to reduce debt, given that we seem to have fallen into a dangerous doom loop of ever higher debt interest payments causing ever lower growth.

Reducing tax and debt – and therefore making it easier for the economy to grow – becomes much easier if we increase the productive capacity of the economy through what economists call 'supply-side' policies, so in the chapters that follow I look at the eight most practical ways to do that. All improve productivity in technical ways – but more importantly, they change attitudes towards risk and wealth creation. That's because, in a theme that recurs throughout the book, economic growth is about mindset as much as individual policies. Those eight areas include how to get more of our working-age population into work. They cover ways to make it easier to build things, whether houses or infrastructure. They examine how to improve productivity in the public sector, which accounts for a fifth of our output. They include analysis and suggestions as to how to make the most of the AI revolution. They then look at how to cut the cost of energy, something very topical, one of the fastest ways to increase growth, without abandoning our climate change responsibilities. They also examine ways to reduce the regional disparities that have long plagued the UK more than other countries. I then consider longer-term changes including improvements to our education system and strengthening our general appetite for risk-taking. For the latter I draw on my own experience setting up and running my own business before going into politics.

It is tempting to think of these solutions as unrelated: what do energy prices have to do with academic standards in schools? In fact, on a very basic level they are all trying to do exactly the same thing: make it easier for entrepreneurs and leaders to start and grow companies. We need more wealth creation, so every one of these reforms reduces the risk of failure for people bold enough to take the plunge. What is clear from the evidence is that the UK isn't struggling because of a lack of talent, innovation or stable institutions. Rather, we have just made it too hard to build, invest, work and take risks. So some of the proposed solutions make it easier to raise capital, others to get a skilled workforce. Some make it easier to get permission to build things, others to keep factories and offices going with lower energy bills. Some keep taxes down by making public services more efficient, others help innovative companies to scale up quickly. Taken together, they are a huge sign on Britain's front door encouraging entrepreneurs, scientists and inventors to go for it.

Growth impact of reforms

Objective	Potential annual GDP growth impact	Potential 10-year GDP impact
Unlocking pension fund investment	0.1%	0.7%
Increasing numbers in work	0.4%	4%
Making it easier to build things	0.2%	2%
Making the public sector more efficient	0.1%	1%
Artificial intelligence	1%	10%
Reducing energy bills	0.2%	2%
Reducing regional imbalances	0.3%	3%
Raising educational standards	0.25%	Minimal but longer-term effect
Increasing entrepreneurship	0.2%	2%

Note: Numbers are rounded. See the relevant chapters for source details. The impact of cutting the tax burden on economic growth is covered in Chapter 1.

In each case, I then try to do something quite challenging, namely to quantify the impact of reform on each area. For that, I have sought out and sourced independent analysis, which is referenced in each chapter. Even though I have used credible sources, their methodologies inevitably vary, which means that all numbers should be treated with a degree of caution. Nonetheless, they are worth looking at because they give a sense of the scale (how big an impact a change makes) and timing (how long it takes to have a measurable effect). That is particularly relevant in light of the current debate about whether the OBR gives governments enough credit for longer-term policies designed to improve growth.

If the numbers in the table are totalled up, they add nearly 3% to annual growth and over 20% to GDP per head after a decade. Sadly, economics is not so simple. Many of the policies overlap and cut across each other – sometimes reinforcing the effect and sometimes counteracting it. Inevitably, some will end up being watered down as they are implemented. But if other global factors remain constant (a big 'if', of course), a determined government could surely achieve half that total impact.

That would be transformational. It would grow our GDP per head by an additional 10% over a decade. It would raise living standards for the average family by around £4,000.[7] It would also allow the Chancellor roughly £120 billion to spend on reducing debt, reducing tax or investing in public services. A big debate, of course, would follow about which of those to prioritise – but given today's circumstances that is a 'nice' problem for a chancellor to have. Budgets could once again become a moment for good news instead of funereal worry.

How, then, do we make all this happen? To deliver such change, we must rediscover British can-do entrepreneurialism in government as well as in the private sector. Ministers and civil servants need to swap their traditionally cautious focus for a much more ambitious mindset. Instead of starting with a problem and trying to move forward, they need to start with a solution and work back. It's what journalist Matthew Syed called a 'growth mindset' in his book *Bounce.* It might sound a tall order but when there are external shocks or international crises, governments have more latitude to act boldly. But we should also remember that the UK has done it before, when we led the way in the industrial revolution. Nobel laureate Joel Mokyr argues that humans emerged from centuries of stagnant living standards only when we developed institutions and norms that actively applied new ideas to the purpose of raising general prosperity. He called it a 'culture of growth'. We need to rediscover the culture of growth that we originally pioneered.

That means optimism – but a credible, grounded optimism which keeps our feet firmly anchored to the ground. For a Chancellor, that means being honest about the many things over which you have no control: unpredictable markets, technology shifts, energy shocks or the discovery of natural resources. But it also means knowing where you do have influence. The Treasury is by far the most powerful Whitehall ministry. It controls not just the budgets of other departments but, through a complicated system of approvals, their ability to spend those budgets. If it wants something, it generally gets it. Budgets can be a highly effective forcing mechanism for getting government agreement for new policies. Most importantly, through the tax system, chancellors can directly shape the social contract between state and citizen. As Margaret Thatcher famously said: 'Economics is the method; the object is to change the heart and soul.'

The trick, therefore, is not to overestimate your ability to shape events but also not to underestimate it. Crucial to success is the ability to communicate a vision that stands the test of time. That's not just because you need to carry the public with you. It's also because many solutions take longer than one parliament to bear fruit, so there needs to be broad support for an approach that extends beyond any one party. That generally only works when leaders cast off an incrementalist mindset and make bolder arguments for radical change. Coming from someone who has been known as a pragmatist, that is partly a mea culpa.

I need to finish this introduction with some disclaimers.

Readers will be relieved to know that in this book I don't intend to rehash the arguments on Brexit. Of course, changing the terms of trade with our biggest partner has an impact on the economy. The OBR says that leaving the single market could reduce GDP by 4%.[8] But I see no reason why a country the size of the UK cannot restore trade to prior levels over time, even outside the single market and customs union. In the longer run, we can surely thrive as an independent country like Australia, Canada and Japan. Whether I am right or wrong, there is little prospect of that debate being resolved quickly, so I do not attempt to do so in this book.

I am also a practitioner, rather than an economist. My perspective is less academic and more hands-on. Rather than dwelling on economic theory, I have looked at areas that have the greatest prospect of rapid, measurable change. It is not a memoir, but as with my previous books, I do use my own experience of trying to get things done in government to illustrate delivery challenges. I also tell the story of setting up my own company because it is relevant to the question of how to create the right culture around risk. In general, I follow Danish philosopher Søren Kierkegaard's view that life can only be understood looking backwards, but must be lived looking forwards.

Finally, I should address the obvious critique: 'If that's the answer, why on earth didn't you do it when you had the chance?' The truth is that no one starting a job can ever know all the answers at the outset. My own thinking evolved, although my principles did not. In some ways, I wish I had been given this book on the day I became Chancellor – but life is never like that.

How, then, do I view my own time as Chancellor? I am proud of a number of things. They include stabilising the economy after the mini-budget, returning inflation to target and nursing the economy back to growth. I was happy to introduce free childcare, raise defence spending to 2.5% of GDP, give the NHS a long-term workforce plan and launch the Mansion House reforms. I also started the painful journey to bring down tax.

But there are also many areas where I did not make progress. I did not put in place a wider public sector productivity plan that would have delivered better services for lower taxes. I did not adopt a fiscal rule to get debt falling. I did not make much progress simplifying the tax system. I did not push through welfare reforms on the scale I wanted to (although, with Mel Stride, I made some progress). I knew some reforms can realistically only happen at the start of a parliament rather than close to an election, and only came to understand the need for other reforms after leaving office. Like many chancellors, I therefore left Downing Street with both pride and regret.

Angela Merkel once said that 'growth isn't everything, it's true. But without growth everything is nothing.' So what matters now is what happens next. This book does not argue that it is going to be easy to get out of our low-growth trap. But it does make the case that the problems we face are solvable and – with political will – the solutions deliverable. Because all parties agree on the need for growth, it is actually easier to make the case for change here than in other countries – so there is no excuse! But any attempt at reform will fail if leaders forget that culture matters as much as policy, and that people matter as much as politicians. It is not ministers and civil servants who create wealth but entrepreneurs and people trying to grow businesses. That's why we need to make life dramatically easier for those willing to take risks, build companies, invest in factories, generate ideas and create jobs. They need to know we value what they do and have their back.

1
Tax

Rachel Reeves and Tate Reeves share a last name. Both have a background in finance. Both hold public office with major economic responsibilities. But apart from that they couldn't be more different. One is the Chancellor of the Exchequer who has raised UK taxes to their highest ever level. The other is the governor of Mississippi who has reduced personal taxes to the state's lowest ever level.

For a long time, Mississippi's GDP per head was not just the lowest in the US but also lower than that of economies like Britain's. But in 2022 it overtook the UK, meaning that the poorest state in the US is now wealthier than one of the richest countries in Europe.

Prices, though, are higher in the US. If you account for that and other differentials (using a metric which economists call Purchasing Power Parity, or PPP), the UK's GDP per head remains just ahead.[1] But over the three years since the pandemic, growth has averaged 3% a year in Mississippi, compared to around 1% a year in the UK.[2] In the Magnolia State, unemployment has fallen to record lows just as it is rising sharply in the UK.

Mississippi has overtaken the UK in GDP per capita

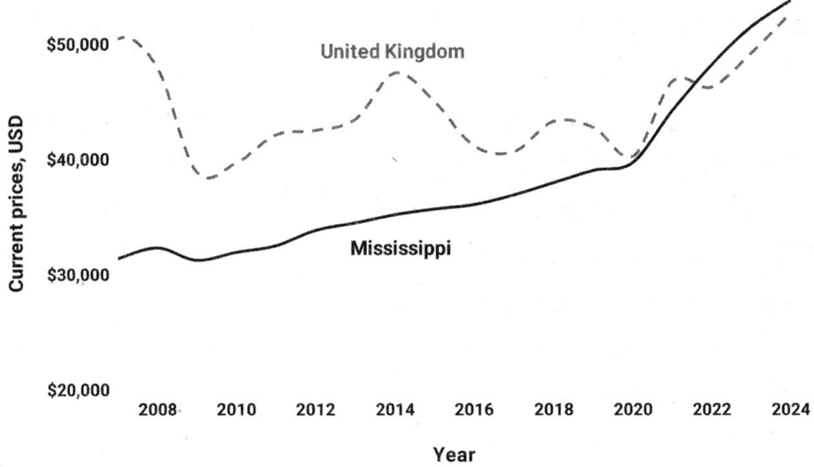

Sources: US Bureau of Economic Analysis,[3] US Census Bureau via FRED,[4] and the IMF[5]
Note: Mississippi's GDP per head was estimated by the author using state GDP and population estimates.

The American Reeves has come from a rather different background to his British namesake. Unlike Rachel, who was brought up in a public sector family (both her parents were teachers), Tate grew up with a father who started his own air-conditioning business. His home was one of traditional Southern Republican values. He became a financial analyst and worked in the private sector, and then served twice as state treasurer and twice as lieutenant governor before becoming governor.

In his first term in 2016, he pushed through the largest tax cut in Mississippi's history, worth $415 million.[6] Because the state has a legal requirement to balance its budget, the reduction was not funded by borrowing and could only be introduced gradually over twelve years. In 2022, he went even further, with a $525 million income tax cut.[7] In 2025, legislators passed a bill that plans to eliminate state income tax by 2040.[8] It wasn't easy. In 2024, individual income tax accounted for nearly a third of Mississippi's general fund receipts.[9] To pay for it, Governor Reeves focused relentlessly on increasing the efficiency and productivity of public services through what he called a 'performance-based' approach.[10] He believed that the economic growth unlocked by tax cuts would increase government revenue over time.[11] So far, he has been right. Tax receipts have increased rather than declined, with a jump in sales tax revenue helping to cover the drop in income tax receipts.[12] Sales tax revenues rose partly because of inflation, but also because over that period Mississippi became one of the fastest-growing states in the US. Its overall growth rate is now higher than the US average, fuelled by more than $35 billion of new private investment since 2020,[13] including $10 billion from Amazon and another $10 billion from Compass Datacenters.[14]

A tale of two politicians called Reeves

Mississippi tax receipts remained stable while the state tax burden fell

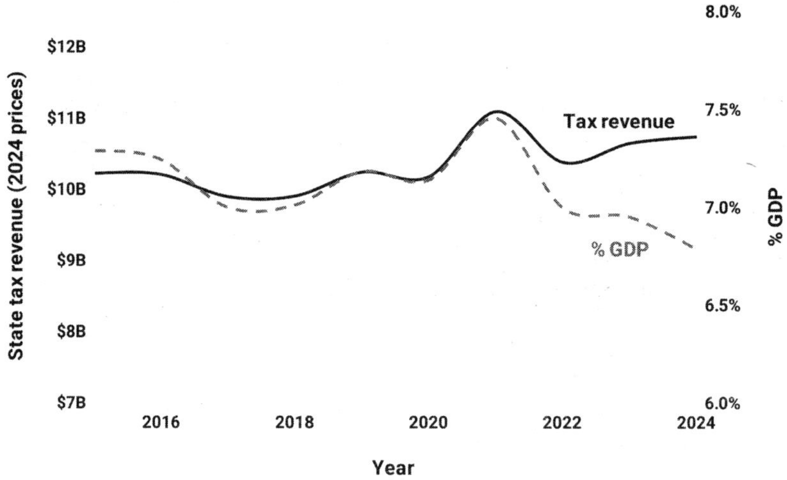

Source: Calculations by the author using data from the US Bureau of Economic Analysis[15] and the US Census Bureau[16]

That said, social outcomes in Mississippi remain generally worse than in the UK. Its infant mortality, at 9.7 deaths per thousand live births,[17] is nearly double the American average and nearly three times higher than the UK's.[18] Obesity is also a major issue: England, with 26% of adults deemed clinically obese, has some of the highest levels in Europe.[19] But in Mississippi obesity is even higher, at 40% of the adult population, one of the highest in the US.[20] Poverty levels are hard to compare, because they're calculated using different methodologies, but Mississippi's appears to be more than double the UK's.

Social outcomes remain worse in Mississippi than in the UK

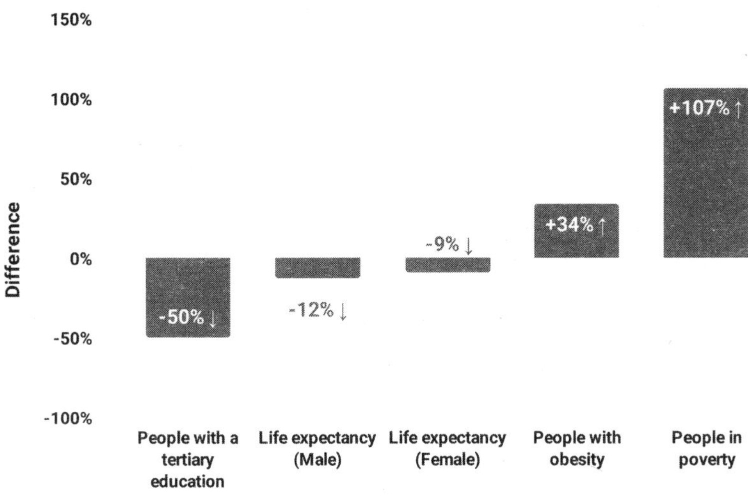

Source: Calculations by the author using the following data: on education – OECD,[21] US Census Bureau;[22] on life expectancy – ONS,[23] NCHS;[24] on obesity – NHS England,[25] CDC;[26] on poverty – OECD,[27] US Census Bureau[28]

Note: For tertiary education rates, Mississippi includes everyone above the age of 25, while the UK's figure includes only 25 to 64-year-olds. The obesity rate used for the UK was England only. The ratio between the national and Mississippi poverty rates was used to extrapolate Mississippi's poverty rate based on 60% of national median disposable income, using the US rate published by the OECD.

But with increasing prosperity, social outcomes in Mississippi have started to improve. A recent report on fourth-grade reading levels shows its children have leapt from the second worst level in America to the top 10 in just a few years.[29] High school graduation rates are up.[30] A public health emergency has been declared to tackle high levels of infant mortality. Most importantly, the proportion of the population in poverty – although still high at 18% – has fallen by a quarter,[31] partly because real median household incomes have risen to their highest level in nearly fifteen years.[32]

Tate Reeves describes Mississippi as 'the best-kept secret in the world'.[33] As he plans to reduce state income tax to zero, Rachel Reeves's move in the opposite direction has been rather more visible. Other low-tax states in the US have performed less spectacularly, so the growth comparison between the UK and Mississippi should not be overstretched. But at the same time other American states that were already more prosperous than us have pulled even further ahead: output per head in New York, Massachusetts and California is now around double the levels in the UK (or France or Japan, for that matter).[34] Have we just got things wrong on tax?

No discussion of tax can avoid considering the public services it pays for. High-quality public services are – for me and most people – an essential part of a civilised society. They also contribute to economic growth. But given that so many countries with a lower tax burden seem to be growing faster, I asked my officials at the Treasury whether there was a link between a country's level of taxation and its growth rate. The advice I got was clear: whatever basket of countries you took – G7, G20, Europe or the OECD – those with lower tax levels had, on average, higher growth. But, officials said, there is a fierce debate between economists as to whether it is correlation or causation. Do low taxes cause higher growth, or is it the other way round? Lower taxes in Switzerland, for example, might be what has fuelled its prosperity – but they might also be just what's possible when you have large numbers of profitable companies. And there are plenty of exceptions to the general trend: low-tax Japan, for example, has been growing more slowly than high-tax Italy.

In this chapter, I explain why I believe there is, in fact, a causal link – namely, that lower tax rates are a cause and not just a consequence of higher growth. I look at why lower levels of tax boost investment and help entrepreneurs and businesses trying to expand. I consider the impact tax has on the broader social contract, in particular the link between effort and reward. Finally, I examine how to fund decent public services even while keeping tax rates down.

The first thing to acknowledge is that not all public spending is bad for growth. Money spent on infrastructure such as new roads or railways can boost productivity, making individuals and companies more efficient. Public investment in nuclear power can bring down energy prices for businesses, offices and factories. Education spending – if done wisely – boosts what economists call human capital. Health spending helps people get back to work after mental or physical illness and reduces the cost of welfare. As a result, organisations like the IMF have long argued that the right public investment – in education or economic infrastructure, for example – stimulates long-term growth more than tax cuts. That is not the case for government spending that purely boosts consumption – such as spending on public sector pay. Such spending boosts demand in the short term, but not the productive capacity of the economy going forward. Pay rises can also lead to inflation if the economy doesn't have enough capacity to absorb the extra spending.

What about spending that serves other social purposes, such as reducing inequality? Some countries do this more extensively than the UK and are also more prosperous. Torsten Bell, now a Labour government minister but formerly head of the Resolution Foundation, notes that if the UK's GDP per head matched the average in comparable countries such as France, the Netherlands and Germany, every British family would be 25% wealthier.[35] That's a big gap, amounting to additional income of £8,300 a year.[36] Most of those countries have higher tax and lower inequality than the UK. Denmark is perhaps the best example: it takes over 10% more of GDP in tax than the UK, and has both lower inequality and incomes that are 20% higher.[37]

The problem is that many of the countries Bell compares us to are stuck in the same low-growth trap as we are. Economic growth in his basket of countries has averaged 1.8% a year over the last decade, not very different to the UK's 1.7%.[38] And with lower growth, all of us will ultimately find social spending harder, not easier. But at the same time as we have been stuck, countries such as South Korea, Israel, New Zealand, Latvia, Lithuania, Estonia, Chile and Turkey have kept taxes lower and grown faster. Many of them also have better public services than us. Some have better social outcomes too.

Why do countries with lower levels of tax tend to grow faster? Because growth depends on investment – and businesses invest more when taxes don't eat into their profits. Conversely, when taxes are higher, businesses make less profit and cut back on future investment.[39] Angela Merkel famously said that Europe has 7% of the world's population, 25% of its GDP and 50% of its welfare spending.[40] The inevitable result of such a choice is higher taxes and lower growth, an outcome made even worse by an ageing population. But the crucial point is that the reverse is also true: lower taxation means more investment and therefore more growth. This has happened after tax cuts in the US (recently), in Denmark (2009), in Sweden (1991) and in the UK (1988 and 2023). The result is a larger private sector and one better able to support the spending needed by the state – a virtuous circle rather than the vicious one we are now dealing with. In the US, the cost of every public sector worker is funded through the taxes of six private sector workers. In the UK it is just five.[41] Inevitably, the burden of paying for public sector employees is higher when it is shared between fewer people.

European countries with a higher standard of living often had smaller states in the year they overtook the UK

Country	Overtake year	Government spend (% GDP)	UK equivalent that year
Switzerland	1946	11%	61%
Denmark	1950	10%	33%
Sweden	1957	22%	33%
Netherlands	1965	23%	35%
Germany	1970	39%	42%
Norway	1975	44%	49%
Finland	1980	40%	48%

Source: Maddison Project Database 2023[42] and the IMF[43]
Note: The table shows the first year each state overtook the UK following the Second World War. It does not account for cases where economic downturns may have resulted in the UK temporarily overtaking them again.

The most influential analysis of the link between growth and tax levels was done by US economist Robert Barro. He was one of the first economists to explain how, when governments spend more, business investment falls – leading to lower growth. Economists call this the 'crowding out effect'. Barro was careful to say that not all government spending is bad for growth – particularly capital spending on infrastructure or investment in education: his models show that investment in public infrastructure in particular supports growth while a country is developing. But over time those returns diminish. After a certain point, a bigger state simply means lower growth. The UK's OBR agrees: in 2024, it said that the tax increases in Rachel Reeves's autumn budget 'deliver a temporary boost to GDP in the near term and some crowding out of private activity in the medium term'.[44] It acknowledged the positive impact of certain types of public investment but said the overall impact of higher tax would mean less investment.

Crowding out is the technical reason why higher tax reduces investment and growth. But an equally important reason is psychological. Capitalism needs what John Maynard Keynes called 'animal spirits' – the entrepreneurial drive that persuades people to work hard, take risks and start a business. Many other economists have studied the role of animal spirits, including Robert Shiller, George Akerlof, Joel Mokyr, Daniel Kahneman and Richard Thaler. They all note that human attitudes and behaviour are a critical driver of economic dynamism. Like many, they conclude that a culture of personal responsibility and reward for effort makes a big difference to a country's growth potential.

Conversely, high taxes erode a country's animal spirits. An economy in which individuals have to calculate whether they can actually afford to accept a pay rise because a higher tax rate will kick in – as in the UK today – is not likely to thrive. But if you get the risk–reward equation right, people are willing to put in the effort. That's one reason why in 2024 the average US citizen worked 1,796 hours, compared to 1,512 hours for the UK and 1,331 hours for Germany.[45] Put another way, Americans work four weeks more than Brits and nine weeks more than Germans. In Europe we tend to look down our noses at the longer hours worked by Americans – despite envying the dynamism of the US economy, often in the same breath. I, too, value precious time with my family. But I also want my children to grow up in an economy with well-paid jobs and boundless opportunities. Have we got the balance right?

Countries with higher taxes work fewer hours

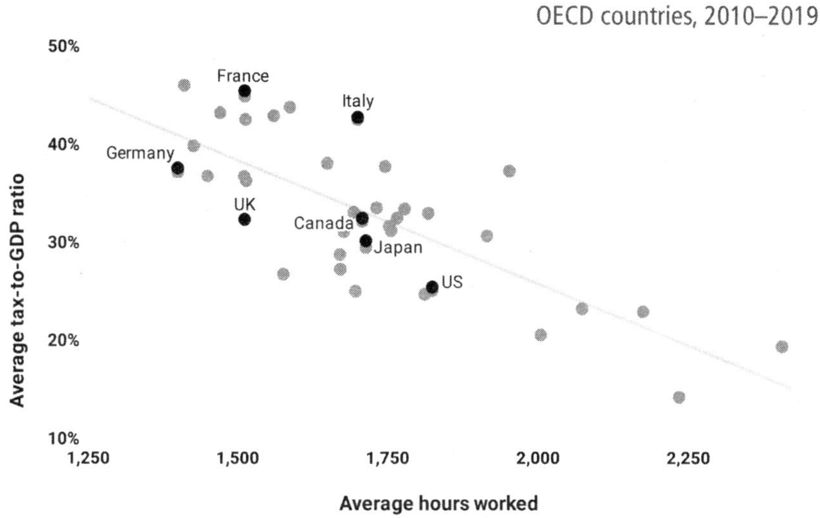

Source: Calculations by the author using data from the OECD[46]

The graph above demonstrates the broad connection between lower tax and more work. Many economists say the biggest impact on work ethic is not the total level of tax but the marginal rate – that is the tax paid for every additional pound you earn. But they are connected: countries with a higher overall tax burden are likely to have higher marginal rates too. That's why the cliff edges in our income tax system are so damaging. They seem to have a particularly large impact on choices by secondary earners, many of whom are women. For people on low incomes, the rules around welfare payments are more important, but again connected: if benefits are withdrawn as you earn more, it makes your effective marginal tax rate higher because you take less home for every additional pound earned.

The impact of more 'animal spirits' alongside higher levels of investment then feeds through into higher growth. The following chart divides the thirty-eight OECD countries into quartiles according to the level of tax as a proportion of GDP. Countries in the lowest quartile, such as Australia, the US and South Korea, grew on average 2% a year faster than those in the highest quartile, such as Germany, France and Italy.[47] During this period, the UK sat broadly in the middle of the pack, but since then it has significantly increased its level of tax. My graph looks at growth between 2010 and 2019 but similar analysis has been done over a longer timescale by Jon Moynihan in his book *Return to Growth*, which comes to the same conclusion.[48] Some will still question whether it's a case of causation rather than correlation, but with such a large difference in growth rates over a large sample of countries it becomes hard to argue that there is no causation involved.

Countries with a higher tax burden grow more slowly

OECD countries, 2010–2019

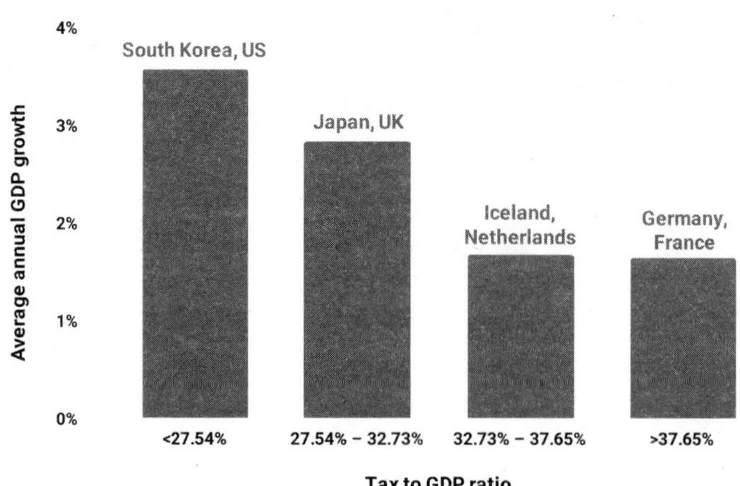

Source: OECD[49] and the IMF[50]

How, then, do many smaller European countries manage to combine higher levels of tax with greater prosperity? Many actually had *lower* levels of taxation when their GDP per head overtook the UK, but then subsequently increased tax, which caused their growth to slow. They have also avoided making other mistakes that we have made in Britain. The Netherlands, Denmark and Finland have been more disciplined in the way they have spent taxpayers' money, putting a greater proportion into infrastructure and education. Many have better-designed welfare systems that pay fewer people not to work. And they generally have more broadly based tax systems which avoid distortion and encourage business investment. As a result, even with lower growth, they have been able to sustain higher absolute levels of prosperity.

More prosperous countries have generally been investing more

Average general government GFCF, G7 plus select countries, 2010–2019

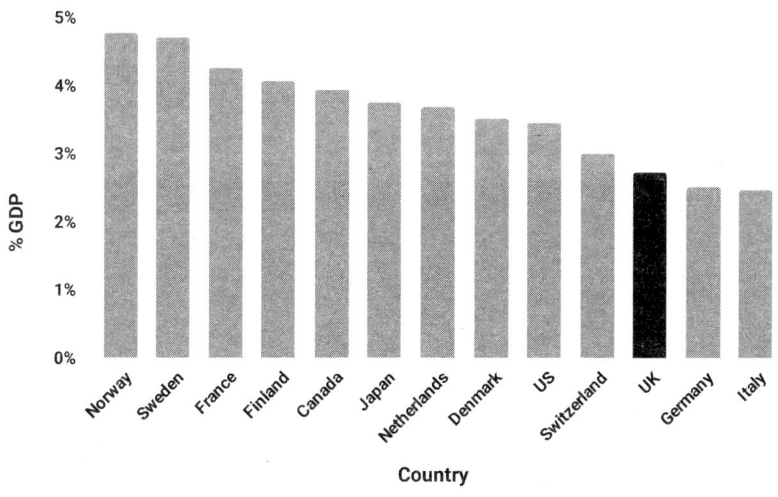

Source: OECD[51]
Note: GFCF = Gross Fixed Capital Formation

Higher GDP per head in some countries with a larger tax burden does not therefore undermine the central link between lower tax and higher growth. But if you want to reduce taxes, you still have to explain how you are going to fund public services. The answer is to secure the economic growth that makes them affordable. An increase of just 1% in GDP leads to higher tax receipts, generating an additional £10–12 billion each year to spend on public services.[52] In other words, we can have our cake and eat it – if we are patient. Countries like Switzerland and Singapore show that in practice you don't need to make a choice between low taxes or decent public services – it is perfectly possible to have both, with the right sequencing. Spending on public services must come *after* economic growth rather than being introduced before it and at a scale that stifles it. Spending should generally grow more slowly than the economy – something that (as I will discuss later) should become one of our 'fiscal rules', the self-denying ordinances chancellors set to reassure markets that they are being responsible with the nation's finances.

Nor is it necessary to accept poorer social outcomes – as in Mississippi or other parts of America – as the price of a low-tax, high-growth economy. In fact, comparisons with the US are more nuanced than many realise. In 2024, its tax burden was 25.6% of GDP, compared to 34.4% in the UK,[53] but although income tax on high earners is much lower in the US, the marginal rate for middle and low earners is often higher. American businesses with more than fifty employees are also obliged to fund health cover, which adds up to 12% to salary costs, making payroll costs higher.[54] Conversely, corporation tax and sales tax (which the US has instead of VAT) are much lower, something which supports both revenue and investment.[55]

That does not mean the UK has made choices that are intrinsically wrong. We have chosen social policies which reduce child and pensioner poverty, lead to better health outcomes and mitigate some inequality (though there is still quite a lot of it). The problem is that funding for such programmes – particularly since the pandemic – has increased faster than the size of the economy. That is having a drag-anchor effect on economic growth, as well as making the funding of further social policy harder. In Britain, a Labour government that would like to increase spending on public services is finding it painful, while in Mississippi, a Republican governor is managing to reduce poverty. Who is more progressive?

How, then, does a Chancellor go about reducing tax? Only with willpower and – sometimes – luck.

If you try to cut taxes without saying how you will finance them, markets assume borrowing will go up. That led to the unravelling of the mini-budget and the fall of Liz Truss. One of my first acts as Chancellor was to cancel nearly all the tax cuts her package contained. I also needed to show the markets how we would fund an extra £350 billion of debt built up during the pandemic. That meant, against all my instincts, higher taxes. But for me and Rishi Sunak it was always meant to be a temporary change: as soon as we had the chance, we wanted to bring tax back down, for the aforementioned reasons.

But for a while, there was just no money to do so. Indeed, after my first budget, I was told the OBR forecasts were likely to deteriorate so badly I would have to put up taxes a second time. Inflation remained higher than expected, which meant higher interest rates and dearer government debt. There were also higher unemployment and sickness benefits to pay, as well as more costly public sector pay awards.

So I was forced to go through the gloomy process of working out where to find the money to balance the books. Freezing income tax thresholds for another year? That was £2–3 billion. Restricting salary subsidies for electric cars and new bicycles? Maybe a billion. Increasing the higher rate of tax by 2p? £3 billion. Raising VAT by a penny? £8 billion.[56] Hiking capital gains tax? £4 billion. Restricting pension tax relief for higher earners? £5 billion. Abolishing the triple lock? Up to £15 billion. Reducing the growth in public spending from 1% to 0.5% a year? £10 billion.[57]

At the same time, I worked up measures that would boost growth without costing anything. We aimed high. I asked civil servants what it would take to increase business investment from 10% of GDP to 12%, the average for similar economies. I got one team to look at whether pension fund reforms could lead to more investment. Another got cracking on a programme of investment zones, designed to boost investment outside the south-east. Other teams investigated ways to boost foreign direct investment and the potential to turn the UK into the world's next Silicon Valley. Increasing annual business investment by 2% would transform growth, and I wanted it badly.

Right in the middle of the planning, something unexpected happened. I found myself rushed to St Thomas' Hospital in the middle of the night with a nasty kidney infection. Lucia stayed up with me all night as I shivered with a horrible fever. The Chancellor being admitted to hospital is big news, but we managed to keep it under wraps. For three days I was brilliantly looked after (though slightly spooked when a doctor told me I would have died in the era before antibiotics). But even better for my morale was some good news that arrived from the OBR when I was in hospital. Rather than having to find what we thought would be £12 billion in tax rises or spending cuts, a recalculation of GDP forecasts predicted a £15 billion surplus. It was only a number on a spreadsheet – but I wanted to leap out of my hospital bed with joy. What a sad human being I have become, I thought.

Nonetheless, I remained cautious. I knew the OBR could take as quickly as it gave. Exactly that had happened to me in the Spring Budget a few months earlier, when their forecasts had moved against me by £20 billion at a crucial moment – nearly derailing my childcare reforms. Another key constraint was inflation, which we were just beginning to get under control. Pumping money into the economy through tax cuts could lead to prices going back up again – the last thing I wanted. It was a tightrope.

A few days later, back out of hospital, it was my birthday. And Richard Hughes, the Chair of the OBR, gave me literally the most valuable birthday present I will ever receive. He came back with new calculations that gave me not a £15-billion headroom but a whopping £32-billion surplus. Sorry Lucia, kids, friends… you will never be able to compete with that one, I thought.

I could have kept it as the buffer many economists were advising. But my priority was growth. That meant boosting investment and starting the long journey to more competitive tax levels. But which taxes should I cut? Business tax cuts would certainly raise investment but income tax cuts were attractive in the run-up to an election. To promote long-term growth, I looked for tax cuts that would boost investment – and the productive capacity of the economy – rather than just consumption.

So I opted for a mixture of business and personal tax cuts. For businesses, I announced a big tax cut known as 'full expensing', which meant immediate tax relief for any capital investments. It was the top ask from business organisations like the CBI, and many economists thought it would do the most of any tax cut to stimulate investment. But at £11 billion a year, it was very expensive. I figured that if I didn't do it then, it would probably never happen. Interestingly, Donald Trump decided to do exactly the same two years later in his Big Beautiful Bill.

Another way to boost growth was to make work more attractive, bolstering Keynes's animal spirits. So I cut employees' national insurance by 2p, followed by another 2p cut in the Spring Budget. The OBR calculated it would lead to the equivalent of around 200,000 more people in full-time work, a number that would fill nearly a quarter of current vacancies in the economy.[58] Overall, it was a reduction in the tax burden of 0.7% of GDP, the largest package of tax cuts since Nigel Lawson's famous 1988 budget. But there was rather less to celebrate, coming as it did right after some horrible tax rises.

Nor was the other work my Treasury teams had been doing to boost growth in vain. We unveiled no fewer than 110 growth measures to stimulate investment.[59] They ranged from a relaxation of planning reforms to speeding up access to the national grid and unlocking pension fund investment. There was also a substantial package of welfare reforms. The Treasury calculated the measures would boost annual business investment by £20 billion,[60] closing around half the investment gap with countries like Germany, France and the US. The OBR said that taken together, the measures would increase the size of the economy by 0.6% – the first time it had ever recognised such an impact. Haltingly, we had started on the path to both lower taxes and higher growth. The CBI said the announcements would 'unleash pent-up investment' into the economy.[61] The following year, factory investment rose to a ten-year high.[62]

The UK tax code is around 21,000 pages long, the longest in the world. It contains numerous illogicalities on income tax, property tax and VAT that often distort the way incentives work in the economy in a way that damages growth. Such complexity can be as damaging to economic growth as overall tax levels. For that reason, there is an unusual consensus between economists from the left and right about the urgent need for tax simplification. In late 2025, the right-leaning Centre for Policy Studies and Adam Smith Institute and the left-leaning New Economics Foundation and Institute for Public Policy Research produced a joint set of proposals to make the UK tax system simpler and more growth-friendly.

They suggest a number of things that are logical albeit controversial. They advocate simplifying and broadening VAT by removing exemptions in areas such as food, children's clothes and travel. That would be a hard sell politically but would allow a reduction in the main VAT rate by up to five percentage points. They rightly say property taxes should be simpler, including reforming council tax, which is based on 1991 valuations. Their most sensible proposal is to abolish stamp duty, which gums up the property market and stops people moving to where jobs are, replacing it with a property tax based on updated valuations. They also argue that landlords should be charged the equivalent of national insurance contributions in return for deducting the cost of debt interest from their tax bills.

Most relevant to this chapter are their proposals to improve work incentives. Marginal tax rates – the amount of tax you pay on the next £1 you earn – matter, as we have seen. Currently, cliff edges in the marginal rate of tax disincentivise people from moving up the income scale. On paper, the rules look simple: 20% tax on income from £12,570 to £50,270, 40% between £50,271 and £125,140 and 45% above that.

But employees' national insurance contributions then complicate this picture by adding 8% to marginal tax rates from £12,570 to £50,270 and an extra 2% on income above that. It gets even messier if you have children, because child benefit is progressively withdrawn around the £60,000 mark, with childcare subsidies completely removed at £100,000. The former can increase the marginal rate of income tax from 42% to 53%, while the latter means that someone earning £99,999 can lose access to £6,500 or more of childcare support if their salary increases by just a pound. I remember being berated by a constituent in Godalming about how difficult life was as a result for people earning just over £100,000. I was later criticised for saying that, in an expensive area, £100,000 wasn't a huge salary for a young couple with kids. I was right, if a little clumsy with my wording.

Tax pinchpoints disincentivise moving up the income scale

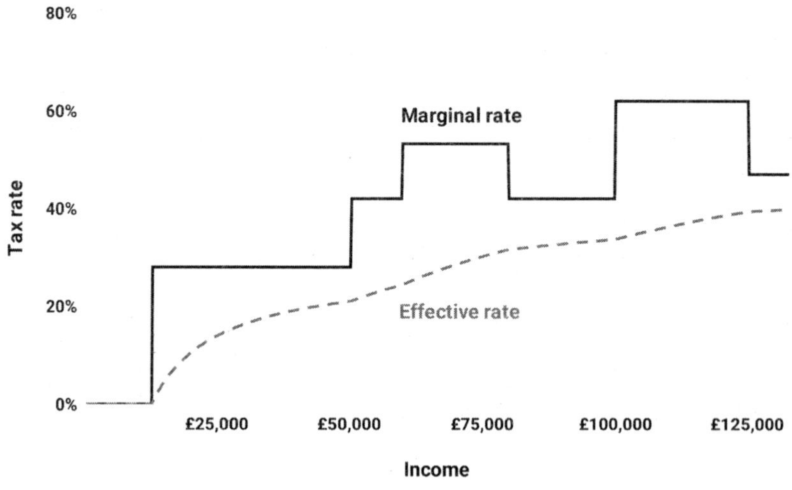

Source: Calculations by the author using UK Government data

Similar issues are even more pernicious lower down the income scale, because of the way benefits are withdrawn as people's income increases. The introduction of universal credit (UC) was designed to address this by allowing payments to continue even if you get a job. But benefit is still withdrawn as income rises, meaning high effective marginal tax rates for people trying to move off welfare. For every extra pound earned above £684 a month (or £411 if you receive housing support), 55p of benefit is withdrawn.[63] At the same time, income tax and national insurance must be paid. The result is that someone earning more can face an effective marginal tax rate of 68%.[64] Allowing people on welfare to keep just 32p of every additional pound earned is hardly rewarding work.

The result of these cliff edges is a system in which some people – often the most ambitious, energetic and productive – decide not to work additional hours or actively request their employers *not* to increase their salary. That is the opposite of what a successful economy needs, namely, people trying to move up the income scale. It is never easy to reduce taxes on better-off groups, so chancellors wanting to tackle such structural issues are probably wise to do so at the start of a parliament rather than in the run-up to an election.

If you are going to take the plunge, the best start would be to abolish employees' national insurance. I hoped such a reform could be achieved gradually, starting with my 4p reduction. But welcome though it was, it was ultimately too incremental: a more radical reform would have been to raise the basic rate of income tax to 25% in order to fund the complete abolition of employees' national insurance. That would have made the tax system simpler and transformed work incentives. We didn't do it, of course, because it would have meant higher bills for pensioners ahead of an election. That dilemma perfectly illustrates the risks inherent in gradual change, namely that it relies on the increasingly rare phenomenon of a Chancellor staying in post and being able to stick to a vision over many years.

But whatever the benefits of a simpler system, pursuing it does not allow you to duck the more fundamental question: do we want to try to reduce the overall tax burden or are we content with it as it is? The evidence from economies around the world is clear: if we want entrepreneurs to take risks, if we want ambitious people to put in extra hours, if we want businesses to invest – then we have to embark on the difficult road of lowering tax. That does not mean inferior public services – quite the opposite, in fact, because economic growth is the only sustainable path to improving them. The immediate pressure to fund health, pensions and defence does, however, mean the process of bringing down tax levels will take time. But as we head in that direction, there are plenty of other ways to boost growth relatively quickly, such as getting more people into work, making it easier to build things and reducing the cost of energy. Before coming to these, there is a further foundation to put in place: we need to tackle our unsustainably high level of debt.

CONCLUSIONS

- ▸ Countries with lower overall levels of tax grow faster.

- ▸ Some public spending, such as on infrastructure and education, supports growth and should be protected.

- ▸ It is possible to have well-funded public services alongside competitive tax rates, providing the sequencing is right: economic growth needs to come first.

- ▸ In order to reduce the burden of tax over time, we need a new fiscal rule stating that public spending will grow more slowly than the economy over time.

- ▸ Tax simplification can make a big contribution to growth by removing disincentives to move up the income scale.

2

Debt

After a record-breaking heatwave over the summer, the rain on that Thursday was welcome. It was 30 September 1976, and Labour's party conference was in full swing. Denis Healey, Chancellor of the Exchequer, hurried to the conference hall. He had flown to Blackpool from London for one reason: to explain why the UK was going cap in hand to the IMF for a bailout. He had a huge challenge: he needed to show markets that the government was still in control, particularly of its own party.[1]

'I come from the battlefront,' Healey declared, with his famously booming voice and bushy eyebrows.

He had seen action in Italy and North Africa during the Second World War, so was more entitled than most to use a military analogy. He was also a highly cultured man, someone who painted and enjoyed classical music. And alongside his highbrow tastes, he had a common touch, mixing easily with ordinary people. He would need that more than ever if he was to persuade left-wing delegates of the need for austerity. The country was in the middle of a major debt crisis, he explained. The markets had lost confidence in the UK. He needed a way of restoring stability. An IMF loan was key.

Many Labour delegates were rightly concerned about the harsh conditions the IMF would demand in return for a fresh loan.

'I am going to negotiate with the IMF on the basis of our existing policies, not changes in policies, and I need your support to do it,' Healey said reassuringly.

The delegates applauded politely. Then he went on: 'But when I say existing policies, I mean things we don't like as well as things we do like,' he clarified.

The room went quiet.

'It means sticking to the very painful cuts in public expenditure on which the government has already decided,' Healey added.

At this point, some of the delegates began to jeer. Healey's ongoing cuts were deeply unpopular among the Labour left. At the time, many were calling for protectionism instead of fiscal tightening.

But Healey had no better options. The previous Conservative government had been plagued by poor industrial relations – resulting in the introduction of a three-day week to ration power. The Chancellor, Anthony Barber, had caused a notorious boom that only led to higher inflation. But after winning power in early 1974, Labour made things worse by failing to resolve the energy crisis. They were forced to introduce cash limits on expenditure and negotiate agreements with the unions to try to stop wage spirals. In turn, the country's budget deficit was getting worse. As the pound collapsed, the cost of debt increased. According to historian Richard Roberts, 'it marked something of a culmination of half a decade of British financial, economic, and political turmoil'.[2]

Healey used the remainder of his speech to explain his plans to tackle inflation and boost exports. By the end, he had won back the support of the room. Healey's final words – 'and I ask this Conference to support me in my task!' – were nearly drowned out by thunderous applause. He had not fallen off the tightrope. A moment of humiliation for the country was also a significant personal achievement.

Denis Healey was notorious for the IMF bailout but walked a political tightrope with great skill

However, Healey's optimism about the impact of 'existing policies' was short-lived. He may have convinced Labour delegates, but the financial markets were unpersuaded. Against a challenging backdrop, the UK started intense negotiations with the IMF in early November. This was not the first loan to the UK – there had been two the previous year – but now the UK was subject to IMF 'conditionality', in other words, it would be forced to accept a loan on whatever terms the IMF dictated.[3]

Negotiations were tough. Healey not only had to reach terms acceptable to the IMF but also needed to convince the rest of the cabinet. Many of his colleagues were vehemently opposed to further public spending cuts. Many wanted to pursue protectionist policies which would isolate the UK from the global economy.

Things were made worse by inaccurate Treasury forecasting. Borrowing requirements had been overestimated, which made the IMF demands even more onerous. But no deal was not an option: without a successful conclusion to the negotiations, lending from other countries would also dry up. Over the course of several weeks there was a succession of breakthroughs and setbacks, all played out very publicly through cabinet leaks. In mid-December, much to Healey's relief, a deal was struck.

In the end, the agreed cuts were relatively mild. Healey later reflected that 'in a sense the whole affair was unnecessary', and suggested that those overestimated borrowing requirements were to blame for the conditions.[4] But without IMF support, stability would not have been restored. A further downward spiral would have ensued, probably involving protectionism and retaliation. Britain's position as the sick man of Europe would have been confirmed, perhaps irreversibly.

This story has been retold many times over the years – usually when markets have wobbled over UK economic policy. Black Wednesday in 1992, the days after the 2010 election, the mini-budget in 2022 and jitters in the bond market in 2025 have all had echoes of 1976. Instability has sometimes been caused by international factors, sometimes by domestic choices. They all demonstrate the wisdom of James Carville, Bill Clinton's economic adviser, when he said that if he was to be reincarnated, 'I want to come back as the bond market. You can intimidate everybody.'

The IMF loan in 1976 was one of the largest in its history. It marked the nadir of Britain's economic performance. Denis Healey's humiliation was also the country's – and it sank deep into the national consciousness. It made the radical reforms of the 1980s politically acceptable for many voters. Margaret Thatcher talked endlessly about the IMF bailout and the 1978–79 Winter of Discontent. 'Never again' was the subtext of her messaging – but her argument was bigger: post-war Keynesianism, which aimed to grow the economy by increasing government and consumer spending, was deeply flawed. It needed to be replaced with tight control of the money supply, to stop inflation. Alongside that would be supply-side reforms that would make business more competitive.

Despite considerable social cost, Thatcher's reforms ultimately worked. For around two decades, Britain's economy grew faster than that of countries like France and Germany. Living standards rose, starting to close the gap with the US. Even during the economic turmoil of the Thatcher years, Britain remained attractive, because it offered political stability and welcomed international investment. But in these last two decades, something has started to gnaw at the foundations of that success. It is something that is not talked about enough as one of the root causes of lower growth, namely our rapidly rising national debt. In this chapter, I look at the impact of higher debt on economic growth, it's impact on public finances and the level of tax. Even though there is no quick fix, I show why it is important to put in place a longer-term plan to tackle it – and worth the political pain involved.

'The United Kingdom will always pay its way.' I used those words in an emergency broadcast to the nation on 17 October 2022. They still ring in my ears. It was only my fourth day as Chancellor. I had accepted the job on a Friday and worked frantically through the weekend with my Treasury team. We knew there was a risk of a further meltdown when the financial markets reopened on Monday morning. So I decided to issue a statement first thing on that morning, followed by another to Parliament in the afternoon. I had watched Boris Johnson deliver numerous broadcasts to the nation, sitting behind his desk with a Union flag behind him. Now it was my turn. It all felt rather surreal.

But it was reality. I had to deal with the consequences of losing the trust of the markets. That can happen very fast indeed, as my predecessor, Kwasi Kwarteng, found out. It can happen as more of a slow burn, as Rachel Reeves found out after me. That early turmoil shaped my whole time as Chancellor. As a result, there was always one person sitting at the table in my office who I listened to more carefully than anyone else: the Treasury's chief economic adviser. Her job was to tell me how markets would react to any announcement. I needed to know I was not tempting fate.

When I arrived, the job was being done by someone called Clare Lombardelli. She had a slightly reserved manner, but I soon realised it concealed a formidable mind and a wicked sense of humour. In the run-up to the 2022 Autumn Statement, she reassured me that markets would be on board with my plans. But with great foresight, she also said that the package to limit energy bills might keep inflation higher for longer. It was a difficult call: I needed to get inflation down but at the same time many people were scared about not being able to pay for their heating and electricity. I went ahead with the energy package, but Clare turned out to be right about inflation. On balance it was probably still right to proceed, but chancellors need to know the risks they are taking. That only comes if you have people around you willing to speak truth to power.

What made the decisions in that Autumn Statement so painful was something previous chancellors had not had to deal with, at least for many decades: the massive cost of the interest payments on our national debt. In the previous two years the level of debt had gone up by £350 billion, to fund support for families and businesses during the pandemic. At the same time, interest rates had risen dramatically following Russia's invasion of Ukraine. The result was that the total cost of servicing our debt had soared to over £110 billion a year or nearly 4% of GDP.[5] That's roughly double what we spend on defence and five times the cost of running the police. It means the average household now has to pay nearly £4,000 in tax every year just to fund debt interest payments.[6] In Germany, which has been more prudent, households pay only €1,100, just a quarter of what we pay in the UK.[7] In the G7, only American households pay more – but from much higher average incomes.[8]

The problem is made worse by the fact that the UK pays a higher rate of interest on its debt than others. We pay more than other G7 countries, and even more than Greece. That is partly because concerns about inflation means markets expect interest rates from the Bank of England to stay high. The markets have also started to question whether the government will be able to both deliver

Debt interest now costs the average UK household nearly £4,000 a year…

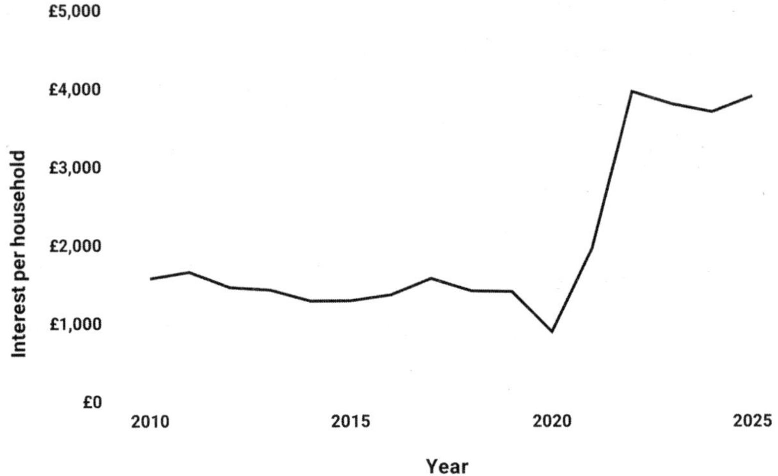

Source: ONS[9]

…more than in nearly any other G7 country

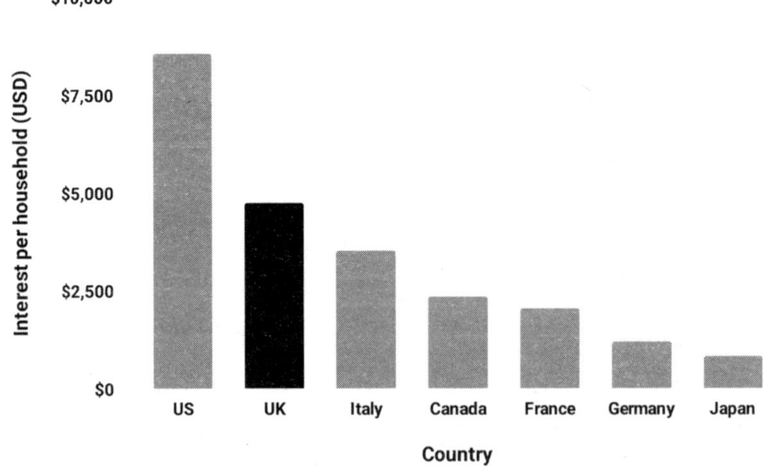

Source: US Census Bureau,[10] US Treasury;[11] ONS;[12] ECB,[13] Eurostat,[14] Government of Canada,[15] Statistics Canada,[16] e-Stat,[17] Ministry of Finance (Japan),[18] OECD[19]
Note: Figures are from the financial year of each country with the largest coverage of the 2024 calendar year.

growth and live within its means – or instead need to come back for more borrowing. UK pension funds are also more willing to buy their bonds from other countries, meaning there is less domestic demand for gilts. But things can go the other way too: as a result of my emergency broadcast promising that we would live within our means, UK bond yields fell 0.5% within a couple of days, reducing our costs by £6 billion a year.

Higher taxes, as we saw in the last chapter, mean less investment by business, lower growth and ultimately lower living standards. Some elements of public spending – building infrastructure or improving the education system – support our longer-term growth potential, but spending on debt interest has little such impact. So having a plan to reduce debt interest payments should be the starting point for any serious attempt to reduce the tax burden. It also reduces the risk of the economy being destabilised by shocks – or, indeed, the whims of James Carville's bond markets.

Why has debt grown so much? The root cause has not been a single economic shock but a succession of them. The global financial crisis, the pandemic and the Ukraine energy crisis were each treated as once-in-a-lifetime emergencies, deserving of special treatment when it comes to borrowing, as with the first and second world wars. But if you increase debt in an emergency, you need to pay it back in the good times. This time, with crises coming thick and fast, that didn't happen. As a result our net debt (which accounts for government assets as well as liabilities) has risen from 32% of GDP at the turn of the century to 95% today. We are not alone: in the US, net debt is 98%, in France it is 108%, in Italy it is 123% and in Japan it is 134%.[20] Across the OECD advanced economies, gross debt has risen from an average of 70% of GDP in 2007 to 110% today.[21] Germany and Canada, who have kept their debt at much more manageable levels, stand out as honourable exceptions.

UK debt is in the middle of the pack but has been growing the fastest

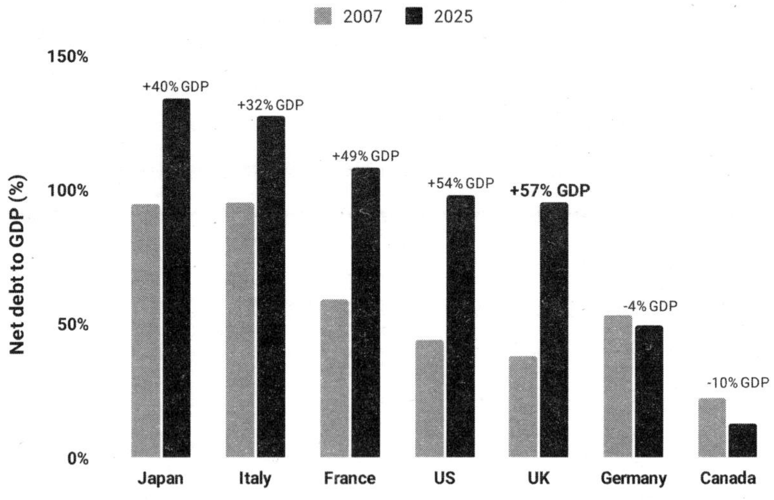

Source: IMF[22]

Nor, unfortunately, is that the end of the bad news, because the official debt number doesn't tell the whole story when it comes to our liabilities. As well as pay back its debts, the state must also fund the pensions of civil servants, doctors, nurses and other public sector workers. For many decades, instead of saving the pension contributions deducted from monthly salaries, governments have been spending them as if they were tax receipts. To their credit, local councils have behaved differently, building up large pension funds which cover the pensions of former employees. But the result of such central government profligacy is that taxpayers have to find nearly £55 billion a year to fund the pensions of retired public sector workers – or £2,000 a year in tax for the average household.[23] If the cost of that liability was added to our national debt as a capital sum, it would more than double it. Again, other countries are in the same boat: France, Germany and Italy are in a similar position to us, with Japan and the US doing only slightly better. Within the G7, only Canada has been properly virtuous in fully funding its public sector pensions. Over time, it will save Canadian taxpayers a fortune.

Finding more than £110 billion for debt interest and a further £55 billion for public sector pensions has made managing public finances extremely challenging. Demography and the need to spend more on defence add further to the pressure. Successive chancellors, including me, have found we have had to raise taxes and cut spending in order to maintain the confidence of the markets. In my 2022 Autumn Statement I had to fill a black hole of £72 billion. My successor has also found things challenging, to say the least.

But the biggest risk of all is not the impact on public finances but what happens to growth. When every household pays nearly £4,000 every year for debt interest and £2,000 a year for public sector pensions, it amounts to the equivalent of 19p on income tax.[24] That is a big anchor-drag on the economy. Imagine the additional spending in the economy, the extra profits businesses would generate and the investment that would flow without families being burdened in such a way. That's why, as well as being in a tax doom loop, we also risk falling into a debt doom loop: ever lower growth generating ever higher debt. How do we break out of it?

In 2003, Warren Buffett wrote the following in an article published in *Fortune*.[25] More than two decades on, his argument has not dated.

Take a wildly fanciful trip with me to two isolated, side-by-side islands of equal size, Squanderville and Thriftville. Land is the only capital asset on these islands, and their communities are primitive, needing only food and producing only food. Working eight hours a day, in fact, each inhabitant can produce enough food to sustain himself or herself. And for a long time that's how things go along. On each island everybody works the prescribed eight hours a day, which means that each society is self-sufficient.

Eventually, though, the industrious citizens of Thriftville decide to do some serious saving and investing, and they start to work sixteen hours a day. In this mode they continue to live off the food they produce in eight hours of work but begin exporting an equal amount to their one and only trading outlet, Squanderville.

The citizens of Squanderville are ecstatic about this turn of events, since they can now live their lives free from toil but eat as well as ever. Oh, yes, there's a quid pro quo – but to the Squanders, it seems harmless: All that the Thrifts want in exchange for their food is Squanderbonds (which are denominated, naturally, in Squanderbucks).

Over time Thriftville accumulates an enormous amount of these bonds, which at their core represent claim checks on the future output of Squanderville. A few pundits in Squanderville smell trouble coming. They foresee that for the Squanders both to eat and to pay off – or simply service – the debt they're piling up will eventually require them to work more than eight hours a day. But the residents of Squanderville are in no mood to listen to such doomsaying.

Meanwhile, the citizens of Thriftville begin to get nervous. Just how good, they ask, are the IOUs of a shiftless island? So the Thrifts change strategy: Though they continue to hold some bonds, they sell most of them to Squanderville residents for Squanderbucks and use the proceeds to buy Squanderville land. And eventually the Thrifts own all of Squanderville.

At that point, the Squanders are forced to deal with an ugly equation: They must now not only return to working eight hours a day in order to eat – they have nothing left to trade – but must also work additional hours to service their debt and pay Thriftville rent on the land so imprudently sold. In effect, Squanderville has been colonized by purchase rather than conquest.

Few countries heeded the moral of this story – which is why many, like the UK, are on their way to becoming Squanderville. Even the US is beginning to look vulnerable. Until recently, it has been able to rely on the reserve status of the dollar to maintain the attractiveness of US debt to investors. But increasingly markets are making the US, too, pay a premium for its rising debt. After the financial crisis, US Treasury yields plummeted to 2.25% as the dollar was seen as a safe haven. Today the yield – and therefore the cost to US taxpayers – has more than doubled. Despite three interest rate cuts in Donald Trump's first year, the price of ten-year US Treasury yields did not fall.

That is leading some commentators to predict a major market correction caused by fears that countries will default on their debts. Ray Dalio, founder of Bridgewater Associates, the world's largest hedge fund, suggests that short-term debt cycles last around six years, after which governments increase borrowing to avoid a recession. But that borrowing in turn feeds into a larger debt cycle, which produces a 'mega' correction every eighty years or so – a catastrophe big enough to end empires or civilisations. The last one followed the Second World War, and Dalio believes the next one is already overdue.

Most people think that is unlikely. Technically, a country's ability to fund its national debt is linked not just to its GDP but to the difference between its growth rate and the interest rate it pays. Theoretically, it can continue to finance a larger debt if interest rates are lower than the economy's underlying growth rate – something that, thankfully, continues to be the case for many. But even if we are not on the brink of a sovereign debt crisis, high debt interest payments push up tax and act as a massive anchor-drag on growth. Boiling the frog more slowly doesn't mean it escapes its fate.

That all came home to me at a pizza-making course in Sicily, of all places.

It was summer half term. I was staying in Taormina with my family. The life of a Chancellor revolves around the two 'fiscal events' you are required to deliver to Parliament every year – a budget and a Spring or Autumn Statement. The March budget was safely behind me and had landed well. The Autumn Statement was a long way off. I had every reason to expect an uninterrupted holiday.

A few days after arriving, we decided to go on a pizza-making course. Early one evening, the five of us arrived at the appointed restaurant and joined a small group of other tourists. We put on aprons and set about the first stage, kneading dough for the pizza base. We then loaded up our ingredients before placing them onto spatulas and sliding them into the wood-fired oven. Just as we sat down with a glass of wine to enjoy the fruits of our labour, I glanced at my phone. There was a message from Prime Minister Rishi

Sunak. He was angry because he thought the Treasury had not supplied him with some information he had requested. His tone rather startled me, because our relations had been generally cordial. All prime ministers and chancellors have disagreements, but we had never exchanged a cross word. What had gone wrong?

The cause of the friction was an inflation shock. A week earlier, April's inflation figures had been published. Headline inflation had fallen from its November peak of 11.1% to 8.7%. But markets had hoped for a bigger drop and noted that core inflation – the underlying inflation rate that strips out energy and food prices – had risen. Clare Lombardelli had turned out to be spot on. As a result, markets had concluded that inflation would be more persistent and interest rates would stay higher for longer. The cost of servicing government debt rose sharply. Both Rishi and I knew this meant trouble for the Autumn Statement. Having just put up taxes and cut spending, we faced the prospect of having to come back for more.

But I had a solution. A few days earlier, I had written a private note to Rishi explaining what I believed we should do. Market movements had pushed up the cost of government debt, leaving us with a whopping £14-billion hole in the numbers. Expected public sector pay awards would add a further £6 billion – the equivalent of having to increase income tax by 3p. So I proposed much-needed welfare reforms to address the fiscal hole and help businesses find workers. Getting back into work would also be good, I strongly believed, for the individuals involved.

However, my letter failed to reassure. Reasonably enough, Rishi didn't want to talk about solutions until he understood the problem. Why was inflation so much stickier than anticipated, and indeed worse than in countries like France, Germany and the US? He had asked the Treasury for information and not got what he wanted. Hence the angry text.

I decided to call him. I extracted myself from the pizza-making class and tried to find somewhere private in the open-air restaurant where I could not be overheard. I ended up perching awkwardly in a corner with my head to the wall. The only people who might have overheard me were an American couple from New York and I was pretty sure they had no idea who I was. Twenty minutes and one cold pizza later, the prime minister realised that the Chancellor and his officials were not being obstructive and had genuinely tried to get him what he wanted. I got a second, friendlier text later that evening to mend fences.

But the truth is both of us were spooked. Our plan to win the next election by getting bad news out of the way early had been spectacularly blown off course. Not by any decision we had made, but by the markets changing their mind about the UK's inflation prospects.

Rishi focused hard on trying to understand the problem. Attention to detail is one of his best qualities, and when I returned to London, we had a series of meetings with the governor of the Bank of England and his team to get to the bottom of things. In order to avoid creating a public panic, the governor, Andrew Bailey, never came in person to Downing Street, and instead video-called in. He was his usual genial self, always knowing how to strike the right note with politicians. The deputy governor, Ben Broadbent, was more dry, but spoke with the steely authority of someone who knew his numbers: on the screen, he pulled up some compelling charts that suggested inflation would start falling soon. It wasn't quite 'don't panic, Captain Mainwaring', perhaps more of a wise owl telling upstart politicians to calm down. It had the intended effect and we did. More importantly, Ben turned out to be right. But our borrowing costs remained high. The damage had been done.

For the UK and many other countries, just as for Buffett's Squanderville, the chickens are coming home to roost. Abnormally low interest rates made debt affordable for the first two decades of this century. Now, that golden period – when many say we should have converted more of our debt into longer-term maturity – is over. If a rise in interest rates causes gilt yields to rise by just 0.5%, government interest costs increase by about £10 billion a year, nearly an extra penny on income tax. The week before my pizza-making course, such an increase had wiped out all my headroom. Exactly the same thing happened to Rachel Reeves in January 2025 (without the pizza).

Before their election, the incoming Labour government assumed that a large majority and a well-publicised belief in fiscal prudence would be enough to bring stability to the markets. But because we remain stuck in debt and tax doom loops, politicians' words are not enough. Markets need to see inflation falling, disciplined public spending and a credible growth plan.

How, then, do we get out of the hole? You can't just wait for economic growth, because even with the right policies, it takes time. So in the meantime, it is essential to control the growth of public spending. As mentioned, demographic pressures and the need to spend more on defence make that particularly hard. For the UK, welfare reform is probably the only area where significant savings can be found in the medium term. The total cost of welfare is currently a little over 10% of GDP, with about half spent on pensioners and half on working-age adults.[26] Its costs have ballooned – and are still growing.

When it comes to working-age and disability benefits, many of the issues seem to date from the pandemic. The overall bill and the number of people claiming were both falling until 2019, but have since mushroomed. If we found a way to return it to 2019 levels, even accounting for inflation the savings would rise to a hefty £56 billion a year after five years.[27] Given we are no longer in a pandemic, that doesn't seem an unreasonable objective for a parliament. But as the current government has found, welfare reform is never easy. In the next chapter, I look in detail at how it can actually be achieved.

The cost of pensions has also risen to an unsustainable level. Some of the increase is unavoidable because of demographics. Some of it is also necessary if we want to stop the poorest pensioners falling into poverty. But with the triple-lock guarantee (the commitment to uprate pensions by the highest of inflation, earnings growth or 2.5%) we have chosen a very expensive way to do so. Pensioners are now the only population group with a guarantee from the government that their basic income will increase significantly more than inflation or earnings.

Ultimately, it is a fake guarantee. Because of the pressures on the rest of the public purse, we effectively end up funding the triple lock by additional borrowing. In other words, its costs will ultimately have to be repaid by the children and grandchildren of the very pensioners who benefit from it. If they knew that their own family was incurring debt to pay for their pension, many would not support it. Far better to replace it with a more modest but still generous guarantee that pensions will increase by either earnings or inflation. That would give pensioners cast-iron protection against prices going up as well as saving up to £13 billion a year. I didn't bite the bullet on this when I was in office and I know it's easy for me to say this with the benefit of hindsight. But we cannot go on ducking a moral and economic necessity.

Proper welfare reform – covering both pensions and working-age benefits – is therefore our best hope of getting out of the tax and debt doom loops that are doing so much damage to our prospects. It would also allow us to commit to a new fiscal rule that really would bring down our debt burden – unlike the current ones, which pretend to reduce debt but don't in practice. That fiscal rule should state very simply that overall growth in public spending will always be less than the growth in the economy. In other words, we will never increase spending beyond our capacity to pay for it.

Economists would describe this as something that committed the government to regular 'primary surpluses', meaning that government spending, excluding debt interest, is less than overall tax receipts. As a new fiscal rule, it would need to be designed in a way that allowed governments flexibility to borrow more in a crisis. It would also need to be robust enough to avoid being gamed by politicians who continually promise, like St Augustine, to be virtuous sometime in the future. But in the process, we would start to move the economy to an Asian model in which growth is driven by investment as much as by consumption. This should ultimately mean better public services – as any visitor to Japan, South Korea or Singapore will attest. But investment has to come from somewhere.

That's why, if we want to grow like Asian tiger economies, we will need to do something else they generally do much better than us: we need to get better at saving.

The most important reason for most people to save is for their pension. That's why in the UK, employees and employers are mandated to save no less than 8% of the employee's salary between them for pension contributions. It's a start, but most actuaries say it's not nearly enough if people are to have the lifestyle they expect in retirement. Other countries agree. That's why pension savings are higher elsewhere: 12% in Australia, 12.4% in the USA and 18.6% in Germany. Although the post-war economic growth of Asian tiger economies is impressive, for cultural reasons Australia is probably a better model for us. Over the last two decades the Aussies have put in place a simple system that both mandates and encourages higher levels of saving. Unlike our complicated system involving a different pension pot for every employer you work for, Australians only have one pension pot. It moves with them when they change jobs. There is then fierce competition between the pension fund providers ('supas' or superannuation funds) to get the best returns for savers who are free to switch whenever they choose.

The simplicity of the system means there is a much larger incentive to top up your own pension. It also has an added benefit for the Australian stock market of turning pension pot-holders into retail investors. Over the last five years, Australian pension funds have generated an average return 1.6% higher than their British counterparts. Over a forty-year working life, this produces a pension pot nearly double the size of those in the UK.

Moving to such a model was the underlying purpose of the Mansion House and Solvency II reforms of 2022 and 2023. Currently, only 6% of the UK's £3.2 trillion pension pool is invested in British 'productive assets', e.g. investments in infrastructure and companies at home rather than bonds or overseas investments. The reforms I introduced were designed to consolidate around thirty thousand often tiny pension funds into a smaller number of more professional funds able to get higher returns for savers. But really embracing Australian-style reform would also involve using auto-enrolment to increase the proportion of people's salaries invested in their pension pots. According to Oxford Economics, doing so could add 0.7% to GDP over a decade by unlocking £220 billion of investment.[28] There are caveats to that number: it depends on the investment being additional and other economic conditions remaining broadly similar. But given it represents less than 10% of the total pension pool, it does not feel over-ambitious.

> £220 billion of additional investment, worth 0.7% of extra GDP, could be unlocked by fully rolling out the Mansion House reforms and increasing pension savings to 12% through auto-enrolment.
>
> **Source:** Oxford Economics

As part of such reforms, we should also follow another close ally, Canada, and start saving the money public sector workers put into their pensions rather than spending it. Such a change could not happen overnight but can happen over time, as indeed happened in Canada. Ten years ago, the Hutton reforms increased public sector employee contributions and linked pensions to someone's career average rather than final salary. It is now time to go further, starting with a ban on new entrants to the current pension schemes. New civil servants should be enrolled in contributory pension schemes, just as employees in the private sector are.

None of these policies are easy. We have accumulated high levels of debt over many decades. Weaning ourselves off the habit won't happen overnight. But, ultimately, following a path to lower debt will be easier for any Chancellor than the alternative, which is being forced into continuous tax rises and spending cuts in budget after budget. And the longer-term benefits are obvious: lower debt, lower debt interest, more investment, more growth and healthier public finances. As well as avoiding the fate of Squanderville.

All chancellors have a moment every year when a public, independent verdict is delivered on their performance. It is rather less glamorous than either *Britain's Got Talent* or *Strictly Come Dancing*. The IMF visits the country, as part of what is called the Article IV Consultation, and gives a press conference on how the country is doing. My moment of truth came on 22 April 2024, just hours before Rishi Sunak announced the July general election.

In the event, the IMF's managing director Kristalina Georgieva was generous: after the turbulence of tax rises, spending cuts, 11% inflation and a technical recession, she said a soft landing for the economy was in sight. Inflation had come right down, the recession was over and growth was coming back. For the reasons we have discussed, she warned that debt was too high across major economies. But she recognised the difficult decisions that had been made and urged us to stay the course. The following month, inflation fell to the target 2% rate and Britain's growth rate rose to become the fastest in the G7. But it was bittersweet news. We were soon to be bundled out of office in the worst defeat for the Conservatives in their long history.

In that election campaign, there was a lot of discussion about tax but little about debt. That was wrong, for the reasons I explain in this chapter. High taxes and debt interest payments reduce investment and penalise risk-taking. That's why the path to long-term growth needs to involve both lower tax and lower debt. With those core objectives established, it is now time to look at the reforms that will make it easier to get there. And we will start with one of the most obvious: getting more people into work.

CONCLUSIONS

- ► The cost of servicing our debt – higher in the UK than in any other G7 country – has itself become a source of instability for both public finances and the economy.

- ► There needs to be a new fiscal rule that says that public spending will never increase faster than economic growth.

- ► We should move to a growth model led by investment rather than consumption. Part of the way to do that would be to adopt Australian and Canadian-style pension reform, with single pension pots, higher levels of saving and better returns through boosting investment into productive parts of the economy.

3

Work

On the evening of 15 December 2022, I arrived back late to Downing Street. I had just been to my son's Christmas carol concert. Before going up to the flat, Lucia and I took our dog Poppy out to the garden. Apart from a few security staff, the building was empty. We walked past the deserted Cabinet Room and a silent prime minister's office. Then, dog in tow, we headed down the famous staircase whose walls are adorned with the portraits of former prime ministers. Seeing them always made my heart miss a beat.

At the bottom of the staircase, we passed an imposing globe gifted to Margaret Thatcher by French president François Mitterrand. Global Britain, I thought. Then I opened the door out into the Rose Garden. It was a crisp, dark evening. I savoured the moment. After a turbulent few weeks, it was now *our* garden. I was still pinching myself at the thought of living in Downing Street – perhaps a dose of imposter syndrome. Like the building, the garden was deserted. Poppy raced around excitedly. We walked around and back up to the Chancellor's flat through a hidden staircase.

I had only just moved in. The flat, previously occupied by Boris Johnson and Liz Truss, had been in a terrible state. Only security-cleared contractors were allowed to work on the building, so after a painfully expensive repaint and new carpets, the Hunt family had finally moved into their new home. My start in the second most powerful job in government could not have been more tumultuous.

But far from switching off ahead of Christmas, my mind was preoccupied with the next challenge. I would soon deliver my first budget. Budgets are the biggest moment of the parliamentary year for one simple reason: their contents affect every single family in the country. However bad the economic news, there is always hope – even expectation – that a Chancellor will produce a rabbit out of a hat, a surprise giveaway for a lucky group of voters. Managing expectations carefully becomes essential if you want to avoid disappointment on the day.

And I had a big problem. There was no money. I only had £9 billion of headroom before I would breach my fiscal rules. That may seem like a lot of money, but it is less than 1% of all government spending – a tiny margin, and far less than the typical swing caused by market forecasts changing from one budget to the next. By leaving behind what was in fact the smallest margin the OBR had ever recorded, I had gambled that things would get better.

But whatever happened, I had to produce a responsible budget. The most scrutinised parliamentary occasion of the year needs to satisfy multiple audiences: MPs, experts in the media, the public and, of course, the markets. I also had a self-imposed stricture of my own: at budgets, chancellors briefly become the most powerful person in the country. I knew I wouldn't be doing the job for ever. So I promised myself I would use those brief moments of power to put in place, by hook or by crook, at least one big, long-term change that stood the test of time. In other words, I would not just muddle through. But with no money, what on earth could I do?

I needed a plan.

In discussions over the Autumn Statement, I had noticed how sensitive economic forecasts were to migration levels. A larger workforce meant more GDP, which in turn meant more tax receipts. At the time, we were anticipating an increase in the official net migration forecasts from 245,000 a year to 315,000 a year. That change alone would add around £7 billion to tax receipts. For that reason, the Treasury – unlike much of the country – has usually favoured migration.

But what would happen, I wondered, if instead of relying on migration we got more of our home-grown workforce into work? Those extra tax receipts were based on the impact of an extra 30,000 people joining the national workforce every year (because not all new arrivals end up working). If I could get the same numbers into work from our domestic workforce, we could boost GDP without the additional costs and concerns associated with migration. It was also the right thing to do on principle. Road haulier boss Eddie Stobart expressed it perfectly when he said that 'the only place that success comes before work is in the dictionary'.[1]

Over the Christmas break, I put together what I called a 'Get Britain Working' budget. In our first meeting of the New Year, I told a group of rather sceptical Treasury officials that I wanted to increase the size of our domestic workforce by no less than one million people. There are 34 million people employed in the UK, so it was a significant jump. Importantly, it would more than make up for the half a million who had dropped out of work during the pandemic.

What made it even more of a challenge was that I didn't want my plan to become reality in the distant future – I wanted it to happen quickly. A fiscal period is defined as five years, so any changes that take effect within that period could end up being counted in the OBR's numbers. And I had done the maths. If we got a million people back to work, it would increase GDP by about 2%. That would mean tax revenues rising by around £30 billion a year, a decent amount even for a Chancellor. I might then be able to afford other things: greater defence spending, perhaps; or training more doctors; or tax cuts to grow the economy. A million more people in the domestic workforce would also answer the post-Brexit question of where new workers would come from once the UK was outside the single market.

So I asked my Treasury team to list all the barriers that stopped people working: a broken benefits system that traps people on welfare; abuse of sickness benefits; pension tax anomalies that make people retire early. Last but not least was the prohibitive cost of childcare. Officials were slightly overwhelmed by the scale of the ambition. They didn't say so directly, but clearly thought I was being unrealistic – describing the plans as 'bold' and 'unprecedented', civil servant-speak for totally impossible. To their credit, however, they were up for the challenge. One formidable official, Vanessa MacDougall, set up teams to look at the four key areas: welfare reform, disability benefit reform, pension tax reform and childcare.

Over a very short period they then did a huge amount of work. Excluding pensioners, eleven million adults are not in work, of whom three million are students. Our focus was on the remaining eight million. How could we get a million of that eight million back to work? We looked at numerous ways to help people not working for health reasons. They included reforming the GP 'fit note' system through which people are signed off work; incentivising employers to provide more occupational health to employees who get sick; boosting enrolment in a programme called Individual Placement and Support; helping people to stop smoking; and even finding ways to prevent obesity, which is linked to unemployment. We also considered tougher measures, such as time-limiting benefits and requiring people to accept jobs they were offered.

For people with disabilities, we considered another set of ideas including expanding a programme called Disability Kickstart and reforming a new benefit called the personal independence payment (PIP). For young parents, we looked into expanding childcare, which had become so expensive that many were simply forced to quit work to look after young kids, perhaps by extending the free thirty-hour offer so that it would start when a child was nine months old rather than three years old. Alongside it, we analysed the impact of paying childcare fees upfront to those on benefit so they could get straight into work when offered a job. For older people, we investigated pension tax distortions which were encouraging many people, especially doctors, to retire in their fifties. For those changing jobs later in life, we looked at mid-life 'MOTs', skills courses and bootcamps. And for those who had already retired, we explored a new type of apprenticeship to get them back to work, called 'returnerships'.

Every option was carefully costed. And those costs varied dramatically. Many cost around £1,000 per person helped into work. Others – quickly discarded – came closer to £100,000. We also looked at the financial benefits that would follow. Getting a disabled person back into work, for example, was estimated to cost about £7,000, but that then turned into £4,000 of additional tax revenues every year, obviously a good deal for the taxpayer as well as for the individual involved.

But there was a catch. In order to afford any of the items in the programme, we had to persuade the OBR to count the longer-term economic benefits in their forecasts. That proved a nightmare. Officials warned me that the watchdog had never previously been willing to take into account new supply-side policies in a budget. Indeed, the organisation had been set up to cast a sceptical eye over chancellors trumpeting the impact of new policies. But ignoring or sidelining the OBR was not an option: we all knew that my predecessor, Kwasi Kwarteng, lost his job after doing just that.

Relations got off to a rocky start when the OBR informed us its forecasts had got worse. We might even lose the tiny headroom I had at the end of the Autumn Statement. That would mean more tax rises or spending cuts. I probably shouldn't have been surprised, as I had been warned that could happen. But this was my first budget. It looked like I had gambled and lost. I felt a bit like Gordon Brown, when he reportedly told Tony Blair: 'You stole my f***ing budget.'

Nor was my 'Get Britain Working' plan making any headway. The granite-hard boffins at the OBR were highly sceptical. They said they would not count welfare reform unless the legislation to implement it had actually been passed – something they knew would be impossible before the budget. For the childcare or pension reforms they demanded academic studies from other countries that proved beyond doubt they would work. That wasn't easy to find, but Vanessa and her team did their best, digging out every possible shred of evidence they could discover from countries like Denmark. I invited OBR delegations to No 11 for breakfast to try and get them over the line. They were courteous, ate the croissants and drank the coffee. But they were not convinced.

Then an even bigger problem emerged, this time from next door. As I've said, Rishi Sunak and I had a good working relationship. But that didn't mean we always agreed – and this was one such occasion. He was deeply sceptical about childcare reforms because of their upfront cost. He made it clear that he wanted them taken out of the package. My first budget was unravelling before it was born.

So against all my instincts, I made contingency plans for a 'boring' budget. I dusted down minor measures that could be 'bigged up' on the day. Perhaps I could extend a temporary full-expensing tax break for businesses by three years? Or I could announce some bold regulatory reforms? Or unveil plans (again) for an east–west rail link between Oxford and Cambridge? We also looked at doubling NHS doctor training places, something close to my heart. I knew a budget with such small measures would sink without trace. But with any luck, I might get through the day.

With just over two weeks to go, we reached the end game. The OBR point-blank refused to count any of the welfare reforms. It was prepared to make only a small increase in workforce projections because of the childcare and pension tax reforms. Instead of the million people into work I originally wanted, it was only prepared to count a measly 110,000. My officials said I should be pleased, as it was the first time it had ever scored a growth policy 'dynamically'. But I was crestfallen.

At the same time, Rishi dug in further on childcare, determined to scrap the package altogether. In a difficult meeting, I headed that off with one reluctantly-agreed concession: we would make our final decision after seeing the GDP impact on public finances of getting more young parents into work.

Then at the last moment, the wind changed. OBR modelling came back showing that the impact on the economy of getting even a miserly 110,000 people into work was actually quite significant. It increased overall output by 0.2%, which added enough tax revenues to reduce the annual cost of the childcare reforms from £5.3 billion to just £600 million. Rishi reluctantly agreed the package could stay in. Many of the other measures Vanessa and her team had worked up were also included, although most of the welfare reforms had to wait until the Autumn Statement. With just six days to go, the budget was saved.

On the day itself, my brother Charlie, bravely battling cancer, came to see me off from Downing Street. Chemotherapy had taken his hair. He watched with Lucia and the kids as I held up the famous Red Box in front of the cameras outside the door of No 11. He then came to see me deliver the budget in Parliament. It wasn't the revolutionary package I had wanted. But it was consequential, the first ever budget focused squarely on boosting labour supply without resorting to migration. And the childcare reforms have stood the test of time.

Nonetheless, it nearly unravelled. After my predecessor's mini-budget, Rachel Reeves, then Shadow Chancellor, was looking for blood. She disagreed with the abolition of the cap on the pensions lifetime allowance and announced Labour's intention to reverse it. As often happens, a relatively small measure – rather than the much bigger childcare reforms – then became the focus of media attention. Would I be pressured into a U-turn, every Chancellor's nightmare? George Osborne had to do one on the 'pasty tax', leading to his budget being described as an 'omnishambles'. Philip Hammond backtracked on the extension of national insurance to the self-employed. Rachel Reeves herself ended up reversing cuts to winter fuel payments and disability benefits. Because such reversals damage a Chancellor's credibility, all of us now spend hours ahead of budgets kicking the tyres of every measure, big or small, to identify any weak links. But we had not predicted a battle on the lifetime allowance.

For a moment, it looked like I too would join the club of chancellors forced into a U-turn. Then, extraordinarily, I was helped out by an old adversary. When I was Health Secretary, the doctors' union, the BMA, had fought my plans with a bitter, year-long junior doctors' strike. It had lost that battle – and to say my name was mud in BMA circles would be putting it politely. But to my astonishment, the morning after the budget, their spokesman told the media that doctors had already been in touch to say they were cancelling their retirement plans and coming back to work because of my new pension reforms. With the NHS onside, Labour's gambit failed. A year later they quietly dropped their pledge to reverse the measure.

I learnt a lot from the process, not least the need to start planning early. Every hour we could get to assemble the evidence for childcare reforms was crucial – without it the OBR would not have counted them in their forecast. I learnt the importance of aiming high: my ambition to get a million people back to work was mercilessly whittled down. Radical ambitions became more incremental improvements. But if I had started more cautiously, there would have been no improvements at all. I also realised how difficult it is to make long-term changes when the OBR forecasts vary so dramatically, often from week to week.

*

In this chapter, I focus on how to get more people into work, the core purpose of that budget. Some of the reforms considered are politically challenging. But they are worth the effort, because doing so is one of the fastest ways to improve public finances and speed up growth. I will consider incentives in the welfare system, and why its failure to support people into work raises demand for migration. I will look at the best ways to reduce poverty, and explain why the way we measure it makes sensible reforms harder. And as with every idea discussed in this book, I will demonstrate that there are solutions that are practical and deliverable. They also have a profoundly positive effect on attitudes towards work, enterprise and risk-taking.

It is important to start by saying that, overall, the UK does not do too badly when it comes to the proportion of working-age adults who are in work. At around three quarters, it is higher than in the US or France, although lower than in Germany, Denmark or Australia. Our relatively flexible labour market has kept unemployment low – though recent increases to employers' national insurance, the national living wage and new 'workers' rights' are eroding a hitherto strong record.

But even though our labour market is still more flexible than in many countries, around a quarter of adults are not in work. Where we seem to do worst is the number of people on long-term sickness benefits, which has now risen to nearly three million.[2] Of those, nearly a million are paid more than someone would earn working full time on the national living wage. On top of which, the UK has also failed to tackle employability issues for school leavers who do not go on to university. A disappointing 200,000 teenagers leave school in England every year without GCSEs in maths and English.[3]

Nearly half of them are unable to read well enough to manage daily life.[4] The result is a continued demand from businesses for migrants: in the last five years, the number of people born outside of the UK in work has gone up by 1.6 million, while the number of UK nationals in work fell by 400,000.[5]

If we want to boost living standards, we need to do things differently. As we have discussed, economists say the closest link to higher living standards is not higher overall GDP but higher GDP per head. A government can boost an economy's overall size by increasing migration, because additional people create additional jobs – but migration also comes with costs: new arrivals will need health care, housing and benefits, and not all of them work. If we want higher living standards, getting more people into work is far more effective.

To see how we can do this better, it is worth looking at some of our neighbours. Denmark, Iceland and Sweden have generous childcare policies,[6] which means fewer mums give up work when they have children.[7] If we increased our female participation rates to the average of those countries, over a million more women would be in work in the UK.[8] At the same time, Scandinavian countries generally have tougher welfare systems. In Denmark, for example, employers are able to hire and fire with relatively few restrictions. There is not even a national minimum wage. But there is immediate support, including retraining, for those who lose their job. The Danish system has seen its employment rate of disabled people get as high as 60% in recent years – compared to a peak of 55% in the UK during the same period. If we were to match Denmark, over 600,000 more disabled people would be in work. That would have a major impact on the morale and life-chances of people coping with disadvantage – as well as being much better for the economy and public finances.[9]

Another near-neighbour, Switzerland, gets to a similar result with more effective vocational training. That means more young people get jobs. The Swiss also make an effort to encourage part-time jobs, something especially helpful for parents. As a result, Switzerland manages to get nearly 5% more of its working-age population into work. If our employment level matched that of the Swiss, just over two million more people would be in work – double the ambition for my original 'Get Britain Working' plan.[10] More people in work generally means less poverty. Ways of measuring poverty vary, but according to national statistics, the UK has 18% of the population below the official poverty line, compared to 17% in Switzerland, 16% in Sweden, 13% in Denmark and just 9% in Iceland. If anything, those numbers understate the difference, when you consider that the poverty line in those countries is set at a much higher level than in the UK because of their higher levels of prosperity.[11]

Greater output per head in certain small European countries is often used to make the case for higher taxes. But a more likely reason many such countries have higher levels of prosperity is that they are better at getting people into work. The proportion of working-age adults in work is 75% in the UK compared to 77% in Denmark and Sweden, 80% in Switzerland and 85% in Iceland. The OECD table below demonstrates how prosperity and employment levels are connected. High employment levels also correlate with higher wages, suggesting a link with productivity. The big exception, interestingly, is the US, where the employment rate is low but GDP per head is high, perhaps caused by higher productivity and longer hours worked by those in work.

More prosperous countries tend to have more people in work…

OECD countries, 2023, select countries highlighted

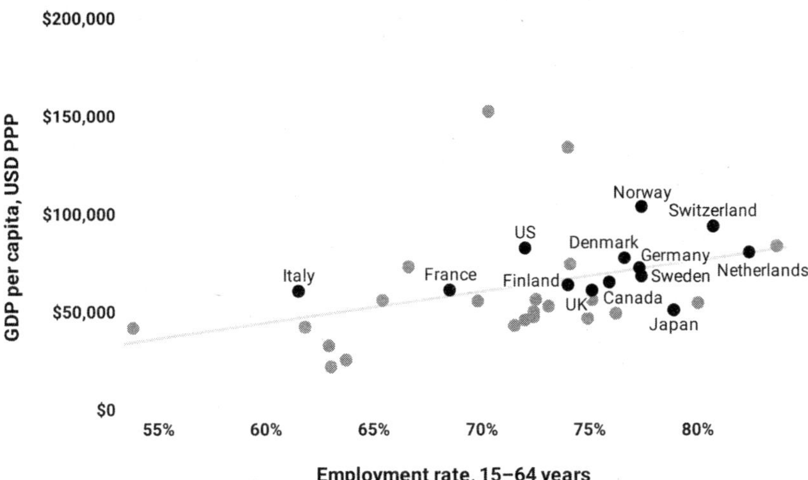

Source: OECD[12]

Note: South Korea not included as some data was not available at the time. GDP per capita data displayed in current prices.

…and also higher wages

OECD countries, 2023, select countries highlighted

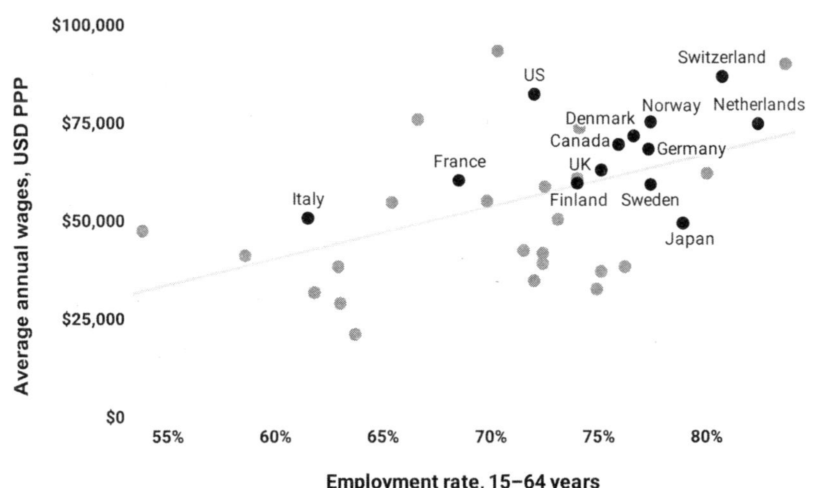

Source: OECD[13]

Note: South Korea not included as some data was not available at the time. Wage data converted by OECD to 2024 prices.

To understand why our welfare system needs reforming, it is worth following the journey of someone who loses their job. Let's take, as an example, a man who hurts his back in a warehouse job. After statutory sick pay runs out, his employer may well let him go. He would then need to sign up for universal credit (UC). It is a stressful process, which requires him to show he is constantly looking for work. At the end of the process, he is awarded £92 of UC per week.

But this is just one of the benefits he will soon be claiming. He could boost that £92 with what is called the 'health component' of UC – an additional allowance for people who find working or looking for work difficult. For that he will need to get a GP to agree that his back condition really does limit his ability to work. If he is then classified as 'Limited Capability for Work-Related Activity' (LCWRA), he won't have to look for work and his weekly income will go up by a further £97.

Meanwhile, the pain in his back also counts as a disability, so he can also apply for the main disability benefit, PIP. Depending on the severity of the condition, this could add between £29 and £187 to his support payment.[14] The extra amount is not means-tested and involves no requirement to look for a job.

Finally, because he is on benefits, he gets help with his rent. This will vary depending on where a claimant lives and the size of the house. In London, rent could be as much as £332 a week for a one-bedroom home. The average across the country is £150 a week or £97 a week in shared accommodation.[15]

Overall, then, his benefits journey has resulted in a package worth up to £377 a week *plus* his rent. In central London that could bring the weekly total to £710, the equivalent of a job with a gross salary of £46,000 per annum.[16] Even in a city with much lower living costs, say Newcastle, the total benefits package could be £491 per week, the equivalent of a job paying £31,000 a year.[17] Meanwhile, someone working forty hours a week on minimum wage would earn less – perhaps significantly less – than that, just £488 a week before tax or £419 net of taxes.[18]

How someone on benefit ends up with more than the minimum wage

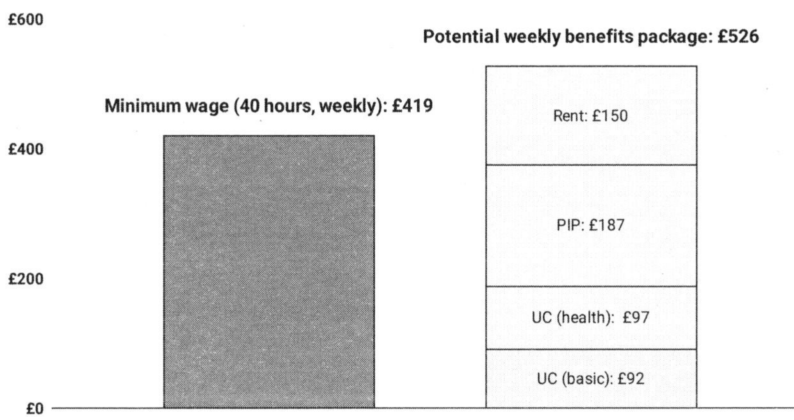

Note: Calculations for take-home pay were based on the tax rates at the time of writing. The benefit figures also do not account for any possible reductions in council tax that may also be granted, which would add to the value of the benefits package.

Our claimant may well need every penny of those awards. Indeed, he would probably prefer to be working (as more than half the people on LCWRA say they would). About one third of UC claimants are in fact in work – which the structure is designed to encourage. But once you are inside the system, it becomes highly risky to look for a job. If that part-time work is taken as evidence that you are capable of more work, you could be moved to a less generous benefits package. If your anxiety or depression improves, you could lose your PIP. In the worst case, you could lose not just your benefits but also your home if the rent subsidy is withdrawn.

For many, it is just not worth the risk. And the longer they are out of work, the harder it becomes to find it, as they lose contact with networks of people who are in work and could help them. So a system designed to offer more help to those genuinely unable to work instead creates incentives for people to classify themselves as incapable of working – and stay that way. Every single day, 1,000 people are assessed as not needing to look for work (e.g. moved into LCWRA).[19] Only 1% of them leave it every month, with most remaining stuck there for years, if not permanently.[20] A well-meaning system has created a self-reinforcing spiral of decline for precisely the people who need it most. It is economically damaging and morally bankrupt.

And it's getting worse. Following the abolition of the two-child cap on benefits, some analysis suggests that a family with three children would now have to earn £71,000 to generate the same after-tax income as an equivalent family on benefits.[21] More than one in five adults in Manchester, Liverpool and Birmingham are on out-of-work benefits. In parts of Glasgow and Blackpool, it is more than half of all adults.[22] Perhaps the biggest tragedy of all involves young people. Some now opt for a life on benefits before ever getting a full-time job, meaning we now have around a million 'NEETs' (under-25s not in employment, education or training). Many cite mental health issues, with a further 38,000 claiming PIP for mental health reasons. Nearly one in five young graduates with mental health issues are not working.[23]

At the same time, government spending rules – or rather, the lack of them – remove any incentive from the Department for

Work and Pensions (DWP) to control its budget. Welfare spending is technically categorised as 'annually managed expenditure' in the government accounts. This means that, unlike the budgets for the NHS, schools and defence, it is uncapped (there is something called a 'welfare cap', but it is routinely ignored). The bizarre result is that the DWP spends more than any other government department, with no institutional incentive to control its costs.

The only budget that *is* capped is the cost of the DWP's own employees, who are therefore encouraged to handle as many claims as possible. Saying 'yes' is much quicker than saying 'no' – and cost-free to the department because the benefits bill will be picked up by the Treasury. Saying 'yes' on the phone rather than in person is even quicker – and since the pandemic, every claimant has the right to apply by phone. Since January 2022, nearly two thirds of those assessed for the health component of UC have been moved into LCWRA (meaning they are not required to look for work) – the maximum possible entitlement. Only 12% have been deemed fully fit for work.[24]

A further problem arises for people with mental health issues, now cited by the majority of claimants.[25] In an attempt to ensure there is no discrimination against people with mental illness, the system ignores one of the key differences between mental and physical illness, namely that mental illness is often not constant but comes and goes. Such conditions therefore need to be managed as a temporary and not a permanent condition. Social contact is one of the best ways to reduce the likelihood of a reoccurrence, but being classified as 'not able to work' does the opposite by reducing social contact. So a benefits system meant to be compassionate actually makes things worse. It also makes no financial sense: treating such conditions would cost a fraction of the bill for parking someone on benefits.

Many welfare recipients are in real need, and it is important to stress that most of the time the issue is not fecklessness or fraud. But when everyone in the system – from claimants and civil servants to GPs – is incentivised to make a classification of 'sick', the numbers inevitably mushroom. And that is what is happening: every year, the total number told they don't have to look for work rises by around 400,000, equivalent to the entire population of a city like Leicester or Cardiff being put on out-of-work benefits.[26]

Reforming such a system is not easy, as the current government has found. It is obviously important to be careful when changing the way support is given to vulnerable families. But we make the process of reform much harder than it should be because of the perverse way we calculate poverty statistics. In the UK, instead of measuring whether someone can afford to buy basic necessities, we use a relative measure of poverty. Any household with an income of below 60% of median income is defined as 'poor'. That means, at the time of writing, an income below £22,000. But measuring inequality is not the same as measuring poverty, and strange things happen when you conflate the two: poverty, as we define it, automatically rises if the economy grows,[27] but if there is a recession, and median incomes fall, the number of people in poverty technically goes down – even though not one poor person has seen their living standards improve.

Defining poverty that way makes welfare reform much harder, because nearly any change leads to a short-term increase in the number of people below that bar of 60% of median income. But over time, if those individuals are helped to find work, they are far *less* likely to live in poverty. They are more likely to be physically healthier and less likely to have anxiety or depression. Most importantly, they have a chance to progress their life in a way that cannot happen on out-of-work benefits. But few politicians want to preside over an 'increase in poverty'. As a result, welfare reform is watered down or abandoned altogether. Labour's 2025 welfare reforms were projected to increase the number of people 'in poverty' by 150,000;[28] it didn't take long for them to be junked.

But progress is possible. Iain Duncan Smith's welfare reforms under the 2010–15 coalition government were the most sweeping in a generation. They merged six benefits into one universal credit: income support, the jobseekers' allowance, the employment and support allowance (ESA), housing benefit, the working tax credit and child tax credit. UC is now a vastly simpler benefit designed to ensure people are always better off in work by removing the penalties from transitioning off welfare. At the same time, the disability living allowance was replaced with PIP in order to offer more targeted help with the additional costs of disability.

Implementing those reforms, however, was far from easy. Duncan Smith was personally targeted by welfare and poverty campaigners. Protesters climbed onto the roof of his house and even took photographs through bedroom windows. But he pressed on – and the reforms had a dramatic effect. There was a significant reduction in the number of households where no one was working. Five years on, one million fewer children were growing up in households where no one was working. Child poverty (on absolute measures) fell. Many more single parents and disabled people found work. Until the pandemic, the welfare roll fell and its cost was coming down. Those reforms have now been accepted across the political spectrum.

But following the pandemic, things went badly wrong. There was a big increase in claimants citing mental illness. Applications for PIP and the UC health component increased dramatically. Undoubtedly the pandemic left long-term scarring on people's health – but in other countries the number of claimants has not increased, suggesting that it is more of a system issue than a health issue. It appears that, while the work incentives in UC have been effective, there are big flaws in the structure of PIP, not least in its assessment of mental health.

As a result, alongside Mel Stride (then Work and Pensions Secretary), I announced a number of welfare measures in the 2023 Autumn Statement.[29] We aimed to help around a million people back to work over five years in a package costing nearly £1 billion. Measures included removing GPs from the 'fit note' process, to avoid a conflict of interest when a GP received a request from their own patient. We planned to stop benefits for those who turned down a reasonable job offer and find work from home for people with mobility issues. We also announced that eligibility require-ments for PIP would be toughened and the 'work-related activity' test would be scrapped. The OBR said the package would lead to nearly 400,000 people moving out of LCWRA, the category which removes any need to look for work.[30] It was not the whole solution, but would have started to turn the tide.

Unfortunately, we were timed out by the 2024 election. The aboli-tion of the work-related activity test was stopped by a court ruling.[31] Many of the other measures were weakened or scrapped by the incoming Labour government. As a result, welfare reform over the last decade has been only partially successful. That has meant that the overall social security bill, including pensions, is higher than the bill for any other government department, and now accounts for nearly £1 in every £5 spent. It is more than we spend on health, more than double what we spend on education and nearly five times the size of our defence budget.[32] Its size is now affecting other government programmes that are themselves vital for people on low income – including skills training for those who don't go to university or social care provision to help disabled people get into work. It is also locking millions of poor and vulnerable people into disability benefits that damage their health, their families and their prospects.

There are significant potential savings on the table…

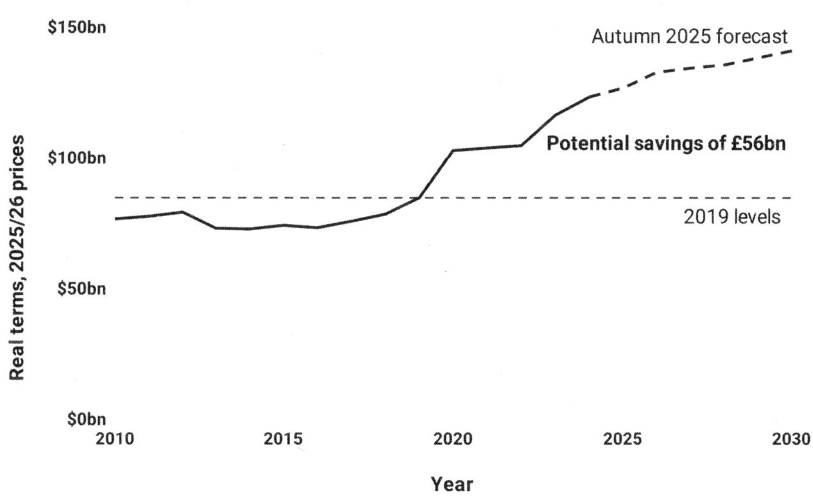

Source: DWP[33]

We therefore urgently need bold reforms.

Firstly, and most importantly, we should not resign ourselves to two million people parked on benefits without any obligation to look for work. Our starting point should be to agree that, with the pandemic behind us, it is time to reduce the number of welfare claimants to pre-pandemic levels. And the first step should be to remove less severe mental health conditions from the benefits assessment process.

As Health Secretary, I changed the law in 2014 to give 'parity of esteem' to mental and physical health conditions. The change was much needed, and two million more people are now treated for mental health conditions every year than before. But giving equal weight to mental and physical illnesses should not mean treating them in exactly the same way. Being in work is beneficial for many people with a mental illness, so our mantra for them should be 'treatment, not welfare'. The cost of doing so would be vastly lower than consigning people with mental illness to out-of-work benefits for the rest of their lives.

At the same time we should do more for the one third of UC claimants who are in work but on low pay. Measures to help them progress to higher-paid work – such as skills training and provision of vocational courses – could help them leave the benefits system altogether. That is good for taxpayers, and would also do far more to reduce poverty in large families than measures like removing the two-child cap (in cases where the majority of affected families have someone in work).

We also need to change the incentives inside government. The DWP should have a budget just like the NHS and the Ministry of Defence. Face-to-face assessments for benefits should be compulsory for all claimants, with assessors rewarded for getting people back into work rather than being incentivised to sign people off.

At the same time, we should ask a fundamental question about the Whitehall-run Jobcentre Plus network. Can national employment programmes ever be as sensitive to local or individual situations as those run locally? The whole system would be far more tailored to individual situations if we devolved responsibility for getting people back into work to elected mayors or unitary authorities. They already bear responsibility for areas that directly connect to employment, such as housing. If they were allowed to keep a proportion of any savings made, we would be likely to see a far quicker rise in the number of adults in work than by relying on a centralised national bureaucracy.

The Treasury also needs to change its mindset about migration. For a long time, it has considered it the easiest way to increase the working-age population as the rest of us age. But as Professor David Miles points out, that is only a short-term fix. To keep what is called the 'dependency ratio' constant would require a population increase of around twenty million additional young people over the next forty years – a totally unrealistic number.[34] And even then, the impact would only be temporary, as the new arrivals themselves would eventually retire. Far better to increase the proportion of the adult population in work.

A sensible labour market strategy also needs to involve employers, who should be encouraged, through the tax system, to step in early when their employees become unwell. This is also something generally done much better in countries like the Netherlands and Denmark. Instead, the UK system does the opposite: if an employer pays for private healthcare, the employee becomes liable for income tax as it is considered a benefit in kind. That needs to be changed urgently – not just to make it easier for people to get treatment more quickly, but also because the cost to taxpayers will end up much higher if delayed treatment means being signed off work and onto welfare.

Get this mix of policies right and the prize is huge. If we increased employment levels to 79% of working-age adults – the average in the Scandinavian countries, Switzerland and the Netherlands – we would increase GDP per head by around 4%.[35] That's a big increase. Inevitably, a number like that needs qualifying: it assumes that productivity levels for new workers are as high as for the existing workforce; it doesn't account for other changes in the economy that affect labour market participation (such as AI, a recession or new employment laws). It is perhaps more accurate to say that with Scandinavian employment levels GDP per head would be 4% bigger *than it would otherwise be.* But it is still worth going for. It is not just a big boost to potential prosperity, but would also generate an extra £40 billion a year in tax receipts for the Chancellor within a relatively short period of time. That's why getting more people into work is one of the quickest ways to get us out of our low-growth trap.

> **Increase the number of adults in work to Scandinavian levels**
>
> Potential impact on annual GDP growth: up to 0.4%
>
> Potential impact on GDP per head after a decade: up to 4%

Even more importantly, doing so changes attitudes to work. A failing welfare state which parks people on benefits doesn't just damage the individuals involved. It also sends a damaging signal to everyone else about the link between effort and reward. If we want a dynamic economy, we need to reward people who behave dynamically – and not sap our national work ethic with a failing welfare state. Sorting out our welfare system would transform public finances, raise living standards and lift thousands out of poverty. It is hard to explain why we are still waiting.

CONCLUSIONS

- ► Increasing the number of people in work is one of the fastest ways to increase GDP per head and therefore overall prosperity.

- ► The Treasury needs to change a mindset that favours migration to one that prioritises getting the domestic workforce back into work.

- ► We should follow reforms aimed to increase the number of people in work to at least the average in Scandinavian countries, the Netherlands and Switzerland, which would see an extra 1.2 million adults in work.[36]

- ► Moderate and low levels of mental illness should not be a criteria for benefits, because doing so incentivises people to classify themselves as such.

- ► Welfare reform should prioritise treatment over benefits for people with muscular-skeletal and mental illnesses.

- ► The DWP should have a capped budget for working-age welfare.

- ► Benefit claims should be made face to face and not by phone.

- ► Jobcentre Plus responsibilities should be devolved to local government, with savings shared.

4

Building Things

Ben the Builder is based in the south-east of England. He lives in a prosperous area known for picturesque market towns, quaint villages and rolling hills. Ben is a property developer who has made a good living since he branched out on his own a decade ago. His current project is a relatively modest proposal to transform a derelict car park on an old field into six detached homes. But it has been delayed by nearly two years.

He has been forced to commission a full ecological survey, because a few years ago someone saw a slow worm there, a snake-like lizard protected under UK law. If any such lizards had been found, Ben would have had to relocate them with great care – and at great expense. He has also been required to complete a 'biodiversity net gain' statement and a Highways assessment, and to endure a fractious public meeting with locals vehemently opposed to his plans. He has long resigned himself to the fact that new housing is never popular with existing residents, who worry about the extra traffic, lack of infrastructure and general overdevelopment. But at the last minute, the local planning officer raised an additional concern: apparently, the proposed brick colour conflicts with the area's 'vernacular heritage'. Ben protested in vain that the site had been a car park for decades.

Less than a hundred miles away, in the north-west of France, someone else is in a similar line of business. Let's call him Claude le Constructeur. He is having a rather easier time of things. His current project is situated in a small town not far from Rennes, the capital of Brittany. His margins are lower, because house prices are lower. But the whole process is infinitely smoother. Claude has just submitted plans to build ten new homes.

The town's local plan, or *plan local d'urbanisme*, has designated areas for residential expansion. Claude has followed the guidelines, including the use of slate roofs and a two-storey restriction on the height of each house. After just two months, the *mairie* gave him the green light. While Ben has to deal with a planning system that is opaque and adversarial, the French system is consistent and transparent. Communes are generally smaller than English councils, which makes them more approachable. They get less in central grants, but unlike their English counterparts they keep all the additional property and business taxes they raise. That means they benefit from all new approvals. As a result, if a proposal complies with the stated specifications, it usually gets the go-ahead. That creates certainty for developers and residents alike. Everyone knows where growth is allowed and where protections will be upheld. There are local objections, but they rarely stop projects in their tracks. Not needing deep pockets for lawyers also creates space in the market for smaller builders, who are often local themselves and more invested in the area.

Compare that to the experience of Ben in the UK. Many planning applications turn into a mini political campaign. Decision-making by local councillors is discretionary and unpredictable. Local communities are slow to release land, because they have little incentive to do so. Even if a proposal appears to fulfil all the necessary requirements, it can be refused on a technicality. Governments generally want more houses built, so often a local refusal ends up being overruled by national inspectors, incensing the local population. The developers aren't much happier: it costs them money, takes up a huge amount of time and destroys relationships in the very community where they want to sell houses.

Geography accounts for some of the disparity. France has much more land to build on, despite a similar-sized population. In the UK, there are over 280 people per square kilometre compared to just 120 people per square kilometre across the channel.[1] Although much of the extra land is in places with little economic activity, it is still easier to release land for development. But the most important difference is that, as we have seen, French communes keep additional business rates and property taxes, giving them a direct financial incentive to encourage new developments. They also have elected mayors as a clear point of contact for decisions. By contrast, English local authorities get little benefit from increasing the business rates revenue base. What they do feel is a lot of pressure from sceptical local residents, who all have votes.

The result has been a stark divergence in the number of homes built. In the 1970s, Britain and France had broadly the same number of dwellings.[2] Since then, Claude has been much busier than Ben: despite similar populations, France now has 24% more dwellings than the UK. Germany's much more decentralised system has delivered 17% more homes even after accounting for its larger population size.[3] English homes are also more cramped: the average person has 38 square metres of living space, compared to 43 square metres in France and 46 square metres in Germany.[4]

And things are getting worse. A recent report by property website Zoopla concluded that because of wage and materials inflation, environmental regulations and social housing requirements, it is not financially viable to build a house in around half of England. It has come to this partly because, since 2022, the cost of delivering a new home has risen by 17% but house prices have only risen 1%.[5] On top of that, there is a structural issue: housebuilding is viable in areas like London and the south-east, where house prices are higher – but those higher prices make the new houses unaffordable for many buyers. Where people can afford to buy, house prices are too low to make building viable. That said, the French planning system is far from perfect. There are problems with urban sprawl; and social unrest in the banlieues is linked to poor social integration, which itself is linked to housing policy. But France has at least found a way to get houses built that young British families can only dream of.

Understanding this difference also unlocks an economic mystery. Over many decades France and Britain have taken radically different approaches to economic policy. The UK has flexible labour markets, Europe's largest financial services sector, its fastest-growing tech and life sciences sectors and some of the world's top universities. France, by contrast, has higher taxes, more regulation, earlier retirement and more employment restrictions. Yet French and British GDPs per head have been almost identical over several decades. Somehow, despite its anti-business, anti-aspiration culture, France has kept up. Why? Partly because its businesses tend to invest more. But also because of how much easier life is for Claude le Constructeur. France is just better at building things.

Britain's failure to build has, however, been good news for one group of people: those who already own a home. House prices have risen by 400% in real terms since 1970, compared to just 150% in France.[6] But that has meant intense disappointment for many young families shut out of the market. In 1970, the average house was two and a half times the average wage in Britain.[7] Now it is around seven times the average wage. Most people born in the 1950s owned a home by the age of twenty-seven; those born later are having to wait more than a decade longer.[8]

In this chapter, we will look at the impact of reforms that would make it easier to build things in the UK. Housing matters because growing companies need their staff to be able to live within commuting distance. But economic development also requires new factories, offices and infrastructure. And new housing itself needs good road and rail connections, as well as access to power and water.

The same challenges that make life difficult for Ben are even more debilitating when it comes to larger projects. Take energy, which is vital to a modern economy, not least to power the data centres necessary for the AI revolution. Many, like me, have long believed we need a big expansion of nuclear power. As Chancellor, I announced in the 2022 Autumn Statement that we were going ahead with the Sizewell C plant. What I didn't know – and would have been rather less proud of – is that when it opens, it will be the most expensive nuclear power station in the world. Originally budgeted at £20 billion, it is now expected to cost £40 billion.[9] A similar-sized plant (based on price per megawatt produced) costs about half that in France.[10] Hinkley Point C, the UK's other new nuclear project, has seen its costs rise even more, to an estimated £46 billion.[11] It was supposed to open in 2025, but that has now been pushed back to at least 2031.[12] While the UK struggles to build two nuclear power plants, France plans to build six. Given how much energy we import from across the Channel, we had better hope they succeed.

The same is true for the construction of hospitals. In September 2019, Boris Johnson famously promised to build forty new ones. By the 2024 election, five years later, only seven were underway. Or reservoirs: the last new one, Carsington Water, was opened in Derbyshire back in 1992. Or prisons, where it is taking years for projects to get planning permission, leading to the early release of dangerous criminals.[13] Nothing better illustrates the haplessness of British political decision-making than our inability to get big projects done.

All this has been detailed in an excellent paper called 'Foundations: Why Britain Has Stagnated' by Ben Southwood, Sam Bowman and Samuel Hughes.[14] In it, they point out that the Lower Thames Crossing planning application alone was 359,000 pages long. Putting the plans together cost £267 million, more than Norway spent on actually building the world's longest road tunnel, which was opened in 2000.[15] Multiple agencies or 'statutory con-sultees' can veto or delay a development, including the Highways Agency, Natural England, the Environment Agency, Historic England, the Health and Safety Executive and utility companies.

It is perfectly sensible for them to have an input, but the process of getting their approval, often one after another, means it can take years or even decades to get building underway. In the case of Heathrow's third runway, there has been little progress since a government go-ahead more than two decades ago. The authors of the paper use the term 'vetocracy' to describe the issue: just one veto by one of numerous organisations can scupper a project. Conversely, streamlined regulation, standardised designs and aligned incentives allowed France to build forty nuclear reactors in the 1970s.[16]

There is another big difference which particularly affects the number of new houses built. In the UK, housebuilders are also developers. They pay high prices for land which either has planning permission or comes with a reasonable chance of getting it. But that in turn means they can only then sell the houses at prices that cover what they have paid. The result? Housebuilders sit on planning permissions for a long time, only dribbling out new homes at the constrained level of demand that exists for higher-priced houses. New developments end up being fully built at about a quarter the speed they would be in France or Germany. In those countries, that issue is avoided by allowing land to be acquired by local development corporations or community interest trusts at much lower prices, without incorporating the 'hope value' of anticipated planning permission. That allows builders – often small, local firms like Claude le Constructeur – to build out and sell the homes in new developments more quickly.

Because we have not learnt these lessons in the UK, we are just not building the homes we need. That is bad for economic growth: it stops people moving to where new jobs are being created and prevents the construction sector from contributing as much as it could to our GDP. What is eventually built then costs too much. When it comes to infrastructure, high-speed rail construction costs double what it costs in Italy and eight times more than in France; underground train lines also cost twice as much per mile than across the Channel, and tram lines can cost up to ten times as much.[17] Given how vital transport connections are to overall productivity, it is hardly surprising that we continue to lag. A failed planning and housebuilding system is one reason why the UK invests just short of 19% of GDP every year compared to the OECD average of around 22%.[18] If we matched that average, there would be an additional £108 billion of investment in the economy every year. That would mean more houses, more factories, better infrastructure – and much more growth.[19]

The UK economy would close much of its investment gap if it built at French levels

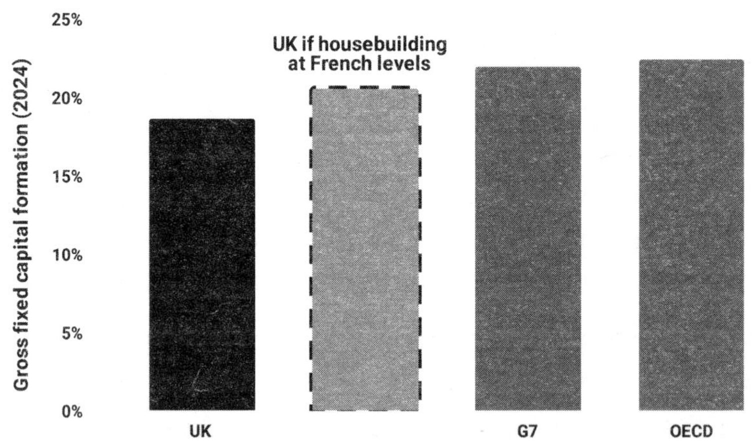

Source: OECD,[20] ONS,[21] Insee[22]

It is tempting to conclude that failure to grasp the nettle on planning reform has been the fault of timid or incompetent politicians. In fact, that is unfair: there have been repeated efforts by politicians of all parties to try to improve things – including in the current Labour government. But if they are going to crack the issue, they should study harder the successes and failures of their predecessors.

Greg Clark, as planning minister and then Housing Secretary, massively simplified planning law by reducing guidance from 1,300 pages to a single fifty-page document which included a 'presumption in favour of sustainable development' and an extension of 'permitted development rights'.[23] The simplified guidance set up local and neighbourhood plans and made it easier to convert offices to residential accommodation. And the reforms worked, with the number of housing units granted planning permission in England rising from 150,000 a year to a peak of over 300,000 a year.[24] Clark didn't even need new legislation to introduce his reforms, showing that ministers often have more power than they realise.

In a 2018 review, Oliver Letwin, a long-time champion of planning reform, took an important step forward by identifying why it was taking so long for sites with planning permission to get built out. He noted that after planning permission is granted, it generally takes more than fifteen years for large housing developments to be completed, a build-out rate of just 6.5% a year. The reason is a combination of high land prices and too much uniformity in the design of the houses being built. One reduces affordability and the other reduces choice.[25] Unfortunately, his recommendations – more development corporations, more community land trusts and greater diversity of housing in large sites – were never fully implemented, partly because of resistance from local authorities and housebuilders.

Then there's Robert Jenrick, hardly someone who can be accused of being timid. He had a big go at radical planning reform as Housing Secretary. His white paper would have introduced French-style zoning, simplified local plans and led to much faster planning decisions. But following huge resistance from backbenchers, his boss Boris Johnson lost his nerve. The reforms were shelved and Jenrick was reshuffled out of his job. Housebuilding targets were then abandoned altogether by Rishi Sunak's government, a change I suspect neither of us is proud of.

The current government is now making some big efforts of its own. It has reintroduced mandatory housing targets. It has promised new towns backed by development corporations. It has reduced the power of local councillors to block applications, reduced the number of statutory consultees and promised to speed up consultations. But it has ducked the opportunity to bring in French-style reforms that would have dealt more decisively with planning delays, misaligned incentives and land-value distortion.

The result is that in London, the largest and richest city in Europe, housebuilding has nearly ground to a halt. Following the mayor's decision to increase social housing requirements for every new development, new housing starts fell to only around 5,500 in 2025, just 6% of the government's target for the city.[26] The UK system remains, in the words of one recent report, 'one of the most complicated legal frameworks ever built'.[27] The same report worried about the democratic implications of governments being unable to get shovels in the ground within a parliament. The losers are not just politicians who see their legacy go up in flames: voters end up angry and disillusioned, with unaffordable prices and creaking infrastructure that no party appears able to sort out.

We are, however, perfectly capable of building things quickly and cheaply – as I found out when I was responsible for the London 2012 Olympics. I was an unusual choice for the role, knowing next to nothing about sport. I told David Cameron about my lack of knowledge before he appointed me, but as so often he was supremely relaxed. I was less so: frontbenchers live or die by their media appearances, and I worried a car-crash interview would expose my lack of knowledge. Others would have been thrilled to sit between David Beckham and Prince William discussing tactics for winning the 2018 World Cup bid in David Cameron's Zurich hotel suite. I was just petrified my lack of knowledge would be exposed.

I came to enjoy sport. But alongside that small miracle, a much bigger one was taking place, namely the construction of the Olympic Park. Under the hawk-eyed leadership of John Armitt and David Higgins, the Olympic Delivery Authority (ODA) was determined not just to open the park on time (about which they had no choice) but also to live within the agreed £9.3 billion budget.

At the start, Stratford was largely a post-industrial wasteland. Derelict buildings littered the area and much of the soil was contaminated. Because it was so heavily polluted, the area had remained underdeveloped for decades, despite being next door to Canary Wharf. On top of poor infrastructure there was high unemployment and deprivation. It was said that for every Jubilee Line station from Westminster to Stratford, life expectancy declined a year.

Before any construction could start, a huge environmental clean-up operation was required. An estimated two million tonnes of soil was cleaned of contamination[28] in an operation costing hundreds of millions of pounds.[29] Only then could the regeneration of the area begin. Both the pre-2010 Labour and post-2010 coalition governments were determined that the 2012 Olympics would leave a legacy in Stratford, breathing life back into the area with a sustainable and attractive development.[30] In addition to the sports facilities, the development involved new Tube stations, housing development and the massive Westfield shopping centre.

The whole project was delivered on time and to budget – in fact, £500 million under budget.[31] The organisers were praised for their effective planning, budgetary efficiency and flawless execution.[32] Since then Stratford has prospered. The area is unrecognisable compared to before: the Athletes' Village has become a bustling residential area; the Queen Elizabeth Olympic Park is now an event hub that regularly hosts concerts and festivals; and the recently opened cultural quarter, called East Bank, has seen major institutions such as the V&A museum, Sadler's Wells theatre, UCL and the London College of Fashion open locations there.[33] Stratford station has also become one of the UK's busiest transport interchanges.

Many things made this possible. The immovable deadline was crucial in focusing minds. Special legal structures ensured the ODA was a planning authority in areas where Olympic facilities were being developed. It passed on those powers to its successor body, the London Legacy Development Corporation. John Armitt and David Higgins's leadership made a big difference. And politicians mattered too: those involved in the project knew they could depend on everyone from the prime minister down to unblock any issues. Perhaps most crucially, the key players' incentives were aligned – everyone defined success in the same way: delivering a spectacular games, for sure, but also one with a lasting legacy.

Stratford before and after 2012 – built on time and to budget

For me, as a new cabinet minister, it felt good to be at the top of a pyramid staffed with smart people. But because it was my first cabinet job, I didn't realise how unusual that was. When I tried to bend the NHS to my will as Health Secretary, or negotiate at the UN as Foreign Secretary, things were very different. And there was no bigger contrast than the fiasco of HS2, which I had to confront as Chancellor.

That project was the opposite of the London 2012 Olympics: the incentives of key players were not aligned – and taxpayers paid the price. The company building HS2 concluded that money was no object, and the Treasury would always cough up. At one point – despite the British weather – they planned to air-condition the platforms, something virtually unheard of in much hotter Saudi Arabia or Japan. The project famously included a tunnel to protect bats at a cost of £100 million. That worked out at about £300,000 per bat saved.[34]

The Department for Transport, supposed to be managing the project, ended up helpless and hopeless. As a result, HS2 has been plagued by chronic delays, huge costs and mounting opposition. A project that was initially planned to cost £33 billion has ballooned to £80 billion and counting.[35] A train line that was supposed to begin the first phase of opening in 2026 will now open well after 2033. Britain, the country that invented railways, still has no high-speed rail. Japan, whose first train line was built by a Scot, unveiled its first high-speed rail line in 1964. China adds nearly 3,000 kilometres to its network every year.[36]

How did Europe's biggest infrastructure project go so badly wrong? Initially, the project was run by David Higgins, who had been responsible for the Olympic Park, so it is hard to pin the blame on leadership, at least in the early stages. Nor is it all the fault of planning law, as special planning powers were granted by Parliament, just as they were for the Olympic Park. What did harm the project was the vetocracy of statutory bodies combined with fierce campaigning by local residents and their MPs. Without the hard deadline and aligned incentives of the Olympic Park, costs and delays mounted.

There was also something else: hubris. The original champions of the plan wanted it to be Europe's fastest high-speed line. That meant it had to go in a straight line from London to Birmingham, whatever the practicality or cost. But because that straight line goes through the Chilterns – a designated 'national landscape' – there was ferocious pressure to put much of it in tunnels. In the end, sixty-five miles of tunnel were built – nearly half the entire route. Had it followed the M40 instead, the journey would have taken ten minutes longer, hardly the end of the world, needing many fewer tunnels. It could also have included Heathrow, massively improving its connectivity. But the perverse way the Treasury calculated value for money meant that a shorter journey time counted as time 'saved' for travellers. This meant that a more expensive route – with tunnels – produced a 'higher return' on public investment.

There are also bigger Treasury issues affecting infrastructure projects. Every time the country faces a financial crunch, the capital budget is much easier to cut back than politically sensitive budgets for schools and hospitals. But that is precisely the budget upon which many infrastructure projects depend. Often, chancellors avoid the pain of cancelling a project by 'moving it to the right', i.e. delaying it. But more delay just increases cost. The Netherlands has worked out a smart way to avoid these issues. Many infrastructure projects are funded not directly by the state but through public corporations, which borrow money funded against future revenue streams. Their cost does not sit on the general government balance sheet, so is less vulnerable to the economic upheavals that force governments to cut spending. Such mechanisms have been used to finance high-speed rail, the Zuidasdok project centred on Amsterdam's railway station, a second tunnel under the North Sea Canal and numerous road projects. Doing that in the UK would require us to change our accounting rules, but it is surely worth doing so: the Netherlands now has a stock of assets a third higher than Britain's, all contributing to greater economic efficiency and healthier growth.

That said, things in the UK have started to improve. Over the last decade a consensus has emerged in British politics not only that infrastructure spending matters but also that we need to do it better. Rishi Sunak increased capital spending plans by an unprecedented 22% when he became Chancellor. I had to reduce that after Covid, but Rachel Reeves has changed fiscal rules to get public capital spending back rising again. Although there is a long way to go, we are starting to close the gap with other countries.

But if we really want to make it easier to build things, we need to overhaul the planning process. Introducing proper zonal planning systems, like the ones that have been operating successfully in Europe and Japan, will speed up approvals in areas designated for development. If we want more mixed-use areas such as the highly successful King's Cross development, we need to make much more use of the development corporations and community land trusts that Oliver Letwin identified. Once set up, they need full autonomy

Having underspent on public capital investment, the UK is starting to catch up

Source: Calculations by the author using OECD data[37]
Note: Investment is defined as gross fixed capital formation of general government

to buy land at pre-development prices so that new developments are cheaper and quicker to build out. When it comes to large infrastructure projects approved by Parliament, we should ban judicial reviews and streamline the consultation process to ensure it lasts a maximum of two years. Statutory consultees – the organisations that form the vetocracy – should be consulted within that period and not one after another.

Most of all, we need to align the incentives for local communities with the country's economic requirements. Local residents in my constituency generally support the principle of building more houses. They have children and grandchildren trying to get onto the housing ladder and know that local teachers, nurses and police officers need to find somewhere to live. If they were given reasonable autonomy to decide where to put new developments and knew their community would benefit from the additional council tax receipts, their calculations would be different, particularly if those with a local connection or working in the area were given priority when it came to buying the new homes. That's why the single biggest way to unlock planning gridlock would be to allow local authorities to keep additional tax revenues generated, as happens in France.

We also need to change the way large infrastructure projects are managed by ministers. Spending authority should always be delegated to those running the project – as it was with the ODA – otherwise ministers end up adding delay and cost with new objectives and specification changes. That authority needs to stand for the lifetime of the project, otherwise the need to renew funding invariably leads to specification changes from new ministers eager to put their stamp on a project. Contracts should also be structured so that the knock-on effects of any changes are minimised. Local mayors and councils should be given the autonomy to fund and build their own large infrastructure projects as well as champion housing developments. Now we have moved to a unitary model of local government across England, there is a perfect opportunity to make that happen.

What would be the impact on economic growth? The OBR has already calculated that the government's so far timid reforms will add 0.2% to GDP growth in 2029. It is difficult but not impossible to quantify the impact of more ambitious reforms: if we built houses and infrastructure at French levels, it would increase annual capital investment by around £60 billion a year. That would add 0.2% to annual GDP growth[38] – a recurring benefit, not just a one-off increase in output. In practice, it would be unlikely to happen smoothly, because of labour shortages that could affect the construction industry. But after resolving any teething issues, the benefits would be widespread.

> ### French-style planning reforms
> Potential impact on annual GDP growth: 0.2%
> Potential impact on GDP per head after a decade: 2%

Businesses would benefit from a quicker, smoother process whenever they needed to get something built, making the UK a country where it would be easier for entrepreneurs to take the plunge. Younger people would then also find it easier to buy a house, unlocking a dream that has slowly been slipping away. For that reason, the social impact of such reforms would be even more important than the economic impact. But to get there, we need to make life as easy for Ben the Builder as it is for Claude le Constructeur.

CONCLUSIONS

- ► Planning reform would unlock massive new investment in the UK and help to close a significant part of the investment gap with other countries.

- ► Local authorities should keep additional council tax and business rates collected locally in order to give them an incentive to support economic development.

- ► Locally elected mayors should be given the power to approve and fund local infrastructure projects, using the model successfully implemented in the Netherlands.

- ► A zonal planning system should offer fast-track approval for houses built in areas designated for development.

- ► To ensure faster approvals and build-out, we should set up more development corporations and community land trusts to buy land for housing at pre-planning-permission prices.

- ► Utility regulators should prioritise investment in infrastructure alongside lower bills.

- ► Judicial reviews for large infrastructure projects approved by Parliament should be banned, with all planning consultations streamlined and reduced to a maximum of two years.

5

Public Sector Productivity

The junior doctors' strike of 2015–16 was the most draining political battle I have ever fought. I learnt the hard way just how difficult it is to improve public sector productivity – even if the need to do so is blindingly obvious. That's not just because we all want decent public services that cost taxpayers as little as possible. It's also because the public sector is a huge part of the country's economic output – around a fifth[1] – so making it more efficient improves our overall productivity. That means higher living standards for everyone.

As Health Secretary, I discovered that was easier said than done. I had noticed that the death rate of patients admitted to hospital over the weekend was 15% higher than those admitted on weekdays. That amounted to around 6,000 potentially avoidable deaths every year. I therefore wanted to get more doctors working on Saturdays and Sundays. Flushed with an unexpected victory in the 2015 general election, I announced plans to change doctors' contracts with great gusto.

In retrospect, it would have been smarter to concentrate my efforts on consultants rather than junior doctors because more experienced doctors would have made a bigger difference to weekend death rates. But the consultants cannily kept quiet, allowing the most vociferous opposition to be led by their younger colleagues. Junior doctor outrage was fuelled by their union, the BMA, which told its members – wrongly – that the changes would mean a pay cut. In their strike ballot, an overwhelming 98% supported industrial action.

Now that I'd started the argument, I had to win it. In politics, backing down publicly can destroy your reputation – and your career. But the leader of the BMA's junior doctors committee, Johann Malawana, was in exactly the same boat. He had marched his troops up to the top of the hill. He knew his firebrand colleagues would summarily eject him if he backed down. Our horns locked.

I thought I would win because I had the full support of Prime Minister David Cameron. But the BMA believed it would win – with equal certainty – because, in the court of public opinion, doctors are always more popular than politicians. It took a year of bitter strikes and massive disruption to NHS services to find out who was right. By then, David Cameron had been replaced by Theresa May. She had kept me on as Health Secretary, feeling that she could not move me in the middle of major industrial action. So in one of history's minor ironies, it was thanks to the BMA that I became the longest-serving Health Secretary in the history of the NHS.

In my book about that period, *Zero*, I wrote extensively about the challenges of health reform. My focus was to reduce the number of avoidable deaths caused by incorrect or poor treatment. Who could disagree with that? But trying to do something about it was often stressful and unpleasant. Having started the fight, I could hardly ask for sympathy. But the physical and mental exhaustion that resulted is one reason why public sector reform often ends up being ducked or dodged by ministers. So far, this book has considered the impact on economic growth of lower tax and debt, getting more people into work and making it easier to build things. This chapter considers how to make our public services more efficient. It looks at what happens if you make space for an entrepreneurial, can-do mentality in the public sector as well as the private sector. It also uses the story of the junior doctors dispute to understand the political challenges involved in public sector reform.

From the outset, the NHS establishment was deeply nervous about my determination to reduce weekend death rates. Even though senior figures had alerted me to the spike in those rates – indeed, had encouraged me to tackle them – they stopped supporting me the moment they realised how unpopular the changes were. They were also very worried about how the system would cope with strikes. One warned me that after Michael Gove's battles with the teaching unions, the Education Secretary became the 'enemy', unable to be heard inside the education establishment – and ultimately reshuffled out of his job. Once I crossed the line, there would be no going back. I might win the battle, but would I win the war?

I crossed that line. But it would be wrong to say I was completely on my own. I had strong support from parliamentary colleagues and even more robust encouragement from the right-wing press.

Many on the right were up for a fight with the unions, their traditional foe. David Cameron and George Osborne were rock-solid in their support, although I never took it for granted. I remembered that my predecessor, Andrew Lansley, had been demoted when NHS reforms got too hot to handle. The only way I would lose the battle was if the prime minister lost his nerve. So in order to make sure he didn't, I sent him a private note just before the strikes started, saying that if he didn't want them, this was the last moment for compromise. As I expected, he told me to stand firm. That support never wavered – nor did Theresa May's when she took over from him.

But the BMA was a clever opponent. Far from being Scargill-style class warriors, they were the bright offspring of proud middle-class parents. Every doctor who appeared in the media was given careful instructions to appear reasonable and sympathetic. They never talked about wanting more pay, instead starting answers with carefully-crafted phrases such as 'As someone who has practised as a surgeon/GP/anaesthetist for five/six/seven years…'. The strategy worked: public support for the junior doctors never wavered. I wasn't overly worried because I had the legal power to impose the new contracts anyway. Instead, I concentrated on appearing determined and unyielding, in the hope that the unions would give up. Part of that approach included imposing new contracts the very next morning after one strike had concluded.

In other words, I doubled down. But so, too, did the junior doctors.

The BMA announced another wave of strikes, this time for forty-eight rather than twenty-four hours. They raised the stakes by threatening to withdraw emergency care. They made sure the strikes were happening on a Wednesday, so that the prime minister would be asked about them at Prime Minister's Questions. I then had to spend hours the day before working out the best lines and briefing him. It was a sign of his confidence in me that I was invited to the preparations for Prime Minister's Questions. But it was not a good sign that the strikes were dragging on, not least because I had been appointed to 'calm things down' in the NHS.

My office also became more nervous. In the street outside, there were daily confrontations. A group of junior doctors protested outside the entrance to Richmond House, the Department of Health building, with placards and an empty chair to signify my alleged refusal to negotiate. Occasionally, I would invite some of the protesters into my office to discuss the issues, but I soon realised that anything I said would get twisted into a social media 'moment'. One evening, I cycled down Whitehall and saw large crowds milling around the entrance to Downing Street. I assumed it was a demonstration against human rights abuses in some distant country. As I got closer, I saw my name on the placards they were holding. I executed a speedy U-turn. Thankfully no one recognised me in my bicycle helmet.

Nor was family life immune. I tried to avoid London over weekends when there were marches of twenty thousand doctors shouting, 'Hunt, Hunt, Hunt must go.' But when I tuned in to Classic FM to try to switch off, I heard the progress of those same marches reported every hour. School holidays also became fraught. On one, our plan was to spend a week with friends in America over Easter. On the day of the flight, the BMA announced another wave of strikes. I rushed back from Parliament to get the family ready for the flight. As I was packing, the doorbell rang. I assumed it was a taxi coming to take us to the airport, but it was a BBC camera crew wanting a comment. I knew it would be disastrous for me to be filmed heading off on holiday. So I went back inside, changed into a suit and called my government driver. When he arrived, I left the house, did a quick clip to the cameras and climbed into the car as if I was going to work. In my hand was a plastic bag full of holiday clothes. Around the corner, I changed back into jeans and waited for my family to pick me up in the taxi. With frayed tempers and just minutes to spare, we only just scraped through security at Heathrow in time. I was not a popular dad.

And all the while, I was becoming one of the most disliked people in the country. A YouGov poll had my net approval at minus 48%, making me the most unpopular politician (of an already unpopular bunch, it has to be said).[2] Radio presenters routinely mispronounced my last name with a C instead of an H. Protesters climbed on top of my car and covered it with flour. Hospital visits were met with whispered insults or pained looks from staff. On one such visit, junior doctors planned to line a corridor and turn their backs to me as I walked past, until we changed the route.

Perhaps most difficult of all was having to put on a brave face for my inner team. You become close to the civil servants and special advisers in your private office because you see them every day – far more often, in fact, than fellow ministers or parliamentary colleagues. Whatever their personal politics, they are staunchly loyal and supportive. But if you reveal any inner doubts, it erodes their confidence. So you keep your worries bottled up, which can make the job feel very lonely. Sometimes, however, you just can't hide what you are feeling. When the third wave of strikes came we were desperately hoping the turnout would fall. During the morning, disappointing news came through that support was still rock-solid at 80%. At that exact moment some junior ministers came into my office for an unrelated meeting. I couldn't hide the tears in my eyes. One of the ministers, Jane Ellison, brought in a pot plant later to cheer me up.

In September, the BMA upped the ante even more. They announced they would strike for a whole week, withdrawing emergency care from A & E departments for the first time ever. Putting patients at risk to such a degree was a step too far for their colleagues. Senior doctors and Royal Colleges spoke out against the strikes. The union lost its nerve and cancelled further action. Johann Malawana had already been ousted from his job for agreeing a provisional deal and now a second junior doctors' leader lost her job. But that warning from a senior civil servant turned out to be right. I had won the battle but turned the NHS against me. Further reform became much harder.

Looking back, I was right to take steps to improve weekend care. But it was also true – as the junior doctors pointed out – that we didn't have enough doctors in the first place. So after the strike collapsed, I increased the number of doctors, nurses and midwives we trained. Nothing changed overnight, because medical training takes many years. When I became Chancellor, I was able to address the issue more comprehensively by putting in place a long-term workforce plan that doubled the number of doctors and nurses we trained. That too will take time to make itself felt on the front line. When it is, alongside the contract changes, we should finally start to see weekend care getting safer. But only after a long, painful and expensive journey.

*

For me, the junior doctors' strike demonstrated why public sector reform is the toughest challenge a minister can face. As Tony Blair famously said, 'You try getting change in the public sector and public services – I bear the scars on my back after two years in government.'[3] But even committed prime ministers make things harder by reshuffling ministers too frequently. I was lucky to have solid support from two prime ministers. But, as mentioned, Andrew Lansley was demoted for his ill-fated NHS reforms. One of my successors as Health Secretary, Steve Barclay, had his own battles with health unions and ended up being reshuffled. To his credit, he didn't back down either – but the incoming Labour government did. It is easy to see why unions think it is worth digging in.

Another good example is the Department for Transport. Train driver contracts are notoriously out of date – not least in the case of driverless trains, which are perfectly safe and indeed operating on London's DLR. We should obviously expand their use, including to Tube lines. Likewise with track repair, where the regulations date back decades: instead of sending one person to do repairs, an electrician and a track engineer are sent, often refusing to travel in the same vehicle as a result of demarcation or safety rules. A job that could take one person three hours can end up costing an eight-hour shift for four separate people. Such Spanish practices are ripe for reform, but it needs a Transport Secretary to be left in post for long enough to see through any battles. Instead, in the last decade, we have had no fewer than seven transport secretaries. Compare that to the train drivers' union ASLEF, which has had just one leader – Mick Whelan – over that period. Unsurprisingly, in 2024 he secured a 15% pay rise with no productivity concessions from the incoming Labour government.

The failure to reform is also the responsibility of my old department, the Treasury. It has often taken a foolishly short-term approach to balancing the books. When a department overspends, the Treasury insists it 'consumes its own smoke' – in other words, finds offsetting savings from its own budget. Cutting popular programmes or shedding staff is politically painful. So instead, less visible modernisation projects get postponed. If the Home Office budget is blown because of a surge in asylum seekers, it might be the new national police computer system that gets the chop. That may be less noisy than reducing the number of police officers but is ultimately far more damaging.

The Treasury also does something that should be the polar opposite of its mission: it incentivises other government departments to waste money. Any budget that is unspent at the end of the financial year is clawed back. Chancellors welcome the 'underspend', which helps them balance their books. But the result is a wasteful and almost comical effort to 'get money out of the door' before a year end. If we want more efficient public services, careful use of money should be rewarded not penalised.

It should therefore come as no surprise that, according to the Institute for Fiscal Studies, public sector productivity declined by 0.3% on average every year between 1997 and 2019. In fact it was a story of two halves, falling sharply in the Blair/Brown years and then increasing during the austerity period. But over those same two decades in which productivity was declining in the public sector, it was increasing in the private sector by around 1% a year.[4] Prior to the 2008 global financial crisis, the long-term private sector growth rate was nearly 2%.[5] How can we get our public services onto a similar trajectory?

Public sector productivity has flatlined whilst the private sector has continued modest growth

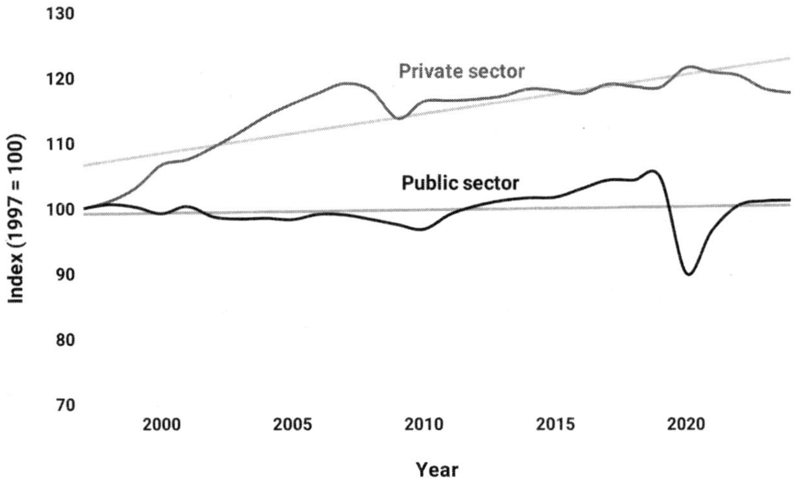

Source: ONS[6]
Note: Multi-factor productivity was used to measure private sector productivity.

However challenging, we need to find a way. Because the public sector makes up around one fifth of our output, more efficient public services keep taxes down, with all the benefits associated with a more lightly-taxed economy. And if raising the country's productivity is a central objective, there is no better place to start than the only part of the economy directly under the control of ministers.

There is a further reason too – a slightly wonkish one, but possibly even more important. As Chancellor, I had seen projections from the OBR that suggested demographic pressures would increase the national debt from around 100% of GDP

118

currently to nearly 300% by the 2070s.[7] That's clearly an unsustainable level of debt which in practice markets would not allow. But it got me thinking: what, I asked Treasury officials, would be the impact on our national debt if we raised public sector productivity to a level closer to that in the private sector? Or, put more bluntly, could more efficient public services help us head off bankruptcy?

When the analysis came back, it was startling. Treasury officials told me that if we raised public sector productivity growth by just 0.7% more a year – still well below the long-term private sector average of nearly 2% – our national debt would stop increasing as a proportion of GDP.[8] Even accounting for demographic pressure, spending on public services as a proportion of GDP would stabilise. If public sector reforms went further and matched private sector productivity growth, debt might even start to go down.

An easy way to think of this is through the prism of the NHS: demographic pressure means demand for its services is rising by around 3% a year.[9] If those services are delivered in the same way, we will need to increase its budget by 3% a year to meet that extra demand. As it happens, that is about the level it has actually been increasing under recent Conservative and Labour governments. But if productivity in the NHS grew 1% faster, spending would only need to increase by 2% a year. If it matched the long-term private sector productivity growth rate of nearly 2% a year, spending need only increase by 1% annually. Repeated across the public sector, such a change would transform public finances, as the next graph illustrates.

A small increase in public sector productivity growth massively reduces its burden on the economy

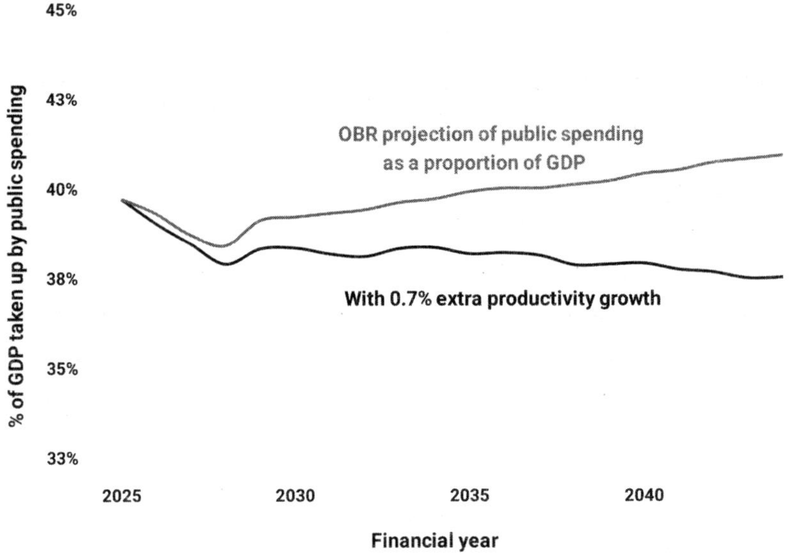

Source: OBR[10]
Note: This graph uses data from detailed spending projections made in September 2024, the latest available data at the time of writing.

So a relatively small increase in public sector productivity has a big impact in keeping both taxes and debt down. It also addresses a more technical issue, known to economists as Baumol's cost disease. If the private sector becomes more productive, wages go up. That then impacts on the wages in the public sector, because the state has to pay more to attract employees of the same calibre. The result is lower productivity and more expensive public services. But if public sector productivity is also increasing, it is no longer an issue because the higher salaries are paying for increased output.

120

But as I found in the junior doctors dispute, theory is rather easier than practice. What makes public sector reform even tougher in this case is that the 0.7% improvement, if it is to reduce the pressure to raise tax or increase debt, has to generate hard financial savings. Any improvements that deliver better services or outcomes to the public (higher-quality teaching, for example, or better weekend care in hospitals) would not count, however beneficial they may be, unless they actually reduce costs for taxpayers. Perhaps the most sensible approach would be to aim for 2% overall annual productivity improvements in the public sector, around the long-term private sector average, specifying that a third of that (0.7%) should be financial or 'cashable' savings.

But change can happen.

Francis Maude made one of the biggest attempts in recent decades to improve the efficiency of public services. Under the coalition government, he focused on digitisation, closing down quangos (large 'arms-length bodies' like the Arts Council or the Environment Agency in charge of key state responsibilities), improving procurement, managing government property, and controlling consultancy and marketing spend.

It was a rough process – almost Trumpian by today's standards. Cabinet ministers like me were required to offer up a quota of quangos for the chop. As Culture Secretary, I was responsible for fifty-five of them in total and was told I needed to find a dozen to abolish. I was not against more efficiency but was more focused on the political challenge of trying to keep the arts and sports world on board during a period of painful cuts. As the deadline crept up on us, we had not made enough progress. I remember a crazy meeting with my permanent secretary when, in just half an hour, we went through our quangos one by one to decide which ones to axe. I felt like the Roman clerk in *Monty Python's Life of Brian*: 'Crucifixion? Good. Out of the door, line on the left, one cross each.'

I am sure we didn't get every decision right. But without a degree of brutality from the centre, nothing would have happened at all. Some cuts in other departments were subsequently criticised, particularly the closure of the Audit Commission, which was respected for its analysis of the performance of local government. But overall the programme led to lasting efficiency improvements: 185 quangos were closed down and a further 165 merged.[11] The current government is now closing down the biggest one of all, NHS England, which employs 13,500 people.

Over that period, the size of the civil service was cut by 20%;[12] procurement was centralised, saving around £5 billion a year;[13] £1.4 billion of capital was released by selling off redundant government buildings, with the number in central London halved;[14] 1,500 websites were shut down and multiple contracts were cancelled, including one under which a government department had to pay £30,000 to change one word on its website; and government services were centralised and streamlined onto a single portal, GOV.UK, reducing cost by 60%.[15] Within five years, the savings amounted to £19 billion a year.[16]

That led to some surprising and unexpected improvements. After the pandemic lockdowns were lifted, people rushed to renew their passports in order to book holidays. With applications around a quarter higher than normal, the Passport Office was overwhelmed. A fast track process was supposed to take five weeks but often took several months. Nearly four hundred thousand people were affected, with many having to pay to reschedule flights or cancel holidays. There was vociferous criticism from MPs, government ministers and the National Audit Office.

Then, almost imperceptibly, things began to change. People started getting their passports back within days. A new online application system called Digital Application Processing (DAP) removed the need to send in a physical passport photo signed by a teacher, lawyer or other professional to confirm your identity. Suddenly, you could upload your photo digitally and verify it by email, with the processing done electronically rather than by human beings. DAP made the new system one of the most efficient in the world. Delegations from other countries started coming to study the miracle, even from more technologically advanced economies, such as Taiwan and the US. How exactly did the Passport Office succeed where so much of Britain's public sector has failed?

Francis Maude's reforms certainly created a focus on digitisation, but good leadership also helped. The civil servant responsible was a highly effective manager called Abi Tierney. She had cut her teeth as an NHS manager and had an approachable, hands-on style. Over many years, she had learnt that improving productivity was not about driving people harder but creating better processes. Like many effective leaders, she credits the turnaround to her team rather than herself. Together, they found a way to turn the pandemic lockdowns into an opportunity. With no demand for new passports, the dead periods were used to speed up the roll-out of DAP. Crucially, they made sure all the IT development was done in-house, avoiding expensive contractual renegotiations with external consultancies. They also focused ruthlessly on 'what would delight the customer' – Abi's own words, and ones rarely heard in the public sector. If a part of the process was not something that would 'delight' people applying for passports, they asked if it was really necessary. If it wasn't, it was chopped out.

Unfortunately, the new service wasn't quite ready when the lockdowns ended, leading to large backlogs for a while. But instead of being scapegoated, the team was supported through the crisis by their ministers, Priti Patel and Kevin Foster, whom they met every week. Abi went on to be the first woman to run the Welsh Rugby Union. Imagine how different the British state would be if people with her can-do entrepreneurialism and calm competence were running programmes to get people back to work.

Inspirational leaders like Abi Tierney at the Passport Office show that radical improvements can be made to public sector productivity

Nor is it just the Passport Office where digitisation has made a big difference. UK citizens can now access nearly all government services online, including registering to vote, applying for a driving licence and even getting a lasting power of attorney. Overall, the UK is ranked third in the OECD for the quality of its online services.

The UK is now a leader when it comes to the digitisation of public services

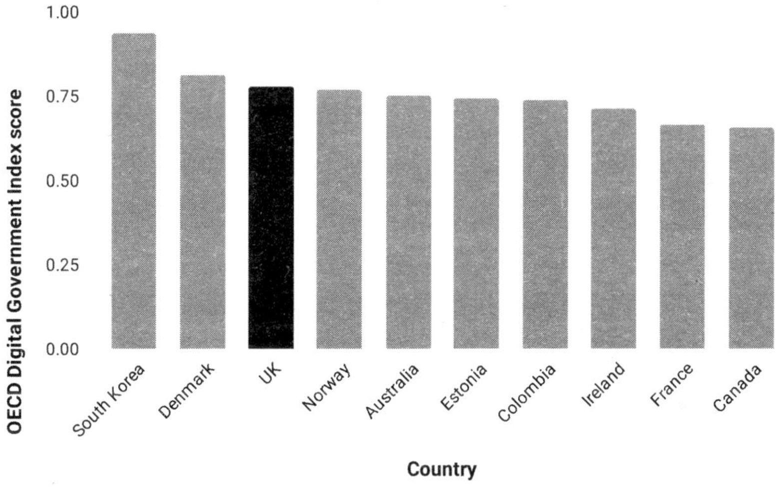

Source: OECD[17]

But digitisation is only part of the story, as we have seen from those rather woeful overall figures on public sector productivity. We also need far-reaching structural reforms.

Those should start with our most powerful ministry. One of the officials I worked closely with during my time as Chancellor was a formidable civil servant called Cat Little. She was the director general in charge of all public spending. With responsibility for over £1 trillion of taxpayers' money, she was probably the most powerful person in Britain you have never heard of. Her power was not just linked to her formal responsibility for public spending, but exercised on a daily basis because of the need for multiple Treasury sign-offs before government departments are allowed to spend their budget. That is a tight leash, unheard of in other countries. It is perhaps justifiable in a financial crisis, but the rest of the time it makes getting anything done very cumbersome.

Treasury micromanagement needs to be replaced with genuine autonomy that rewards ministers who make savings. In return for agreeing to increase productivity by 2% annually, they should be released from having to get their budgets signed off before they can spend them. They should be allowed to roll over underspends at the end of a financial year. With a 2% annual productivity target, they would then have a strong incentive to deliver Passport Office-style transformations, crucially with the autonomy to make them happen. Proper autonomy would also make it much easier to attract high-flyers like Abi Tierney.

Nowhere does this matter more than in the NHS, the world's largest and most bureaucratic health service. Health service micro-management comes not from the Treasury but from NHS England and the Department of Health. Hospitals, for example, have eighteen monthly operational targets, and GPs have forty-four annual targets,[18] far more than in any other health system. As a result of such a tractor-factory obsession with targets, patients are too often treated like statistics rather than human beings. And managers end up being box-tickers, focused on internal processes rather than outcomes for patients.

That is why, after reflecting on my time as Health Secretary, I concluded that all national NHS targets should be abolished. Instead, we should use the accountability mechanisms used in nearly every other health system around the world. The most important of these is clinical accountability: making sure there is an individual doctor responsible for every patient. That used to be the case with the old GP list system, when local doctors had a personal list of around two thousand patients for whom they were responsible. But in 2004 those lists were abolished, replaced with a system that is less personalised and more expensive. A recent study in Norway showed that patients who see the same GP on a regular basis are 28% less likely to go to hospital and even 25% less likely to die. That is because doctors who know their patients are less likely to misdiagnose and more likely to keep them at home. Conversely, doctors who don't know their patients are more likely to send them to hospital, increasing the number of procedures and operations the system has to deliver. Even inside hospitals, the priority given to impersonal targets means less accountability, more mistakes and ultimately more money spent trying to put things right. We now spend nearly as much on settling litigation claims for maternity services as the entire cost of running them. Until we scrap structures that turn patients into numbers, we will pay the price with demoralised staff, distressed patients and disappointed taxpayers.

And we already know that the right combination of autonomy and accountability works. Decentralisation has been highly successful at driving productivity improvements in both the police and schools. Crime fell after policing targets were scrapped in 2010. Standards rose in state schools after major education reforms empowered academy heads.[19] Autonomy is not always the right answer: when it comes to back-office functions such as procurement or property management, centralisation of services can be very effective. But for operational delivery on the front line, it is usually far better and cheaper to empower professionals to use their judgement to innovate and improve. You need to get the 'tight–loose' balance right.

Other reforms could also make a big difference. One would be to get better at measuring productivity. In some ways, by international standards, the ONS does this well. I asked them to make further improvements when I was Chancellor. But even now, for rather bizarre reasons, any increase in public sector productivity does not count towards our national productivity numbers. When a French hospital – generally not state-owned – becomes more efficient, it shows up in France's productivity numbers. When an NHS hospital makes identical improvements, it does not.

But at least a hospital does know key productivity details, such as the number of operations performed by each surgeon. In many parts of the public sector, we don't even capture the most basic information. If the Ministry of Justice reduces reoffending rates, the cost of the additional rehabilitation services counts as a cost in its budget – even though lower levels of reoffending actually save the taxpayer much more, because of reduced crime, less pressure on policing, less court time and fewer prisoners. The problem is no one knows how much. Until we work that out, the Treasury won't really be interested. If we did, people would be motivated to implement reforms and get the support to do so. Being better at measuring productivity improvements would also allow governments to link them to above-inflation pay awards, something ministers always want to do but find difficult in practice.

Something else that would make reform easier would be more consistent direction from the top. Francis Maude believes the way to do this is to copy government structures used in Ireland, Canada and Australia, where there is a specific department focused on government efficiency that reports to the prime minister: the finance ministry continues to make the final decisions on tax and spending levels, but financial oversight of government departments – including the correct 'tight–loose' balance – is given to an independent office for budget and management. If we were to adopt a 2% public sector productivity objective, that new department would have the responsibility for measuring it and spreading best practice in a way the Treasury has never been able to manage.

Even with the flawed numbers we currently have, we can estimate the impact on economic growth of improving public sector productivity: given that the public sector accounts for around one fifth of our GDP, 0.7% additional annual productivity growth over a decade would add 1% to GDP.[20] As mentioned earlier, such improvements would need to deliver actual financial savings. The impact of any reforms might be reduced by knock-on effects such as higher salaries or a shortage of IT contractors. But even so, it would be worth the effort: at the very least, public services will end up better and more responsive than before – as we saw with the Passport Office.

Boosting public sector productivity

Improve public sector productivity growth by 0.7% a year

Potential impact on annual GDP growth: 0.1%

Potential impact on GDP per head after 10 years: 1%

In my final budget in March 2024, I tried to show how this could happen in practice. And I did so with our most expensive public service – my old friend the NHS. As the country's biggest employer, it accounts for around 40% of all government spending on public services. As we have seen, it's also probably one of our most inefficient services, with productivity still nearly 8% lower than pre-pandemic levels.[21] Could I get better results second time around, hopefully with less confrontation?

I started by agreeing with Amanda Pritchard, the NHS England chief executive, to more than halve the number of operational targets. NHS planning guidance (the document where the targets are spelt out) was reduced from forty-one to twenty pages, a significant improvement if not the more radical abolition of targets I now advocate.[22] I then asked Amanda a very specific question based on that same Treasury analysis: what investment in technology would allow the NHS to deliver annual productivity growth of 2%? She told me it would need a whopping £3.4 billion to transform the NHS's creaky IT systems. That was a big ask in the run-up to an election, not least with tight public finances. But I decided to go for it.

After difficult negotiations with No 10, I found the requested £3.4 billion. In return, the NHS made a public commitment to increase productivity by 2% annually for five years. It would then be matching the long-term average for the private sector, as well as far exceeding other parts of the public sector. Part of the deal was to measure productivity carefully, not just at a national level but in every local NHS organisation including hospitals, GP surgeries and community services.

On Budget Day, the NHS productivity plan became the rabbit I pulled out of my hat.[23] Predictably, it was drowned out by a debate over the tax cuts that were also in the budget. The few who did notice it were somewhat sceptical, dismissing it as yet more distant 'efficiency gains'. But the new government has kept the plan in place. And there is some evidence it is starting to work. All GP practices now have digital telephony, meaning that patients don't get an engaged tone and can ask for an automatic callback. Most hospitals either have or are in the process of installing modern IT systems. The NHS app has grown to thirty-nine million subscribers, delivering more than five million repeat prescriptions a month.[24] Genomic testing is now being used to scan for two hundred cancers and seven thousand rare diseases.[25] There are plans to decode the genome of every baby born in the NHS.[26]

A total of £9 billion was saved through efficiencies in the first year of the programme. According to NHS England, hospital productivity went up by 2.7%, more than double the previous rate.[27] Early gains were flattered by the ending of strikes over pay, so the momentum may not be maintained. Nonetheless, independent experts believe the NHS will achieve 0.7% annual productivity gains, potentially rising to 2.2% if new technology is fully embraced.[28]

If the NHS, with all its pressures, can engineer that kind of change, so too can other public services. Of course, it will need political courage. Health unions will always try to block changes to doctors' contracts. Rail unions will never like driverless trains. Teachers will oppose innovations from AI. Many will welcome efficiency improvements in theory, but oppose them in practice – especially if they involve workforce reductions.

But if we take a longer-term, more strategic approach to efficiency in public services, the prize is more fulfilling jobs as well as better value for taxpayers. Unlocking a positive can-do mentality in our public services would make work far more rewarding for people on the front line who are often as frustrated by their inefficiency as the people who use them. It would fire up dynamism in the 20% of our economy that the public sector represents. Most importantly, we would finally start to escape the endless cycle of governments running out of money and forcing austerity cuts on services that are already stretched. If that sounds too much like another politician dangling the prospect of more efficient services sometime in the distant future, the next chapter discusses one reason why it may be different this time. Having looked at boosting the employment rate and reforming planning, we now turn to the unfolding revolution in AI.

CONCLUSIONS

- If public sector productivity grew just 0.7% more every year, it would stabilise our national debt.

- Because public services are around one fifth of our output, they are the biggest opportunity for productivity improvement directly under the control of ministers.

- Oversight of government efficiency should be passed on to a new office for budget and management reporting directly to the prime minister, with the objective of delivering 2% annual productivity improvements across all public services of which one third should be cashable.

- There needs to be clear 'tight–loose' demarcation of government spending, in order that functions which are best delivered centrally remain so, but much greater autonomy is given to those on the front line.

- Accountability should be through transparency rather than targets.

- Prime ministers should reshuffle ministers less frequently, to allow them to see through difficult reforms.

- The NHS needs to be decentralised, with all national targets and micromanaging abolished.

- When money needs to be saved, it should not be taken from projects that improve productivity, such as new IT systems.

6

Innovation

The weekend before a budget is sacrosanct for a Chancellor. Although there is feverish media speculation about 'putting final touches' to the measures it contains, all decisions have long been made. They need to be submitted to the OBR well in advance, so that it can make its all-important independent judgement on the budget's economic impact.

Any decisions worth more than a billion pounds – major tax cuts or spending increases – have to be finalised around two weeks before Budget Day, when they are submitted to the OBR on what the Treasury calls Major Measures Day. It is a big milestone but passes largely unnoticed by the media. A few days later, the watchdog returns with a preliminary forecast showing whether you will meet your fiscal rules.

Then there is about a week to finalise smaller measures, ahead of what is known as Minor Measures Day. The convention is that these should not amount to more than £1 billion in total. But what is 'minor' for the Treasury can actually be a very big deal. My decision in March 2023 to give a permanent tax break to theatres, galleries and orchestras, for example, was widely welcomed in the arts world but technically 'minor' – and only included at the last moment. Sometimes last-minute changes do end up breaching the 'billion threshold', but officials always advise chancellors not to do so, because it risks incurring the wrath of the OBR. No one wants to do that before the OBR chair delivers their independent verdict on your efforts straight after the budget speech.

So if all the decisions have been made, why does the weekend before the budget matter? Because that's when you write your speech. In politics, performance matters. Hundreds of journalists assess not only the substance of what you announce but your body language, jokes and delivery. As will an equally important audience: your colleagues in the House of Commons. A good speech is one that delivers the headlines you want. It makes it more likely, in Westminster jargon, that the budget will 'land' rather than 'unravel'. You get help from a speechwriter, but politicians know that speeches need to come across as authentic. That generally means doing much of the writing yourself. I was lucky enough to have an excellent Treasury speechwriter. After I left office, he did the same job for Rachel Reeves – even writing the infamous speech in which she claimed I left behind a £22 billion 'black hole'. Being able to write a speech that directly contradicts all the claims of the last speech you drafted is a fascinating example of civil service impartiality.

I was very careful to keep the weekend before the budget clear. But ahead of my first budget, those plans went up in smoke. That was because, for a scary few hours, it looked like the central plank of my vision for the UK economy was going to be blown up. And all thanks to a Californian bank I had never heard of. I tell that story here because it shows both the opportunities and the vulnerabilities inherent in the UK's growing technology sector.

Silicon Valley Bank (SVB) was a Californian bank with a good reputation that had flourished for many years. But it was caught out by the rise in interest rates following Russia's full-scale invasion of Ukraine. Depositors began to worry whether SVB could survive a fall in the price of US Treasury bonds and their customers started withdrawing funds. Soon, there was a classic run on the bank, and US regulators were forced to close it down just days before my budget. I read a rather dry submission from Treasury officials about the UK subsidiary, which stated that 'Silicon Valley Bank London will close this weekend and the Bank of England has publicly announced it is considering placing the firm into insolvency'.

It slowly dawned on me that the demise of a bank I had never heard of could be disastrous for the UK. The issue was that SVB's London subsidiary held nearly £9 billion of funds for our most promising tech and life sciences companies. Seven 'unicorns' – companies worth more than $1 billion – held their assets with the bank alongside countless other rising stars across biotech, fintech, gaming and streaming. If the bank went under, it could take up to four thousand such companies with it, and all but wipe out a key growth sector.

Erin Platts ran the London branch of SVB. She is a modest, easy-going American who fell in love with the UK and had made it her home. Never in a million years did she imagine she would find herself at the centre of an international banking storm. She was first told there was a problem on a Thursday night. At 11 p.m., she dialled into a Zoom call and realised the US parent business was in deep trouble. She didn't sleep that night (or over the next four days) as she worked through a series of deeply uncomfortable options. After meeting her UK board, she made the first important decision: because the London business was solvent, they would open for business the following morning. That meant they would continue to open accounts, approve loans and allow withdrawals throughout the day.

But at the close of play on Friday, it was announced that in the US, the regulator had taken over the parent bank. Because of the time difference, the London branch was closed, meaning that it was too late for a run on it by anxious depositors. But UK regulators were worried, because the London subsidiary's technology was managed from California. At 6 p.m. on Friday evening, Erin received a call: she had the weekend to find a new owner or regulators would step in and she could lose the business. She commissioned Rothschild to help her find a buyer.

One of Erin's customers had passed her my WhatsApp contact details, so she got in touch. She told me SVB London were inviting prospective buyers to examine their books. At the same time, I hosted a succession of crisis meetings in the oak-panelled dining room of No 11. It is called the Churchill Room because it has a picture of Britain's most famous Chancellor on the wall. What would he make of our problems? I wondered to myself, as I looked up at his glowering face.

Joining the meeting by video were the governor of the Bank of England and Sam Woods, head of the Prudential Regulation Authority (PRA). Also on the screen was Rishi Sunak, on a plane on his way to a G7 leaders meeting in San Diego. No one wore ties. Dialling in to the prime minister's official jet from a seventeenth-century dining room summed up both the charm and the contradictions of the British state.

The line to Rishi's plane was terrible, but together we worked through the options presented to us. The easiest option would be a private sale of the bank. Much trickier would be what to do if that didn't happen: should we sanction a taxpayer-funded multi-billion-pound bailout of a foreign bank?

As a former banker – and Chancellor – Rishi had a feel for the situation. But it was not straightforward. The global financial crisis of 2008 had forced the UK government to commit to spending up to £1.2 trillion to stop a banking collapse – nearly three quarters of the country's GDP at the time. That huge sum was necessary to shore up confidence in the system and stop a run on the banks that would have collapsed the economy. But it came at an eye-watering cost: Gordon Brown and Alistair Darling put up the equivalent of £43,000 for every household in the country to bail out the banks. The final cost ended up lower – but still a whopping £33 billion.[1] Many voters were understandably furious, not least because bank chief executives continued to pay themselves large bonuses. So bailing out a Californian bank just over a decade later would not have been popular. But the future of the fastest-growing part of the British economy was at stake and it was a sector that I had personally championed. If there was a solution that avoided a bailout, I wanted to find it.

And we did. Following the 2008 crisis, many changes were introduced to make the financial system more robust. In the end our bacon was saved by one of them – a technical change that required foreign banks to set themselves up as legally separate subsidiaries. That meant that if the parent company collapsed abroad, the assets of UK customers had to stay here. Just eight months earlier, SVB London had become a subsidiary. Its customers' money stayed in London.

We could therefore sell the London branch as a going concern. But would there be any buyers? We needed to know, and fast. If companies could not withdraw their funds on Monday morning, there was the risk of a bank run – which could only be avoided with a bailout. So we started ploughing through approaches from potential buyers. Some were corporate raiders. Others were start-ups we had never heard of. The most promising offer was from an overseas sovereign wealth fund. By midday on Sunday, we felt a deal was achievable. I asked Sam Woods what would happen if the deal fell through. 'HSBC has made an approach,' he told me. 'Keep them warm,' I said.

Noel Quinn, chief executive of HSBC, had worked at the bank for thirty-six years, starting at a branch of Midland Bank in Birmingham before it became part of what is now Europe's largest bank. He was considered the ultimate steady hand on the tiller. He had long wanted HSBC to get more involved in the tech sector and sensed an opportunity. But could a large, complex and inevitably bureaucratic bank get its act together quickly enough?

We soon found out. Early on Sunday evening, the overseas sovereign wealth fund started to play tricks. Thinking they were the sole bidder – and that we were desperate – they started making unreasonable demands. Sam Woods refused to blink. Assuming he was bluffing, the buyer walked away. But Sam had kept HSBC in the wings as I had asked. He and his team worked through the night to deal with regulatory hurdles. Just before midnight, Erin realised her efforts had paid off.

At that stage, I still didn't know whether we had a deal, so I went to bed with my phone next to me. I even took it on my morning run, which meant that I finally sealed the deal with Noel Quinn jogging around Hyde Park. HSBC paid just £1 to buy SVB London. Quinn had shown a large business could move fast. Now retired, he describes it as the most satisfying moment of his entire career. But if it was a bargain for HSBC, it was also brilliant for the UK. At no cost to taxpayers, our fledgling tech sector had been saved. That was of profound importance for the UK's economic future.

There was little media coverage, because most journalists were focused on the budget. But it probably mattered more to our long-term prosperity than many of the budget measures. And the businesses that were saved are now giving the UK the opportunity to be one of the biggest winners from the revolution being driven by AI. This chapter looks at how realistic it is for Britain to aspire to be the world's next Silicon Valley. It looks at the impact on the economy if we succeed and the obstacles that stop us getting there. It shows that our issue is not a lack of talent but a hesitant mindset. Luckily, it is a mindset that can be changed.

One of the customers of SVB in London was the Oxford-based fusion company Tokamak Energy. It was set up in 2009 by three physicists whose dream was nuclear fusion – unlocking the energy that powers the stars. Its potential is enormous: unlimited, clean, cheap energy. But so too are the technical obstacles the company is trying to overcome.

Over a short period, Tokamak has turned heads globally with the progress it has made. To generate steam at the temperatures needed for fusion, they have found a way to do the equivalent of boiling a kettle at temperatures higher than the core of the sun. They have done this by building a doughnut-like chamber, called a 'spherical tokamak'. Inside it are high-temperature superconducting magnets that keep superheated gas – or plasma – confined in a way that allows fusion reactions to happen.

The three founders – David Kingham, Mikhail Gryaznevich and Alan Sykes – had to persevere for a long time with a dream that was far from an overnight success. But it turns out that the magnets they have developed have much wider uses: they could revolutionise MRI scanners, maglev trains and nuclear-powered submarines. They also demonstrate that Britain is no longer a country of inventors that leaves the dirty business of commercialisation to others. Tokamak's origins are in the UK Atomic Energy Authority, where the three founders have roots, but its future is focused on the commercial exploitation of their innovations. As a result it has attracted over $335 million of global investment to date as well as supplying fusion companies around the world.[2] It is based in the Oxford Science Park, where its story is far from unique. And not just in Oxford: many British universities now have US-style science and business parks where tech and life sciences start-ups are thriving. As part of the broader tech and AI revolution, they have the potential to transform the UK economy.

Sir Demis Hassabis is perhaps one of the five most influential AI names on the planet. He is a Nobel Prize-winning Brit who set up the AI lab DeepMind, which he sold to Google in 2014. As a result, Google's AI research is now headquartered in London. I told his remarkable story in my book *Can We Be Great Again?*, but his insights are also relevant for a book on economic growth. He believes the technology revolution we are about to experience will be ten times bigger than the industrial revolution and ten times faster. That is because for the first time in history, we will have computers that don't just replicate but surpass the functions of a human brain. Not only will they think autonomously with something that looks like human consciousness – but they will do so with unlimited processing power. Scientific and technological advances will speed up at a dizzying pace, including in medicine: Stanford professor emeritus Dr Stuart Kim speculates that the first human to live to the age of two hundred may already have been born.[3]

AI will also transform our relationship with work. Elon Musk once told me that over time work will become a lifestyle choice rather than a necessity. This would make the AI revolution different to previous technology shifts, which have tended to create new types of work rather than eliminate it altogether. If he is right, the question will then become whether the benefits will accrue to everyone or just a lucky few. Theoretically, vast increases in productivity could lead to extraordinary prosperity – an age of plenty. But it is also possible that the extra wealth ends up concentrated in the hands of a small number of very fortunate people. American economist Tyler Cowen described this as a 'bifurcated labour market', in which there are lots of low-paid jobs at the bottom with just a few highly paid ones at the top.

Such a two-tier economy is already emerging in some advanced tech economies. A fifth of Israel's economy and half of its exports are now linked to technology. Israeli taxi drivers live in a totally different world to the tech bros they ferry around, but both are aware that the number of high-paid jobs is beginning to shrink as companies invest in automation to increase productivity. In the UK, the number of graduate jobs on offer has fallen by 32% in just one year, partly attributed to the launch of ChatGPT.[4] One UK employment agency boss described the looming graduate jobs crisis as the inverse of the blue-collar jobs recession of the 1980s, even telling middle-class families to encourage their children to pursue careers involving manual labour.[5] At the same time, the rewards for some are already astronomical: in 2025, Meta reportedly offered an AI engineer it wanted to attract a package of $300 million over four years.[6]

Cowen's bifurcated labour market is likely to spread well beyond a few tech hotspots. Fewer traditional jobs in consultancy and accounting will leave many graduates wondering how they will pay back loans or buy a house. Retail automation and self-driving cars will reduce service sector employment. The social care sector is already starting to use remote monitoring to replace visits by care workers. Even doctors are finding AI models can be more accurate at diagnosing illness. Although ultimately AI is more likely to be combined with existing jobs than wholly replace them, the upheaval will be huge: research by McKinsey suggests that half of American jobs could be replaced with AI or robots. Goldman Sachs believes that three hundred million jobs are at risk globally from AI-driven automation.[7] Even the normally cautious IMF says 60% of jobs in advanced economies will be affected.[8]

The UK has experienced similar transitions in the past, but it has previously been a slower process. For decades, the reality of the Industrial Revolution was a terrible quality of life for those working in mines or factories. Eventually, new laws and social reforms improved working conditions and evened out the benefits of modernisation. This time those left behind are unlikely to be as patient. If thousands lose their call centre or service jobs overnight and graduates are unable to find work, there could be widespread social instability. It will impact our appetite for welfare reform and the government's ability to reduce tax, both of which are essential for economic growth. Political instability could follow on an even greater scale than we have seen to date. Of course none of this may come to pass. But the risk that it might needs to be carefully weighed as we plot our path through the technology revolution. One thing, though, is beyond doubt: countries that make the technology others have to buy are more likely to come out on top. Could the UK be one of those?

As so often, Britain has the pedigree. In the nineteenth century Charles Babbage, who is seen as the father of modern computing, invented the first mechanical computer. Shortly afterwards Ada Lovelace, daughter of the poet Byron, published her algorithm for a 'theoretical computing machine'. A century later, Alan Turing's work led to the building of Colossus, the world's first programmable electronic digital computer, used to decrypt the Nazis' Enigma code at Bletchley Park. The University of Manchester then built the world's first stored-program computer, the Manchester Baby, in 1948. The world's first business computer was developed three years later for the British tea company J. Lyons and Co.

But our biggest contribution to the technology revolution has probably come from someone alive today: British scientist Sir Tim Berners-Lee, who is credited with the invention of the World Wide Web.[9] Born in London in 1955, he grew up surrounded by technology. His parents were both mathematicians and met while working on the world's first commercially available general-purpose computer, the Ferranti Mark 1. Not long after, Berners-Lee developed

Sir Tim Berners-Lee, the inventor of the World Wide Web

his own interest in electronics. After leaving school, he won a place at Oxford to study physics. During his time at university, Berners-Lee remained interested in electronics, even building his own computer using junk parts and an old television set.[10] Following graduation, he pursued a career in computing, and after holding several roles elsewhere, moved to Geneva in 1984 to join CERN, the world's pre-eminent centre for particle physics research. It was there that he became frustrated with how difficult it was to share information across incompatible computer systems.[11] As a solution, he proposed a hypertext system that could be used to share information across networks. He outlined these ideas in a historic memo published in 1989 that laid the foundations for the World Wide Web.[12] A year later, the world's first website went live. Soon, thanks to Berners-Lee and his collaborators, everyone had adopted HTML, HTTP and the URL.[13]

What made Berners-Lee's invention world-changing was that he convinced CERN to make the new technology freely available.[14] It helped that he has, rather impressively, never been financially motivated. As he once said, 'People are what they've done, what they say, what they stand for, rather than what they happen to have in the bank.' In 1994, he moved to MIT, where he founded the World Wide Web Consortium.[15] Despite numerous accolades, he remains modest about his achievements and continues to champion an open, ethical internet.

Even if the UK has made an outsized contribution to the internet revolution, history is not destiny. Looking forward, do we have what it takes to be an innovation superpower? Many are sceptical, partly because we have become so used to a narrative of decline. We may have a few brilliant boffins and Nobel Prize winners, the thinking goes, but the future belongs to other countries with more resources and bigger markets. The facts suggest something different: despite fierce competition, our tech sector has quietly become the largest in Europe.[16] We have nearly eight hundred venture capital-backed companies turning over more than $25 million in annual revenue.[17] Nowhere else in Europe has more AI start-ups or more graduates with AI skills. The UK remains the only European country with more than one hundred 'unicorns', with London alone home to more of them than Berlin, Paris and Tokyo combined. It has now become the world's fourth-largest venture hub (and largest outside the US),[18] sitting alongside San Francisco and Beijing as one of the world's leading centres for AI research and development. In 2022, the UK became only the third tech ecosystem in the world, after the US and China, to be worth more than $1 trillion. That's why, as Chancellor, I said with some confidence that our ambition should be to become the world's next Silicon Valley.

University spin-outs have helped attract more start-up capital to the UK…

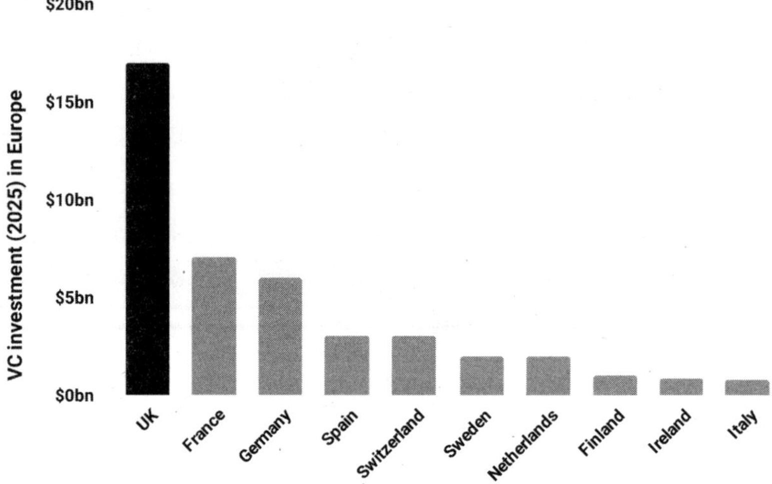

Source: dealroom.co[20]

…meaning it now grows large numbers of unicorns

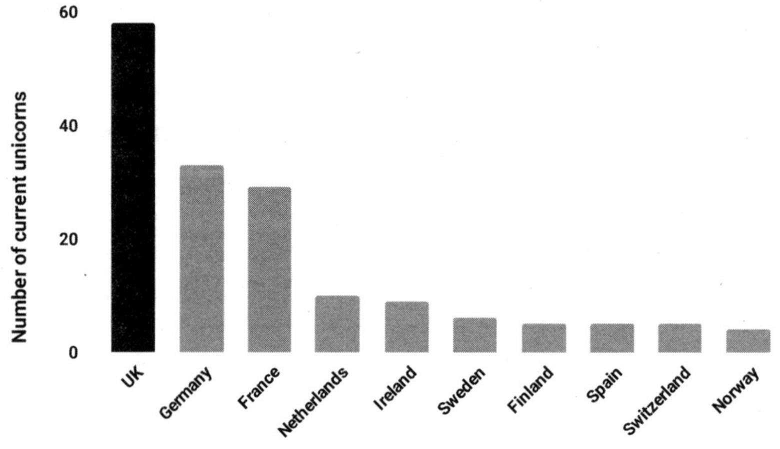

Source: CB Insights[19]

That doesn't mean the UK will overtake the US or China. Nor should we underestimate the competition from countries such as France, Israel, the UAE, Taiwan and South Korea. But when it comes to being the best of the rest, the UK has some key advantages. We are ranked fifth globally for innovation, ahead of any large European country. Outside the US, Britain has the most respected universities in the world, including three of the global top 10 (Oxford, Cambridge and Imperial). As we saw with Tokamak, many have created an ecosystem of Stanford-style spin-outs with close links to venture capital and private equity backers. UK universities continue to file more patents and win more Nobel Prizes than those in most other countries. One third of those prize-winners were born overseas, demonstrating our long-standing ability to attract the best minds from all over the world.

The UK's tech ecosystem is especially attractive for its breadth. Its science base means that life sciences, creative industries, gaming, fintech and clean energy are all able to tap into the latest advances in quantum and AI in a way that encourages the cross-fertilisation that scientists value. Sir Demis Hassabis himself combined gaming and neuroscience to unlock the mysteries of protein folding. The intersection of financial services and technology has created one of the world's biggest fintech sectors. Big increases in defence spending are likely to fuel a reinvigorated defence tech sector, the motor that drove the original Silicon Valley expansion in the 1950s. At the same time, despite its woes, the NHS has become a magnet for life sciences research because of its fifty million electronic health records. A parallel attraction is the UK Biobank, which offers open access to the anonymised genomic data of over five hundred thousand patients[21] – more than anything available elsewhere. It plans to collect data from every baby born in the NHS.

Another advantage for British start-ups is access to capital, at least in the early stages. On their doorstep is one of the world's top two financial centres, the City of London, which offers an ecosystem of private equity, venture capital and angel investors attracted by tax advantages such as Enterprise Investment Scheme (EIS) and Seed Enterprise Investment Scheme (SEIS). One of the key foundations for any Silicon Valley ambition is the availability of capital, and UK tech start-ups attract more of it than those in France and Germany combined.[22]

But if Britain really does want to become the world's next Silicon Valley, it needs to address some significant weaknesses. A cautious mindset among UK-based investors makes it harder for our most promising businesses to access the larger sums of capital necessary to become global giants. As a result, there are only a few UK-domiciled, globally significant tech companies. DeepMind is our most important – but it is owned by Google. The next is Arm, which designs the chips used in iPhones. It is headquartered in Cambridge and the only UK company in the world's top 100 tech companies – but listed on the New York Stock Exchange.[23]

Even when UK companies do manage to access large amounts of capital, it is more likely to come from overseas than home. Elsewhere, local pension funds are big investors in domestic growth companies. In the UK, however, our fragmented pension funds – thirty thousand in total – often lack the expertise to invest in private businesses.[24] Following the Maxwell scandal three decades ago, they have remained highly cautious investors. As a result, even though UK pension funds constitute the second largest pension pool in the world, they invest only 1% of their assets in unlisted UK companies.[25] That measly level of investment means that half the money raised by British venture capital firms comes from US and Canadian pension funds.

IPOs in the UK cannot access pension fund capital as easily as those elsewhere

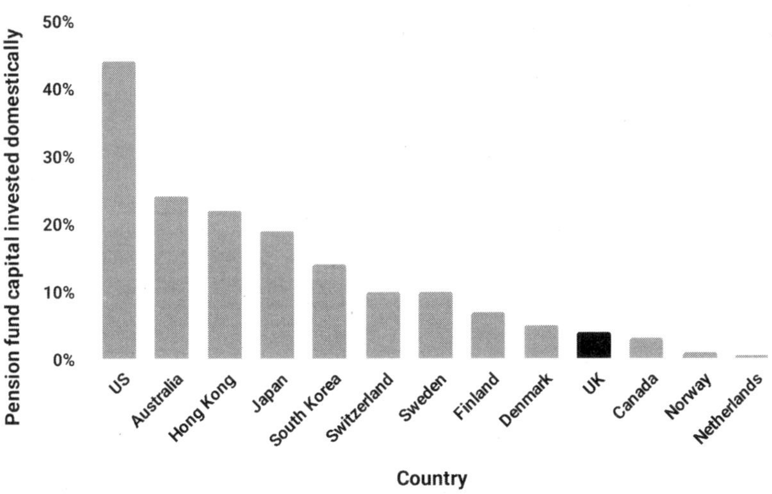

Source: New Financial[26]

Domestic investors, it must be said, do supply the vast majority of the capital for funding rounds smaller than £1 million. But by the time funding rounds surpass £10 million, foreign investors supply the majority of it. For rounds above £250 million, fully 85% of the money comes from abroad.[27] That means that the most successful British tech entrepreneurs are far more likely to get investment from a North American pension fund than a British one. With the UK's £3.2 trillion pension pool, nearly the size of the entire British economy, it doesn't have to be that way. But a cautious mindset means less capital for our most promising businesses and lower returns for savers.

If UK start-ups can still access the capital they need, does that matter? In one way it doesn't, as long as good companies are able to grow. In the early stages, they generally can secure the funding they need, something that was not always the case. The issue is the later stages: if funding comes primarily from overseas, fast-growing companies begin to feel a strong gravitational pull to cross the Atlantic. Most tech giants are based on the West Coast, so the investments they make tend to fold smaller companies into their ecosystem rather than ours. The biggest tech firms are listed in New York, making the NASDAQ the most attractive market in which to raise capital. It's true that many New York funds and NASDAQ-listed companies are happy to invest in UK businesses because of the inherent strengths of our tech ecosystem; but that ecosystem would be far bigger, more profitable and more influential if it was led by a group of British-owned and British-based 'hyperscalers'. Not an easy thing to achieve, but certainly not impossible. And if we pulled it off, the contribution to both tax revenues and economic growth would be enormous. The UK would also have more influence on global tech regulation and more leverage in increasingly frequent trade and tariff disputes.

For that reason, I introduced the 2023 Mansion House reforms. They are a comprehensive set of changes designed to unlock capital from UK pension funds for our most promising growth companies. They are designed both to raise returns for pension fund holders and to support economic growth. They do that by encouraging the consolidation of the fragmented pension fund market, making sure funds are judged on overall returns and not just cost, and making London Stock Exchange listing rules competitive with NASDAQ. As part of that, they also secured a commitment from most large pension funds to invest a larger proportion of their assets domestically. To her credit, Rachel Reeves has continued with these reforms, but there is a long way to go.

The next step is to copy Australia's more radical pension fund reforms. As discussed in the chapter on debt earlier, Aussies have just one pension pot that follows people throughout their working life, and pension savers rapidly turn into retail investors, following the value of their pension daily through an app on their phone. This results in intense competition between superannuation funds fighting to get the best returns. On average, they generate returns nearly 2% higher than their sleepier British counterparts. Over forty years of saving, an Australian pension pot is now likely to be worth double a British one.

To get there, there is lively debate about whether the government should mandate more domestic investment as a quid pro quo for the tax advantages pension funds receive. Some worry this would compromise a fund's fiduciary duty to invest wherever it can get the best returns for its fundholders. But given that the health of our pensions sector depends on the health of the economy, it is surely reasonable to ask it to play its part in supporting economic growth. And it doesn't necessarily have to be done through mandating: a good alternative would be to require defined contribution pension funds to have a default policy to invest a minimum proportion of their equity domestically – but give their savers the right to opt out if they choose. According to analysts at New Financial, doing so would generate an additional £76 billion of investment in domestic equities, making a big contribution to addressing the gap in the supply of equity finance, estimated at around £11 billion a year.[28]

Regulatory pressure also needs to be applied to pension funds that are just too small to pursue a balanced investment strategy. They should be encouraged or required to opt in to 'superfunds' or use vehicles like the British Business Bank or Pension Protection Fund to achieve the same end. We need institutional investors to develop an approach to structured risk that is closer to that of their equivalents in the US, Canada and Australia. In doing so, they would help solve the fundamental paradox at the heart of Britain's tech ecosystem: we are brilliant at creating frontier companies and have large pools of capital, but have yet to find a way to combine the two strengths.

Other more practical changes would also help the UK's Silicon Valley aspirations. The data centres that process AI are extremely power-hungry, but British electricity costs are the highest in Europe. This is an entirely solvable problem, as the next chapter will show. But doing so quickly really matters for our tech sector: even though large language models (LLMs) are unlikely to be trained outside the US, UK businesses and consumers will still need to access them. That requires abundant cheap and secure energy for locally-based data centres.

We also need a smarter approach to regulation given the regulatory autonomy that the UK now enjoys following Brexit. Leaving the EU was initially opposed by most of the tech sector because of concerns about their future ability to attract talent. That has now been replaced by a degree of relief that the UK is not part of the EU's heavy-handed AI regulatory regime. If we regulate in a light-touch way, the UK has a big opportunity to lead in future AI cycles, as the technology moves beyond LLMs. Britain's science base, its research into new medicines and (thanks again to Sir Demis Hassabis) its role in unlocking protein structures all suggest there could be significant opportunities for the UK in the crossover between AI and scientific research. We should therefore use our autonomy to agree mutual US–UK recognition of technical standards. We should allow more regulatory 'sandboxes' that allow start-ups to test innovations without having to get approval from multiple regulators. We should also digitise the approval system for NHS clinical trials to support our life sciences innovators.

But the most obvious way to support our growing army of tech unicorns relates to the public sector productivity challenges considered in the previous chapter. If we made the UK public sector a world leader in the adoption and diffusion of AI, we would be offering talented British start-ups the chance to tap into a huge new market right on their doorstep. Adoption potential is different from innovation potential – and while we excel at the former we should use the public sector to show we can also do the latter. Doing so, though, would require a complete overhaul of the cumbersome and bureaucratic procurement processes that currently make it much harder for dynamic, smaller companies to win contracts with the state. Too often our civil servants seem to believe that 'no one ever got fired for hiring IBM'.

At the same time, we must be careful not to backslide where we have existing strengths. The UK's openness to the brightest and best talent from around the world has been a major source of competitive advantage. It has been the foundation of the City of London's success in financial services and the secret sauce for our universities. It has turned our creative industries into major exporters and made the UK into Europe's largest TV and film producer. More than a third of our fastest-growing companies were set up or are being run by people not born in the UK, so maintaining a pipeline for the world's best talent to come to the UK is critical.[29] Our visa rules are reasonable enough by international standards, but we could do much more as part of an ambition to make the UK the easiest place for global AI talent to move to.

None of these reforms will bear fruit immediately. But if we keep the momentum moving in the right direction, there is really an opportunity to build a giant domestic tech sector. Changing the risk-averse mindset of British pension funds would help develop a class of UK-based technology giants. Faster adoption of AI in the NHS, schools or the defence sector could make the UK a leader in its public sector applications. Our regulatory autonomy makes us nimble – as demonstrated by the SVB rescue – which is why organisations such as the IMF single out particular opportunities for the UK from the AI revolution, describing the 'greater benefits from AI adoption as an upside for growth over the medium term given the UK's robust technology ecosystem'.[30]

It won't, however, give us a free pass when it comes to any social dislocation that may also be around the corner. So alongside technological innovation, we will need social innovation. But there, too, our roots run deep. In the nineteenth century, Edwin Chadwick championed clean water and sewage systems, Robert Owen improved factory conditions, Elizabeth Fry reformed prisons and Lord Shaftesbury campaigned against child labour. Such social pioneering transformed not just the UK but other capitalist economies too, saving us all from the implosion predicted by Karl Marx. Once again, we will need to be imaginative and inventive in order to make sure the benefits of an economic revolution are spread fairly. That means ensuring that opportunities for the best tech jobs spread beyond the London–Oxford–Cambridge triangle. It means making sure school leavers have the education and skills they need to profit from new jobs and industries, even ones of which we have little knowledge at the moment. It means a social contract that reassures the wider public that the unfolding changes will benefit everyone, not just a chosen few. Most of all it means facing into the future rather than trying to delay it.

> ## Make the most of the AI revolution
> Potential impact on annual GDP growth: 1%
> Potential impact on GDP per head in 10 years: 10%

And if we succeed, the prize in terms of economic growth is enormous. Analysis from Microsoft estimates that AI could help boost output by 2% a year.[31] Accenture's forecast puts the number at between 1.6 and 3%[32] – more than returning us to the growth rates we enjoyed before the global financial crisis. PwC agrees, saying it will increase the total size of our economy by up to 15%.[33] French economist and Nobel Prize-winner Philippe Aghion is more cautious, and says the impact on annual growth is likely to be between 0.7 and 1.3%. I have taken the mid-point of his range as my benchmark.[34] But it is not impossible to imagine the UK's tech sector becoming as big as California's today (even as California's becomes bigger still). That would put us well on the path to being Europe's largest economy. It would ensure the UK is an actor in the upheavals ahead rather than simply swept along by them.[35]

Perhaps the most practical step to help us get there would be to sort out Britain's high energy prices – to which we turn next.

CONCLUSIONS

- ► Unlocking UK pension fund capital provides a big opportunity to nurture British-based hyperscalers that could help the UK become the world's next Silicon Valley.

- ► We need fewer pension funds with more professional investment strategies that include infrastructure projects and early-stage companies which offer some of the highest and most reliable returns.

- ► UK pension funds should invest a default minimum proportion of their assets in UK assets – but give savers the chance to opt for different investment strategies.

- ► Copying Australian-style pension reforms, with a single transferable pension pot, would attract more savings and generate higher returns for savers.

- ► Britain should use its post-Brexit regulatory autonomy to make its technology and life sciences regulations the lightest, most nimble and most pro-innovation in the world.

- ► We should actively nurture innovation in AI that goes beyond LLMs, particularly in the public sector and at the interface between science and AI.

- ► We should pioneer social reforms that ensure all citizens benefit from the extraordinary innovations in science and business coming down the track.

7

Energy

In July 1887, James Blyth was working in his garden in the village of Marykirk in Aberdeenshire. He was not tending to the plants. Instead, the Scottish professor was conducting an experiment to see whether electricity could be generated from wind power, something never done before. Could he get an experiment in his garden to work?

We tend to think of renewable energy as a new phenomenon. In fact, the opposite is true: the first factories in the Industrial Revolution used water rather than coal-fired steam engines to generate their power; and six years before Blyth started experimenting in his garden, the town of Godalming in Surrey (part of my constituency) set up the world's first town-wide system of electric lights – powered by a turbine on the River Wey. But drawing energy from water proved expensive and unreliable. It also meant factories had to be located away from the cities where people worked. As a result, the factories switched to coal, and pioneering Godalming switched to gas.

To get a windmill to generate electricity, Blyth constructed a wooden tripod that was ten metres in height and had four

Scotsman James Blyth built one of the world's first wind turbines

four-metre canvas sails attached.[1] It drove a generator, which was then used to charge a set of battery cells. Despite some design flaws, the experiment worked.[2] He used the electricity generated by his amateur wind turbine to power lamps in the evenings and run a small lathe in his workshop. He continued to improve his design and later patented the invention.

In 1895, a version of Blyth's turbine was installed as a standby generator at the nearby Montrose Asylum, where it stood for thirty years. He offered to light the streets in Marykirk, but his generosity was rebuffed – his fellow villagers still thought electricity to be 'the work of the devil'.[3] Then, as now, the biggest drawback of wind power is what is called 'intermittency'.[4] When it's windy, you generate so much electricity that you need to find a way to store any excess, but when it isn't windy, you can run out. Nonetheless, Blyth was convinced of its potential. He imagined a time 'when each house has its own little windmill'.

His experiment was one of the first times wind was used to generate electricity – around the same time, American Charles Brush and Austrian Josef Friedländer were conducting similar experiments.[5] Over a century later, Britain has once again become a global pioneer in wind energy. In the late 1980s, the country opened its first commercial wind farm, and it has since become a world leader in offshore wind energy generation:[6] it overtook Denmark in 2008 to become the largest in Europe, and is now second only to China globally.[7] The Dogger Bank Wind Farm in the North Sea, which started producing electricity in 2023, is the biggest single offshore wind farm in the world. It will generate electricity for six million homes.[8]

Dogger Bank's story began in 2008,[9] when the UK government was attempting to harness its untapped marine energy and opened a number of offshore zones for lease bids.[10] (The name Dogger is derived from the Old Dutch word *dogge*, a type of fishing boat.) The Dogger Bank Zone was one of the biggest such zones in the world.

Things were no easier then than today. One of the early challenges was navigating a very complicated and lengthy environmental impact assessment, mostly because of Dogger Bank's designation as a special area of conservation.[11] Developers had to address multiple concerns about harm to habitats and wildlife. This was in addition to other challenges, most notably the monumental engineering task of building such a large project 130 km offshore.

Whatever your views on wind power, the scale of the project is extraordinary. When its three phases of construction are complete, it will have a total of 277 turbines, each standing at a height of 260 m with blades measuring 107 m in length. Every turbine is nearly thirty times the size of Blyth's original experiment – and together they will cover an area larger than a thousand football pitches. With three offshore substations, Dogger Bank will supply high-voltage direct current into the UK's national grid – the first time ever for a UK wind farm.[12] So confident are the wind farm's operators of its success that they have already proposed adding an additional 1.5 GW of capacity via a fourth construction phase.[13]

Dogger Bank exemplifies the transformation of Britain's energy sector. In 2010, 28% of UK electricity was generated by coal. Now none is. Instead, renewable energies including wind and solar have risen from around 7% to half of the total amount of electricity generated.[14] On a windy day, over 50% of UK electricity can come from wind.[15] Though not every house in the UK has its own little windmill, as Blyth imagined, the UK now has more than twelve thousand wind turbines generating electricity.[16] Quite a legacy for an unknown Scottish inventor.

Cheap, reliable energy is essential for economic growth as we discovered after the invasion of Ukraine and during the recent crisis in Iran. This chapter considers how well the UK has been doing at securing it. It recognises successes, such as investment in renewable energy and a new push for nuclear power, but doesn't shy away from an ugly truth: the British economy remains hampered by some of the highest energy prices in the world. We will look at the impact of those prices and whether things can be done differently while still meeting our climate change obligations. The good news is that it is a fixable problem. Even better, unlike many growth reforms, that impact would be almost immediate.

Let's start, though, with a positive when it comes to the UK's record. The impact of wind farms like Dogger has made a big difference to an issue Blyth had never heard of – climate change. Partly thanks to those twelve thousand turbines, Britain has reduced emissions by more than any other large country. Our carbon footprint is down 48% from 1990 levels compared to a 46% reduction in Germany, a 17% reduction in Japan and a mere 4% reduction in the US.[17] The UK's numbers are, it has to be said, flattered by deindustrialisation: we have started importing a lot of our more carbon-intensive products instead of making them at home. Nonetheless, when independently assessed for its commitment to tackling climate change, the UK ranks top in the G7 and second overall.

The UK scores better than any G7 country for commitment to tackling climate change...

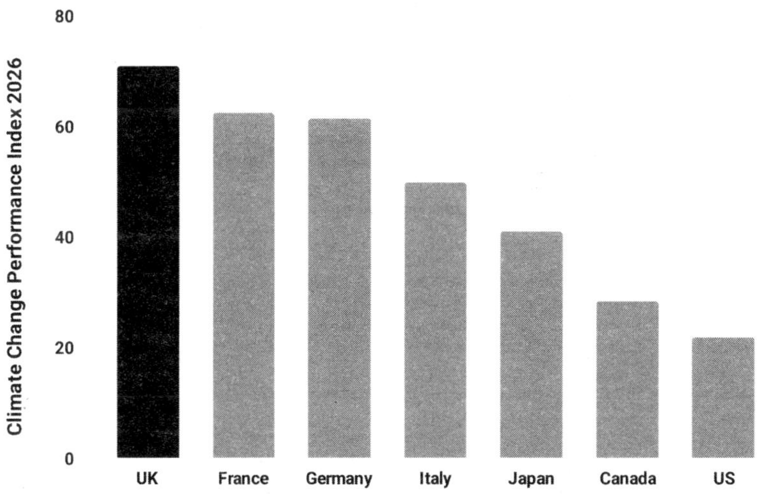

Source: Climate Change Performance Index 2026[18]

…but also has the highest energy prices in the G7.

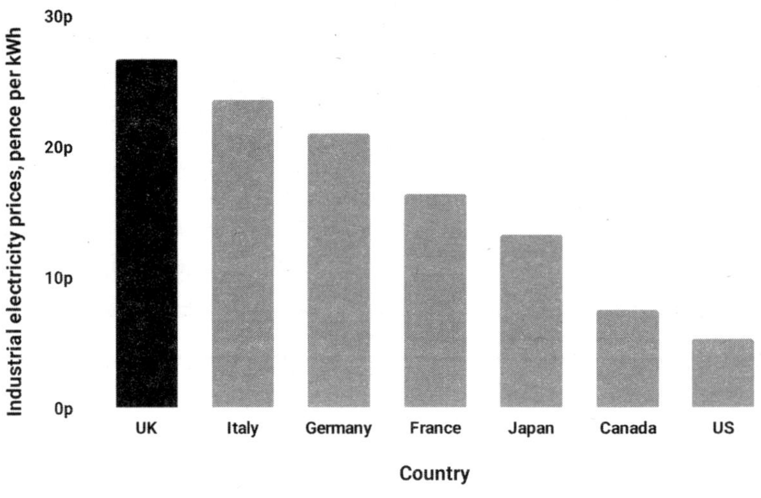

Source: DESNZ[19]
Note: Prices inclusive of taxes and are all from 2024, except for the US, where the latest available data is for 2021, although it looks like the number hasn't shifted much.

But it is a flawed revolution.

The large investments involved – £9 billion for Dogger Bank alone – have been largely funded through higher energy bills. This has made UK energy costs not just the highest in Europe, but higher than those in any other large economy. German businesses pay 24% less for their energy, French businesses 35% less and American businesses 75% less. The picture is more complicated when it comes to domestic energy, but American household electricity bills are less than half those in the UK.[20]

High energy prices damage economic competitiveness. They reduce business productivity and deter investment, particularly in manufacturing sectors that use a lot of energy such as steel, chemicals and ceramics. Even sectors with relatively low energy use suffer: restaurants, pubs and shops rely on consumers having money in their pockets, but there is much less of that if household electricity bills are high. OBR analysis suggests a 10% increase in energy prices reduces GDP growth by about 0.2% a year over the medium term.[21] Given that energy prices in the UK have doubled in real terms over the last decade, the total detriment to our growth is likely to be much higher.

High prices also put at risk the key emerging sectors discussed in the last chapter. The computing power needed by the tech industry has doubled every six months since 2010.[22] Large language models like Gemini, Claude and ChatGPT are particularly hungry for energy: Google says that AI-enhanced searches consume thirty times more power than regular ones.[23] That means more data centres globally, which, taken together, will consume as much electricity as the whole of India by 2034.[24] If the UK wants to be an AI superpower, having some of the world's highest energy prices puts it at a significant disadvantage. Nor will people want to switch to electric cars if electricity is too expensive.

UK energy prices are also more volatile. Because they are set by international markets, they spiked following Russia's full-scale invasion of Ukraine and are highly vulnerable to events in the Middle East such as the US/Israeli 2026 attack on Iran. I had to deal with the consequences of the Ukraine invasion and saw that it was not just bad for energy bills, but had even bigger knock-on effects for the economy: higher inflation, a slower recovery from recession and a wave of damaging pay strikes. A previous consensus in favour of decarbonisation was shattered as consumers became angry at the green levies on their bills.

The UK also has some of the most volatile energy prices

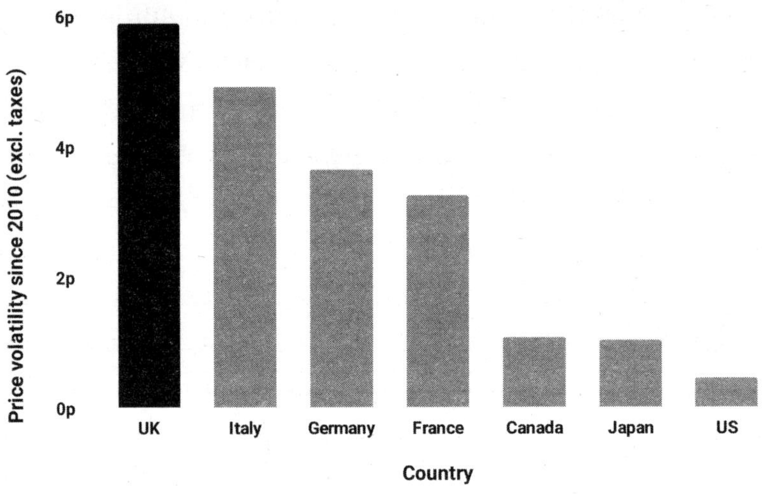

Source: DESNZ[25]
Note: Volatility in this case is measured by one standard deviation of annual prices (per kWh). Prices exclude taxes.

Those levies, which raise around £12 billion every year, have helped to attract around £200 billion of investment into the clean energy sector, a huge sum that the Treasury would never have been able to find from public funds. But the contracts that went alongside the new investments mean we will be paying higher bills for a long time. Both Dogger Bank and the Hinkley Point nuclear power station have been guaranteed above-market prices for their electricity in what are known as 'contracts for difference'. Purists prefer levies to direct government subsidies, because they encourage households to invest in energy efficiency. But they also raise the cost of living, cut growth and damage competitiveness. Is there a way to do things differently?

*

Tackling some of the many distortions and inefficiencies in the UK energy market would be a good starting point. One of the biggest reasons for high bills is that UK consumers pay for a lot of electricity they never actually use. At the moment, electricity is bought by National Grid at a single price irrespective of where it is generated. Often, the grid can't cope with surges of provision in particular parts of the country – if, for example, there is a windy day in the North Sea. It then has to ask wind farms to switch off their supplies – but pays for them anyway through what are called 'constraint payments'. It then has to buy the electricity that was switched off from somewhere else – often at last-minute premium prices.

In other words, we pay twice. Over half of the income of our biggest wind farms now comes not from supplying electricity but from constraint payments. The Seagreen Offshore Wind Farm opened in 2023 off the east coast of Scotland, with 116 turbines designed to supply electricity to 1.6 million homes.[26] But two thirds of the power it has generated has been switched off because the grid can't handle it. Constraint payments to Seagreen and other wind farms, alongside the cost of buying replacement electricity, amounted to nearly £1.5 billion in 2025, adding £52 to a typical household bill. This is likely to increase further in the next few years.[27]

The issue has been compounded by a broader failure to increase demand for electricity in a way that matches the increase in supply. Most people assume that with electric cars, hot summers and computer equipment, demand for electricity has soared. In fact, since 2011, while installed capacity has gone up by 10%, overall demand has fallen by 15%.[28] But again, because we have promised to buy the additional electricity, we still end up paying for it.

UK bills are higher because we do not use the extra electricity capacity we have installed

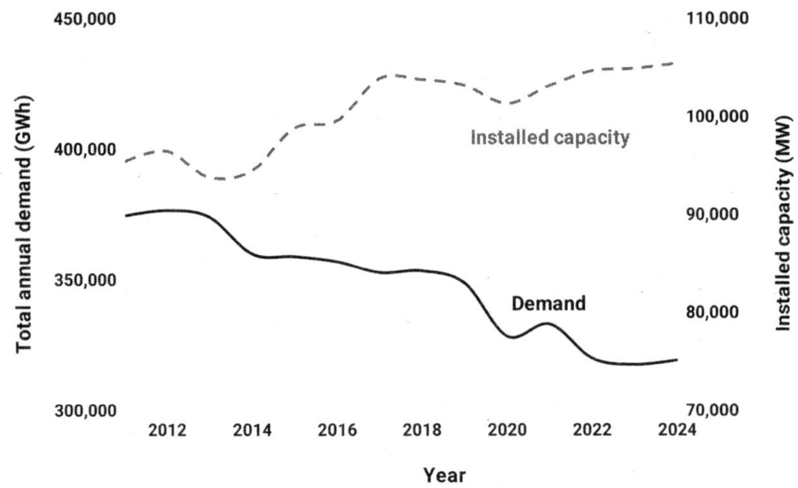

Source: DESNZ[29]

Why has demand for electricity fallen? Because until recently, increased use from new areas such as electric cars was outweighed by reductions from factory closures – such as the tragic closure of the Honda car factory in Swindon in 2021. Consumers have also got better at energy efficiency, prompted in part by soaring bills. Putting in insulation and installing smart meters are perfectly sensible things to do, but weaning people off gas would have had a greater impact on emissions. Yet instead of encouraging greater electricity use, the government puts a £140 levy on electricity bills, compared to just £50 on gas bills.[30]

Then there is the way prices are set. In theory, the energy generated from wind farms should be cheap because its marginal price (the cost of generating power once the farm has been commissioned) is zero. But we allow its price to be determined by

168

global gas prices. If we decoupled domestic energy prices, our bills would be less susceptible to international events (such as the war in Ukraine) and more likely to fall as renewable and nuclear energy come on stream. Spain has done just that with a mechanism called the 'Iberian exception', which started in 2022. It had to compensate gas generators for lower prices, but over time the wholesale price of electricity fell by between a third and a half, and bills came down.[31] Spain's economic growth picked up and is now significantly outpacing the UK's. We should do the same.

France has kept energy bills down a different way – by sustained investment in nuclear power. Their nuclear programme has had plenty of hiccups, including corrosion in its nuclear plants, which took most of them out of service in 2022. But after many decades of investment, its business energy costs are among the lowest in Europe. As in the UK, electricity is more expensive than gas – but only double the price, compared to four times higher here. But even with its lower prices, the French government is still worried that they are not competitive with the US; in 2022 my then G7 colleague, French finance minister Bruno Le Maire, said, 'Our industry is already suffering from a competitiveness deficit linked to the differences in energy prices between the United States and Europe.'[32] Despite being Europe's largest producer of nuclear power, France now plans to build six additional power stations. The absurdity of Britain's energy policy was brought home to me in the Autumn Statement of 2022. I had come to office following the unravelling of my predecessor Kwasi Kwarteng's mini-budget. Most of the media focus had been on unfunded tax cuts. But what really spooked the markets was the promise to cap energy bills at £2,500 per household. That pledge put the UK government on the hook for massive future liabilities. To remove what looked like a blank cheque being offered by the British state, I pared back the plans. But even my scaled-down version cost a staggering £78 billion – the equivalent of nearly £3,000 of extra borrowing for every household. If only we had invested that huge sum of money in building new nuclear power stations a few decades earlier.

Governments can't control oil and gas prices but they can make an economy less vulnerable to when they spike. Doing so will require radical changes to our energy policy, including planning and regulatory approval reforms, measures to eliminate constraint payments and better grid access. Most (but not all) of them are rather technocratic changes which ordinary voters will not notice. What they will see, however, is a reduction in energy bills. That ought to be very popular.

Starting with planning and regulatory reform, the government needs to implement the recommendations of a recent review of nuclear power by economist John Fingleton. His analysis is sobering: new projects are often forced to deal with six different regulators, who take overly cautious decisions that are quite disproportionate to the risk being managed. Laws and regulations prioritise process over outcomes, leading to a lack of urgency and a culture of box-ticking. Alongside indecision by ministers and a lack of competition, that has led to cost increases which make British nuclear power some of the most expensive in the world.[33]

One of the biggest reasons is the time it takes to get a new nuclear power station built. Final approval to go ahead takes at least five years, followed by a further decade to build it. The government says it will implement the Fingleton recommendations, which should make a difference. But as discussed in the chapter on building things, we should go much further and reduce the time it takes to get approval for any critical national infrastructure project to no more than two years. If a project gets the green light at the start of a parliament, it should surely be possible to start construction during the same parliamentary term. That way governments will have an incentive to get on with difficult decisions early – and retain the confidence of voters that their elected politicians can actually get things done.

Regulators are also too relaxed about requiring changes that delay new projects. Hinkley Point C, for example, is based on a template used successfully by EDF in France. But that wasn't good enough for the UK nuclear regulator, which insisted on no fewer than 7,000 design changes. One of them was to add a non-computerised backup system, probably the first time ever for a nuclear power station.[34] Safety is especially important when it comes to nuclear power, but that kind of additional complexity actually increases risk, because problems become harder to fix. And the more you move away from standardised designs the more you increase cost and delays: changes at Hinkley entailed the use of 25% more concrete and 35% more steel, contributing to a delay of more than a decade.[35] Worst of all, such gold-plating undermines the main rationale for building a nuclear power plant in the first place – namely, cheaper power. As a result, when Hinkley finally opens, its electricity will be double the price per megawatt than in France or Finland and six times more than in South Korea. We need to do things very differently, not least with the new small modular reactors coming on stream.

As well as planning and regulatory reform, we also need to speed up access to the national grid. Often, companies planning new off-shore wind projects are told that a new grid connection will take fifteen years.[36] Building new transmission lines only takes about two years, so the culprit is once again a laborious planning process for new pylons and substations.[37] But is it really in the interests of people whose homes are blighted to face such a long wait for a decision? In 2023, I introduced measures to halve grid connection delays that were estimated by Treasury officials to unlock an extra £90 billion of investment. Bolder reforms would release much more.

One thing that would speed up access is for Ofgem to scrap its policy of only allowing grid investment at the last moment. It is an old policy designed to make sure investments are really needed before they are approved. But when we know our demand for electricity will double in the decades ahead, it makes much more sense to plan strategically and allow National Grid to invest in anticipation of demand rather than in response to it. Doing so would also help reduce constraint payments.

But could we go further and eliminate constraint payments altogether? At the moment, investment is concentrated in the North Sea, which makes it difficult for the grid to absorb and transport the energy it produces. Zonal pricing – allowing different prices for electricity in different parts of the country – could achieve more balanced geographical investment and potentially eliminate constraint payments altogether. As part of that, we should also consider the most radical reform of all, namely allowing energy companies to build their own transmission connections to the grid – as happens in Australia, India, the US and Brazil. AI companies should also be allowed to do the same for their data centres, something regulators have so far refused. Operators built their own infrastructure in the steam and energy revolutions of previous centuries. Broadband infrastructure was transformed in the UK when we opened up the ducts and poles owned by Openreach to third parties. Why not find a way to do the same for energy?

Given we are paying for so much electricity that we do not use, we should also encourage more people to use it. A more comprehensive national network of electric car charging points would boost electric car take-up, as would other measures, such as making it easier to recharge on residential parking streets. Over time, green levies should be switched from electricity to gas, taking care not to disadvantage low-income households.

Most of all, we need to be more pragmatic when it comes to net zero ideology. The 2030 target date for decarbonising the grid is entirely arbitrary. It is not necessary for our 2050 commitment to net zero but does increase energy costs by forcing through expensive, hurried investment. At the same time, instead of cancelling new licences for North Sea oil and gas, we should continue to source domestic fossil fuel while we still have it. Net zero is a commitment that our *net* impact on the environment will be zero by 2050 but it does not ban the use of fossil fuel. We and others will need it for many decades after 2050 – so we should make the most of the reserves we have.

Planning and regulatory reform, more balanced decisions from regulators, investment in the grid, eliminating constraint payments and boosting electricity use alongside exploiting North Sea oil and gas are just some of the things that could bring energy bills down. It is hard to quantify by how much, but industry analysis suggests that a modest package of reforms along such lines could reduce bills by around 10%. A bolder package, including the two-year limit on new infrastructure approvals and fully restarting North Sea oil and gas exploration, would surely double that impact.

What would that do for economic growth? As mentioned earlier, OBR data suggests we have already paid a huge price for our higher energy bills, which have doubled over the last decade in real terms. Analysis of other OECD countries broadly backs up the OBR claim that a 10% rise in energy costs knocks 0.2% off annual GDP growth.[38] It is difficult to gauge how long such effects last and whether reducing bills would increase growth by exactly the same amount, although earlier Bank of England and OBR analysis does suggest there would be a direct effect. Overall, though, it is not unreasonable to assume that a 20% reduction in energy prices would be likely to add around 0.2% to annual growth rates for several years.[39]

> **Reduce energy bills by 10–20%**
>
> Potential impact on annual GDP growth: 0.2%
>
> Potential impact on GDP per head after 10 years: 2%

What makes doing so particularly attractive is the immediate impact of any reduction, given that the cost of energy has such a direct effect on every part of the economy. The effect would not, however, last for ever and is not guaranteed: many other factors influence economic growth, including wars, strikes and tariffs. But it would be the single policy most likely to lift us quickly out of our low-growth trap.

That said, the mistakes in energy policy should not be overstated: £200 billion of investment since 2010 is a big achievement by any standard, and has made Britain's renewable sector one of Europe's most successful. Despite the nightmare of getting planning approval, we are finally building new nuclear power stations; David Cameron's support for Hinkley Point C was the first government approval of nuclear power for nearly two decades, and since then plans have progressed for Sizewell C in Suffolk and Bradwell B in Essex. Together with Grant Shapps, I announced a competition for small modular reactors, which was won by Rolls-Royce. They plan to build the first one in Anglesey within the next decade, and we remain just about on track to generate a quarter of our energy from nuclear sources by 2050.[40] We just need to make sure that the increased supply of clean energy translates into lower bills.

Grasping the nettle to bring down our high energy costs would not just translate into economic growth. It would help insulate us from ongoing instability in the Middle East and increasingly volatile oil and gas prices. It would also reassure the public that we are taking a balanced approach to our climate change responsibilities which takes account of the pressure on family finances. It would secure the UK's place in the AI revolution. Most importantly, it would reduce cost – and risk – for everyone starting up or growing a business. By making life easier for them we would be sending the clearest possible signal that their success is the country's top priority. What better way to convince them that there is a growth mindset at the very top of government?

CONCLUSIONS

- ► Energy policy should focus on cheaper bills as much as climate change.

- ► Scrap the 2030 grid decarbonisation target.

- ► Exploit North Sea oil and gas while we have it.

- ► Reduce the time for planning approval to two years to make clean energy – especially nuclear power – much cheaper.

- ► Nuclear regulators should take a risk-based approach rather than gold-plating safety regulations.

- ► Improve the infrastructure for electrification, especially electric cars.

- ► Allow National Grid to invest proactively rather than wait for formal grid connection requests.

- ► Reduce costly constraint payments by encouraging more investment nearer to where power is needed, including through zonal pricing.

- ► Allow energy companies to build their own transmission connections to the grid.

8

Regions

Andy Street does not come from a gilded political background. He was raised in the Midlands by a salesman father and a pharmacist mother. He studied politics, philosophy and economics at Oxford before applying to become a social worker for Birmingham City Council. Perhaps surprisingly, he was turned down, and ended up as a graduate trainee at the John Lewis Partnership. His first assignment was in their Brent Cross store, where, in line with the company's egalitarian culture, he was kept busy stacking shelves, manning checkouts and counting stock. Over two decades, he quietly rose through the ranks, earning respect for his low-key but determined management style. In 2007, he became managing director. Under Andy's leadership the company increased its sales by half, doubled its stores and pioneered the move to 'bricks & clicks' shopping.

In 2016, he put himself forward for election as the first ever mayor of the West Midlands. Being a Tory businessman was not the easiest sell in a Labour-voting region with an unpopular national government. But he won, albeit by a tiny margin of less than 1% of the vote. As mayor, he applied the same no-fuss approach to leadership he had shown at John Lewis. Over seven years, he patiently broke down doors and knocked heads together to bring investment and jobs into the area. I saw him in action when we worked closely together to set up a new investment zone at Coventry Airport.

Andy championed improvements to transport infrastructure, and was a vocal supporter of HS2 – indeed, he nearly resigned from the Conservative Party when its northern leg was cancelled. He also put a lot of effort into boosting skills among young people, opening job hubs and launching an ambitious plan to tackle youth unemployment. He promoted not just housebuilding but affordable housing, which grew to a third of all new houses built on his watch. He also focused on homelessness, with an initiative that took four hundred rough sleepers off the streets. He was re-elected in 2021. Although he was eventually defeated in 2024, the narrowness of the margin was a marked contrast to the landslide loss suffered by the Conservatives nationally two months later.

During his time, the West Midlands attracted £10 billion of inward investment, the most successful region in the UK outside London.[1] It had the UK's fastest-growing tech sector outside the south-east. Sixteen thousand homes were built annually,[2] and big infrastructure projects, including the new Camp Hill railway line, were prioritised. Even his critics conceded that no one could have done more to promote economic growth.

Austin, Texas has a comparable population to the West Midlands. Over the same period, it also had dynamic civic leadership under Mayor Steve Adler. He came from a legal rather than a business background, but like Andy Street he saw the potential of big transport projects to revitalise development. He championed Project Connect, a $7.1 billion transformation of the city's transport networks, which involved building new light-rail lines and expanding bus routes to reduce the numbers driving to work. He set up a bold initiative to eliminate traffic fatalities. And he, too, worked hard to attract more investment into the area, particularly from the tech sector. Austin boomed and was soon ranked the best city in the US to start a business.[3] Other surveys placed it fifth for tech talent and seventh among the country's top 100 tech cities.[4]

Both the West Midlands and Austin were badly affected by the pandemic; but even accounting for that, the West Midlands economy expanded by 3% in real terms under Andy Street.[5] But the Austin economy grew by a massive 53% over the same period – nearly twenty times faster.[6] Why such a big difference? In this chapter, we look at why regions in the UK find it so much harder to close the gap with more affluent areas. We then consider the impact on our national prosperity if we found a way to do things differently.

A tale of two cities: Mayor Street and Mayor Adler

What's interesting about the comparison between the West Midlands and Austin is the similarities as well as the differences. Both had strong civic leadership determined to fire up economic growth. Arguably, the West Midlands should have had an advantage, being led by an experienced businessman rather than a lawyer. But Steve Adler had something Andy Street could only dream of: extensive autonomy and executive authority. He chaired the city council, through which he was able to control the city budget. He could offer tax incentives to new businesses. He had control over local planning decisions. He could even issue municipal bonds, subject to voter approval. He was effectively the city's CEO. To fund Project Connect, Austin residents voted to approve a 4% increase to their property taxes[7] – 58% in favour to 42% against.[8]

Mayor Street, on the other hand, had virtually no executive power. His budget came not from voters but from bureaucratic negotiations with local councils and national government. The former were generally under the control of a different political party, which made the process fraught. Unlike Mayor Adler, he had no power to set or waive business taxes and no control over planning. Borrowing was subject to Treasury caps and controls, effectively making it impossible. Neither mayor had power to set local income tax, but in two crucial ways Steve Adler had the stronger hand: firstly, he had control of the city council, which set many local taxes; and secondly, the city received 12% of local sales tax revenues, which boosted its coffers as business boomed. Andy Street, on the other hand, could only add a small precept to council tax bills. He got only a small share of the increase in business rates, which he used to fund his administration costs in order to keep taxes down.

Perhaps the simplest way to compare the two mayors is their spending power: Mayor Street had the ability to direct spending of about £800 per household in the West Midlands; Mayor Adler had roughly ten times that amount – £8,000 per household.[9] Project Connect would have been utterly impossible in the West Midlands, because 95% of tax revenue in the UK goes to central government.[10] Birmingham is probably the biggest city in the developed world unable to fund its own infrastructure projects.

That is not to say that everything is better in Austin than in the West Midlands. Homicide rates remain about six times higher.[11] One in seven people don't have health insurance.[12] And not all of Austin's spectacular growth was down to local government freedoms – at a state level, Texas charges no income tax, compared to up to 13.3% in rival California.[13] But its autonomy meant that strong civic leadership made a much bigger difference than in the UK.

This chapter looks at the economic growth that could be unlocked if we tackled the regional imbalances that have long held back Britain's economy. It's a problem that has existed for a long time and is often called 'the north–south divide'. It didn't start in the 1980s, but got a lot worse in that period, as many manufacturing businesses closed. Productivity per hour worked in Manchester is today 34% lower than in London.[14] That means lower salaries – a median salary of £36,500, rather than the £46,400 in the capital – and ultimately lower living standards.[15] In France, the gap between Lyon and Paris is nearly half that, at just €7,000 (£6,000).[16] Japan does even better, with virtually no difference in salaries between Tokyo and Osaka.[17] And in Munich, wages are actually higher than in Berlin.[18] In a comparison with twenty-six other OECD countries, the UK ranks fifth worst for regional income disparity.[19]

There are many reasons for this, but the hobbling of civic leadership, as Andy Street found, is one of the biggest. That combines with ineffective infrastructure and housing policy – both again largely dictated by London. A lack of high-speed rail services makes it harder for businesses in the north to do business in London. It also makes it more tempting for talented individuals to up sticks and move south. Compare that to Osaka: it is nearly two hundred miles further away from Tokyo than Manchester is from London, but you can still get there and back in a day on a reliable and comfortable bullet train. Meanwhile, we are still waiting for HS2.

Another reason for entrenched regional disparity in the UK is London's runaway success. Despite the recent exodus of non-doms, it remains Europe's richest city, one of the world's two great finance centres and a global centre for arts, culture and education. That creates enormous gravitational pull. Talented young Mancunians are far more likely to earn a six-figure salary if they move south. Over decades, that migration has contributed to unaffordably high house prices in the south-east, something that has further increased the north–south gap.

That has several damaging consequences. Because benefit rates are set nationally, their level has to take account of the cost of living in expensive as well as lower-cost areas. The result is that in more depressed parts of the country, rates are set at a level which makes it difficult for private sector jobs to compete. Fewer businesses means fewer jobs. Lower-income families then do less well than in countries with less stark disparities. In the UK they are 20% worse off than families in France or Germany at a similar position on the income spectrum.[20]

Such a large imbalance creates problems in the south of the UK as well. For sure, baby boomers have seen a huge increase in their wealth as house prices have soared. But many of their children are forced to move away in order to get onto the housing ladder. The average age at which Londoners buy their first house or flat is now thirty-seven – eleven years older than they were in 1980. Many wait even longer or give up altogether, frustrated and excluded from the property-owning democracy they were promised. Market economies remain the best way ever invented to generate wealth. But unless they give everyone a fair crack of the whip, democratic legitimacy erodes. Social instability can follow, leading to a drift towards extremes. If we want to keep the benefits of the system we have, we need to make it work better.

Which is what, in fairness, many politicians have tried to do. Gordon Brown introduced the minimum wage and tax credits, of particular benefit to people living in areas where salaries are lower. George Osborne brought in the national living wage and increased income tax thresholds. Rishi Sunak increased those thresholds to £12,570 – meaning that for the first time, anyone could earn £1,000 a month without paying any tax or national insurance.[21] As a result, contrary to what many believe, people on low pay are now taxed more lightly in the UK than in any other G7 country.[22] Regular increases in the national living wage have further boosted living standards: I increased it to two thirds of median income, a measure which again has the biggest impact in regions where pay is lower. Those on median pay (about £39,000)[23] have not done too badly either: following cuts to employees' national insurance contributions, they now have the lowest personal tax rates for half a century.[24] Take-home pay for those on median pay has increased four times faster than for those on the highest salaries.

All such measures were well-intentioned. By redistributing the tax burden away from the poorer north to the more prosperous south, they have had some impact on reducing both regional pay disparities and the numbers living in poverty. But in a crucial way, they missed the point: instead of putting our faith in levers we can pull from Downing Street, we should be giving local communities the tools to transform themselves. Ultimately, that is a far more lasting way to reduce regional disparity. How can we do that – and what would the overall impact be on economic growth?

Regional imbalances are far more entrenched in the UK...

Labour productivity per worker as a % of capital city equivalent (2021)

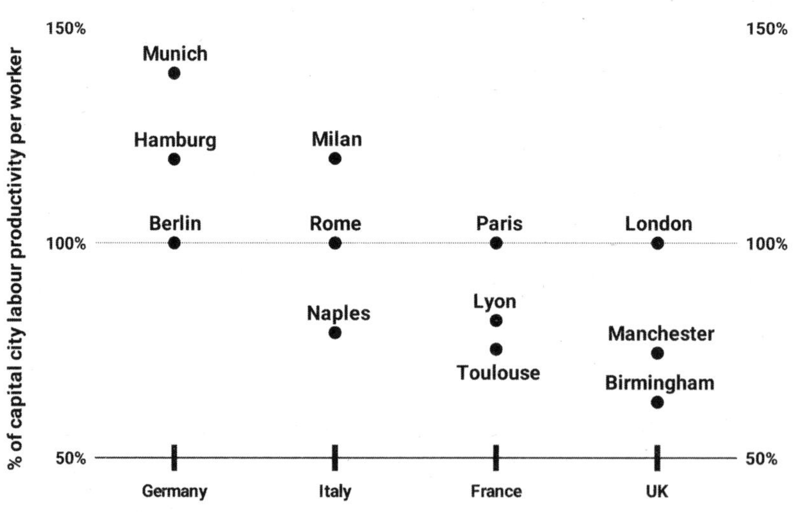

Source: OECD[25]

...despite a big effort by governments to improve incomes of those in regions where pay is lowest

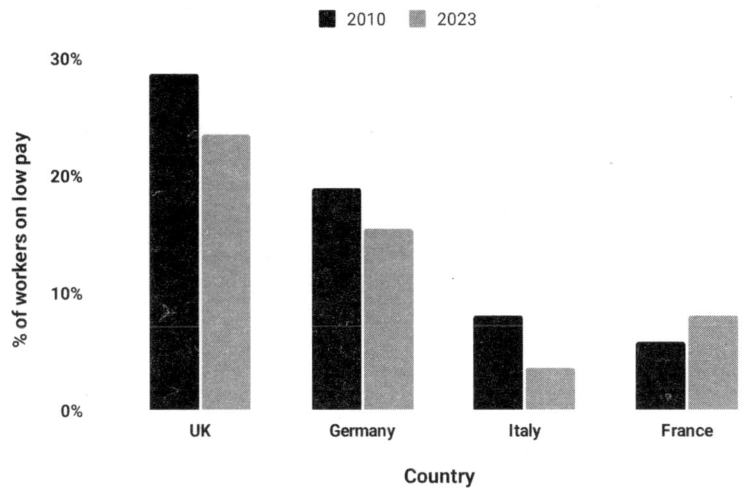

Source: OECD[26]

Despite being one of the richest countries in the world, Switzerland has many less prosperous regions. One of them is the canton of Jura in the north-west of the country. Local citizens voted to split from Bern in 1978, making it Switzerland's newest canton. Jura is rural and relatively undeveloped, with higher unemployment than its neighbouring cantons. But Switzerland is one of the world's most decentralised democracies, and the newly independent canton used its freshly acquired freedoms to impressive effect.

A big priority was to improve poor transport links. So one of its first decisions was to build a new motorway, known as the Transjurane, to provide better connections to France and the rest of Switzerland. In most countries, new roads or railways are highly controversial. Angry residents do everything possible to get routes

185

changed, leading to court cases, delays and increased cost. But in Jura, it was different: the decision to proceed was put to a referendum and was backed by 71% of voters, giving the project strong democratic legitimacy right from the outset.[27]

Because of the extensive tunnelling involved – two four-kilometre tunnels which were necessary to get through the rugged Jura mountains – it took sixteen years for the first stretch to open.[28] The final section didn't open for a further two decades. But when it did, it transformed access to nearby economic hubs such as the capital, Bern, the pharmaceuticals city of Basel and the watchmaking city of Biel. Tourism also took off.

The Transjurane: Switzerland skilfully uses referenda to secure support for infrastructure projects

Jura's economic development has been supported by a raft of local initiatives. People have been consulted in referenda on issues including support for the watchmaking industry, investment in technical education, new industrial parks and improvements to digital infrastructure. Strong leadership from Jura's president, Rosalie Beuret Siess, and Federal Councillor Elisabeth Baume-Schneider has made a difference. But asking people to show their support through regular ballots has maintained momentum and built consensus.

The result is that Jura has started to close the prosperity gap with the rest of Switzerland. Its unemployment is now only marginally higher than the Swiss average. Pride in its social and economic progress has fostered a much stronger regional identity. And even accounting for Switzerland's higher prices, Jura has a GDP per head 40% higher than the UK.[29] Not all of that is down to local autonomy: other factors such as excellent technical education, strengths in advanced manufacturing and geographical location have been crucial. But as with Austin, local empowerment allowed the region to take greater control of its economic destiny and drive faster progress.

Switzerland is the world's most decentralised advanced economy as well as being one of its most prosperous. Interestingly, there are a number of other smaller European countries with successful economies including Ireland, the Netherlands, Iceland, Denmark, Sweden, Norway and Finland. On average, their GDP per head is a striking 40% higher than that of larger European countries.[30] They also tend to have higher well-being scores, better governance[31] and more social trust.[32] Those of us from larger countries sometimes dismiss their success as not relevant because of their size.

But shouldn't we ask a different question: namely whether we can replicate their economic success and democratic stability by decentralising our own politics?

In a smaller democracy, power is automatically closer to ordinary people, partly because leaders have to reach out to fewer citizens. But the most successful ones don't stop there: Switzerland, which has a population of just nine million, has given its cantons enormous autonomy. It encourages them to engage their own citizens as much as possible with direct democracy. Higher civic participation rates have also prompted more sophisticated debates than in other countries: a referendum proposal to reduce the working week to thirty-six hours was rejected by 75% of the population.[33] Swiss suspicion of concentrated power means that even their presidency is rotated every year.

There are plenty of elements of this model that would not work elsewhere. Referenda have been less successful in California, where they tend to be highly politicised, with mixed consequences for growth. In a more combative political culture, the questions people vote on are often framed as constraints on government action – what would you like to stop the government doing? – rather than seeking positive consent for a long-term reform. But there is still much we can learn about the link between decentralised political structures, social stability and economic prosperity.

We can also learn from our own, rather mixed experience in the UK. Since 1997, power has been devolved to Scotland, Wales and Northern Ireland. Yet economic growth in all three countries has been lower, albeit marginally, than in England. If they had performed like Jura in Switzerland, it would have been the opposite. The reason it didn't happen is that the devolution settlements – and the politics that came with them – were flawed. Instead of giving devolved governments a funded mandate by which they had the authority and the ability to fund their own ambitions, continued dependence on national government handouts has fostered grievance politics, which allow problems to be blamed on 'London' or 'Westminster'. Compare that with French cities, which receive very little from Paris but are allowed to keep all the business taxes raised locally. Or the US, where cities receive no federal 'operating grant' but collect property taxes and a share of sales tax. Unlike in Scotland, Wales or Northern Ireland, their future is squarely in their own hands.

We have seen the same pattern when it comes to devolution within England. Local authorities get a significant chunk of their income through a central grant that comes from the Ministry of Housing, Communities and Local Government. They have to hand half of the business rates they collect back to the Treasury. Even when they are promised a share of the uplift in any business tax collected, it is only temporary. And if an authority collects more council tax from approving a new housing development, it often ends up being clawed back by the Treasury through complicated local government funding formulae designed to be 'fair'. Fairness in this context means equalising a council's 'spending power' with that of poorer councils – by transferring tax receipts from one to the other. The result is that the strongest incentive for local coun- cillors responsible for planning applications is to secure votes from residents who want to block them. Instead we need councils who are willing partners in nurturing growth in their areas. The irony is that the very policies designed to promote 'fairness' have the effect of entrenching regional inequality.

*

Arguments about inequality are generally conducted through a partisan prism. Those on the left argue that it is an issue of social justice which should be tackled as a matter of principle, ahead of considerations about economic growth. Those on the right tend to see prosperity as an absolute good which trumps inequality. Does it matter if the 1% get very rich if the other 99% are also getting richer? It does – and not just because of the need for social cohesion. A country's productive potential depends on tapping into the skills, ideas and energy of as many of its people as possible. If large chunks of the population are left behind because of poor skills, disabilities or a flawed welfare state then everyone loses out. Fixing social issues costs money, but investment in education, skills and economic infrastructure adds to economic potential.

But it needs to happen everywhere. That's why one of the biggest opportunities to unlock economic growth in the UK is through being better at harnessing the potential of its regions. International evidence suggests that devolution works when it is done with the consent of the local population and involves transferring power to competent local leaders. Most crucially, it needs to be a funded mandate which gives locally elected politicians the ability to raise their own resources rather than just spend money allocated to them from the centre.

Part of that, as discussed in the chapter on building things, is to make sure local authorities benefit financially from growth that happens in their areas. As mentioned, in the UK half of the main local business tax – business rates – is returned directly to the Treasury. In France it is all kept locally. As we saw in that earlier chapter, that is why they have 24% more dwellings across the channel than we have in the UK.[34] It's also why France was able to build an astonishing forty nuclear reactors in the 1980s: the prospect of a major, permanent increase in local revenue rapidly eroded nimbyism. Avoine, in the Loire region, hosted the first nuclear reactors; its residents saw revenues jump by millions of francs. They gave themselves the nickname 'the Kuwait of Indre-et-Loire'.[35] Other areas with nuclear power stations offered their residents free high-speed internet and free TV subscriptions. All reduced property taxes.

In fairness, governments of all parties have spent time and energy trying to boost regional growth. Tony Blair's government set up the Scottish Parliament and Welsh Assembly. George Osborne championed the Northern Powerhouse. Theresa May talked about an 'economy that works for everyone'. Boris Johnson championed 'levelling up'. The current Labour government says it will introduce elected mayors and unitary authorities across England. The trouble is that all these initiatives have suffered from one central flaw: they have devolved decision-making authority, but not funding autonomy. The devolved governments and metro mayors have ended up with legitimacy but not agency. The result is that after several decades of reform, the buck still stops at Whitehall. I found that out in my final budget in March 2024, when I rather ridiculously approved funding for a tiny bridge in Scotland, Cloddach Bridge just south of Elgin. There were cheers in the House of Commons when I did.

Nonetheless, there are signs that the tentative devolution we have embarked on so hesitatingly is actually starting to work. Greater Manchester was given a higher level of devolution than other English regions in the 'Devo Manc' deal of 2014. In 2017, it was allowed to choose its own mayor. Andy Burnham then took responsibility for housing, strategic planning, transport and skills. In 2023, I went further and authorised a single funding settlement for Greater Manchester similar to those given to Scotland, Wales and Northern Ireland. It was not proper funding autonomy, but gave it much greater discretion over the use of funds received from the government. Over the last decade, the area has taken advantage of all those freedoms to generate the highest productivity growth in the UK, higher even than London. As a result, more young Mancunians are staying rather than moving south. Manchester is finally starting to close the gap with London.[36]

But it is still not Austin or Jura. Nor have other regions in the UK been given Manchester's still limited freedoms. If we continue to put our faith in benevolent dictatorship from Whitehall, we will never cast off the learned helplessness that has become prevalent in our regions. Andy Street left office frustrated he was not able to achieve more. Despite massive efforts, a centralised system meant he could only achieve a fraction of what he wanted to do. If we want more people like him to go into politics – local champions focused on transforming their region, city, town or even village – we need to trust them with the same powers they would have in a US city or a Swiss canton. What, then, needs to change?

Every city and county should have an elected mayor with full authority over those areas that have the biggest influence on economic growth, including planning, local transport and crime. In order to align incentives, we should take a leaf out of France's book: local councils should keep the entirety of any increase in business rates and council tax created by their planning decisions without any threat that it will be clawed back in the name of 'equalising spending power'. That simple reform would change the attitude of planning authorities from 'How can we stop this?' to 'How can we make it happen?'

In order to give local leaders both agency and accountability, they should also be given genuine freedom to raise or reduce tax. At the moment they only control one – council tax – and even then substantial changes require a referendum. How much extra effort would be put into promoting tourism if local areas received a share of the extra VAT receipts generated? How many more local transport projects would get underway if local mayors could issue municipal bonds, like Mayor Adler in Austin? How much more energy would go into attracting business investment if the local authority kept business taxes? How many more houses would be built if local authorities knew it would permanently increase their council tax base?

Of course, devolution also involves risk – which is why finance ministries generally dislike it. Not all civic leaders are effective. Some would put up taxes and drive business away. Others are incompetent or corrupt. It is never possible to guarantee no failures – but Westminster politicians are hardly a shining example of how to get things right either. And the system we have in the UK actually makes failure more likely, because straitjacketed town halls are less likely to attract capable politicians. In other countries, talented national leaders often start their career in local politics – such as Alain Juppé, who became French prime minister after transforming the city of Bordeaux. Municipalities then become a breeding ground, allowing politicians to earn their spurs before moving up to the national parliament. Proper local autonomy also attracts able people who may have no such ambitions, but want to make a difference where they live. And if they fail, accountability at the ballot box means local voters can try someone else.

We know it works in the UK, because for many years we, too, had a strong tradition of effective, autonomous local leadership. Joseph Chamberlain was a hugely influential figure in shaping the growth of Birmingham in the late nineteenth century. James Kay-Shuttleworth pioneered public health and schools in Manchester. William Rathbone was a big civic figure in Liverpool, as was James Kitson in Leeds. Their energy and vision did not just transform the cities where they lived but also inspired and supported hugely successful local industries. We now need their twenty-first-century equivalents to transform the growth prospects of our regions. Structural changes to make that possible would have been one of my top priorities in the unlikely event that my party was re-elected in 2024.

> **Halving the regional productivity gap over a decade**
> Potential impact on annual GDP growth: 0.3%
> Potential impact on GDP per head over 10 years: 3%

The impact of sorting out the UK's regional imbalance is relatively straightforward to quantify: according to PwC, if regions with below average productivity closed half the gap with the UK median, it would add 3–4% to overall GDP.[37] The RSA City Growth Commission has estimated that if the fourteen non-London metros were to grow at the UK average, it would add 5% to overall GDP.[38] Research from the LSE/Resolution Foundation says that combined with other reforms it could be as much as 7%.[39] Even the lowest of these estimates would increase living standards by more than £1,000 a year – but in the regions doing the catching up the increase would be much higher. There are some important caveats: such estimates do not always account for the full costs of the improvements in infrastructure that would be necessary, and, unlike the changes in the cost of energy discussed in the previous chapter, they would take time. But it is surely reasonable to aim to halve the gap between the lowest-performing regions and the UK median within a decade, which is why I use the lower number as the benchmark.

Such a transformation would happen more quickly in some places and more slowly in others – real autonomy means an element of trial and error. Not every local leader will be a star. But surely the size of the prize makes it worth the effort to try. And if we did succeed in unlocking an entrepreneurial mindset in our local civic leaders, it would help do the very same for local business leaders too – indeed, they would often be the same people. Nor should we forget the intrinsic value in giving people more power to tackle their own social and economic challenges. If it restored a bit of faith in our battered democracy, good economic policy would be good social policy as well.

CONCLUSIONS

- ▶ Allow local authorities to keep revenues raised from business and council tax to incentivise a pro-enterprise approach in their decisions, especially on planning.

- ▶ Replace often toothless local authorities with elected mayors who have real power to tax and spend (although not to run a deficit).

- ▶ Genuine funded autonomy for all locally elected mayors, giving them the agency and authority to solve their own problems rather than having to get in the Whitehall queue.

9
Education

On a grey autumn morning, I got off the Jubilee Line at Wembley Park. I had been there many times before to go to matches and concerts. However, this time I was not heading for the stadium but to a nondescript 1960s office block across from the station. Outside, it could not have been more ordinary. But inside was something extraordinary: the Michaela Community School. Its story has come to symbolise a revolution in English state education which will, in time, be of huge economic significance. Even though it is a slower-burning reform compared to – for example – reducing the price of energy, its impact will ultimately matter more than nearly anything else.

Katharine Birbalsingh is the unlikely architect of that revolution. Born in New Zealand in 1973, she grew up in Toronto and didn't move to the UK until she was fifteen.[1] Her Indo-Guyanese father was an academic and her Jamaican mother was a nurse. Her father started life in extreme poverty, but received a good education. Katharine has stated that 'the old-fashioned British education in British Guiana that helped my dad rise out of poverty is being denied to children in schools in this country'.[2]

Katharine won a place at Oxford, where she read French and philosophy. Drawn at that stage to the radical left, she flirted with the Socialist Workers Party.[3] But after visiting state schools as part of her plans to become a teacher, she changed her views. She later reflected: 'Like any student, you know, leftism seemed to be the way of pursuing justice for the poor. Life has taught me that that was wrong. And that, actually, "small c" conservative values are what will bring justice for the poor.'[4]

After graduating in 1996, Katharine began working as a teacher. Over the next fifteen years, she taught at a variety of schools in London, first as a French teacher, before progressing to head of languages and then deputy head.[5] She experienced the reality of British state education at first hand.

The author with Katharine Birbalsingh, the unlikely hero of a revolution in English schools

In 2010, her life changed for ever. At the Conservative confer-ence that year, Katharine was thrust into the national spotlight thanks to a passionate speech on education. She argued that the state education system was broken because it kept poor children in poverty. She blamed a culture of excuses, low expectation and weak discipline. In the conference hall her speech went down a storm. But back at her school it was a disaster.[6] She had just started a new teaching role but had ruffled feathers in a major way. She became a target of online abuse and her job became untenable.[7] She was effectively forced out of the state system and told that if she wanted to teach it would have to be at a private school. She had been 'can-celled'. Speaking at the Conservative conference, she said at the time, ruined her life.

But the experience only strengthened her resolve to fight for change. She was determined to confront what she believed was fun-damentally wrong with the modern approach to teaching – namely, progressive doctrines in education that focus on self-esteem rather than the acquisition of knowledge. She decided to open her own school.

The coalition government had just introduced a new policy allowing parents and teachers to set up 'free schools:' new schools with more freedom when it came to both culture and curriculum.[8] That gave Katharine the chance to put her vision to the test. She embarked on a three-year marathon to get the school up and run-ning. She had to overcome both practical challenges and ideological opposition, but pressed on. Eventually she found a site in Wembley and in 2014 the Michaela Community School opened.

Katharine believes that strict discipline and high standards are an act of love.[9] Students, she says, respond well when they are held to account.[10] And her tough love has worked. In 2019, when the school's first set of GCSE results were released, Michaela's grades were four times better than the national average.[11] Since then, the school has risen to become one of the highest-ranked secondary schools in the country, according to key government performance metrics.[12]

When I gave a book talk to a mainly adult audience at the LSE, some Michaela students were present. They were the first to raise their hands and asked questions with confidence and eloquence. Hence my visit to their school – I was intrigued. After being buzzed through security, two eleven-year-old girls, Ifra and Summer, met me for a tour. I have a daughter the same age, so my first question to them related to a topic that was being hotly debated in our family: 'Do you have a phone?' I asked. 'No, sir,' Ifra replied. 'There is too much to learn and screens are a distraction. When I have time off, I would rather play with my little sis or the other kids in the block than look at a phone.' Summer, the other girl, did have a brick phone, but only for safety when walking to and from school. 'Do you ever get asked to research things on the internet for homework?' 'No, sir. We are given booklets. Everything we need is in them. We learn that reading is a superpower skill you need to pass English GCSE.'

Then I was shown into a classroom of thirteen-year-olds, Year 9s. 'Sir, just to remind you, please don't say anything when you go inside.' As an MP, I have visited numerous schools in my constituency, and normally there is a bit of a stir when you enter a classroom; but not this time. Every child's eyes remained fixed on the teacher as they went through *Romeo and Juliet* line by line. Each had a personal whiteboard on which to scribble the answers to constant questions asked by the teacher. They were kept busy and engaged. I saw biology students told to write the word xylem (the vascular tissue in plants) five times.

Michaela is often referred to as the strictest school in Britain. Compared to many schools, 'strict' would be an understatement.[13] Students walk through the corridors silently, in single file.[14] They are taught the acronym SLANT, which stands for 'sit up', 'listen', 'ask questions', 'nod' and 'track the speaker'. They receive demerits for relatively minor infractions such as forgetting a pen or taking too long to get out a textbook. Two demerits get a detention.

Time is precious inside the school. Lessons are timed down to the second. On my tour, I got a constant sense of the clock ticking: teachers would ask a question and then count down 'Five, four, three, two, one,' after which an answer was expected. 'They want us to be fast so we can get through as much education as possible,' my guides explained. Both of them had stopwatches to make sure the tour finished in the allotted twenty minutes. Even at lunch, not a second was wasted: before sitting down, more than a hundred children recited Shelley's 'Ozymandias', which happens to be one of my favourite poems (and one, by the way, every politician should learn by heart). After that, everyone sat down in groups of six. But instead of chit-chat, they were given a topic to discuss. It was St Andrew's Day, so everyone had to think about what they knew about Scotland. Amusingly, I was introduced as 'Mr Jeremy Hunt from the Conservatory Party'.

Katharine's goal is to teach children not just skills, but knowledge. That creates a very regimented atmosphere, which is not to everyone's taste. 'What about special needs kids?' I asked her. 'There are lots here – we don't select. But in other schools, standards for special needs children are too low. We ask more of them and create an atmosphere where they find they can keep up.' Part of that comes from the school's ethos, which is about giving its children a culture of agency. The banner in the playground proudly quotes 'Invictus' by William Ernest Henley: 'I am the master of my fate, I am the captain of my soul.' And despite the regimentation, I found the children full of character. One wanted to be a surgeon and said she fancied 'Dr McDreamy' from *Grey's Anatomy*.

Michaela's story is remarkable – but far from isolated. Free schools and academies like Michaela have helped to raise standards in England's state schools to some of the highest in the Western world. The OECD has been measuring this for twenty-five years, with an independent comparison of educational attainment across advanced economies called PISA. In 2009, England was ranked twenty-fifth of sixty-five countries for reading, twenty-seventh for mathematics and sixteenth for science.[15] Today, it ranks thirteenth for reading and science, and eleventh for mathematics.[16] This is partly due to absolute levels falling in other countries. But it isn't just the PISA rankings that show England pulling ahead: according to another study, PIRLS, our reading standards are now the highest in western Europe,[17] and in the 2023 TIMSS study, English performance in Grade 8 maths sat behind only Singapore, Taiwan, South Korea, Japan and Hong Kong.[18] That is very important for Britain's economic prospects, as we will see.

The best-known reform of recent years is the introduction of academies – chains of independently run state schools which are granted extra freedoms to innovate. Until recently any school that failed an inspection was forced to join an academy group, which then took responsibility for turning it around. But Michael

Gove and Nick Gibb, both appointed education ministers in 2010, made a wide range of additional, radical policy changes.[19] They tackled 'grade inflation' – the gradual weakening of A level standards – and introduced phonics, a proven way to improve reading results. They overhauled the national curriculum to emphasise the teaching of knowledge and tackled numerous cultural problems, including what George W. Bush called 'the soft bigotry of low expectations'. Crucially, they were able to see through their reforms, because they were in post for longer than normal – Gove was Education Secretary for four years and Gibb schools minister for a decade.

But the foundations for England's success in education were actually laid earlier. Since 1992, failing schools have been identified with brutal transparency through an Ofsted inspection system established by Ken Clarke when he was Education Secretary. For years, it ranked schools as 'outstanding', 'good', 'requires improvement' or 'inadequate'. An 'inadequate' rating put the school into 'special measures', which usually involved the dismissal of the head and governing body. It was a tough system, but it transformed standards at the lowest-performing schools. To their credit, Tony Blair and David Blunkett kept the system in place when they came to power in 1997. To the disappointment of teaching unions, which opposed the system, they signalled their support for academic rigour by keeping on Chris Woodhead, a pugnacious and unpopular chief inspector of schools.

At every stage, there were political battles. Blunkett called teachers who opposed his efforts to raise standards a 'miserable bunch of sneering cynics'. He faced down unions with the introduction of performance-related pay. Gove was so unpopular within the teaching profession that David Cameron felt he had to move him before the 2015 election. But the cumulative result of all those reforms was a stark divergence between outcomes in England and outcomes in Scotland and Wales, where the devolved governments stuck with the old system. While England's results climbed the rankings, Scotland's PISA performance for both mathematics and science is now below the OECD average.[20] Students in Wales score more than 5% lower across all three categories compared to English students.[21] The IFS says that the best explanation for this difference is 'longstanding differences in policy and approach'.[22] To avoid continued embarrassment, the Scottish government decided to pull out of PIRLS and TIMSS, although they did eventually rejoin.[23]

Standards in English state schools have soared to become some of the best in the world

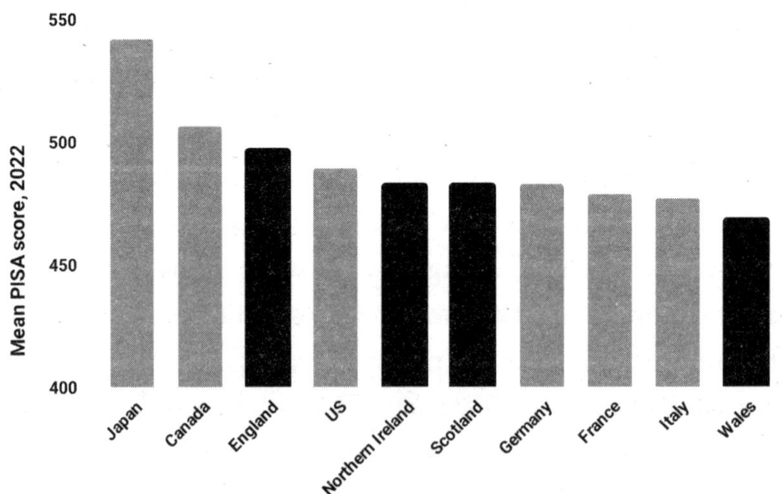

Source: OECD[24]

Raising standards in state schools is the best single way to improve opportunities for the most disadvantaged children. But at the time, the reforms in England were tough and deeply unpopular with teaching unions. This came to a head in 2023 when Ruth Perry, a head teacher in Caversham, Berkshire, killed herself following a downgrade of her school's Ofsted ranking. Rather than trying to find a balanced way to avoid such tragic outcomes, the incoming Labour government of 2024 scrapped Ofsted's one-word ratings and set about dismantling the freedoms that had allowed academy chains to flourish. Katharine Birbalsingh is worried that the consequences will be extremely damaging for children from poor families.[25]

Nonetheless, for now, at least, England has an education system that is the envy of other countries. Many have sent delegations to study our reforms, including China, Saudi Arabia, Ghana and the Dominican Republic. Australia, New Zealand and the Flanders region of Belgium have also taken a keen interest (its parliament has voted through a knowledge-rich curriculum based on English reforms), with New Zealand and a number of Australian states adopting England's phonics screening check.

Nor is it just state schools where the UK is doing well when it comes to education. We have a highly competitive independent school sector, where boarding schools successfully attract thousands of children from other countries (despite being pummelled by the introduction of VAT). Three of the world's top 10 universities are British and the overall strength of the UK's higher education sector means we outperform similar-sized countries when it comes to the most frequently cited research,[26] the number of patents[27] and Nobel Prize-winners.[28] Every year around four hundred thousand international students come to the UK, making it the second most popular destination globally.[29] Britain churns out more AI-literate graduates than anywhere else in Europe.[30]

Interestingly, many of these improvements happened during the austerity period. Despite leaky roofs and crumbling buildings, standards rose. English schools have therefore shown it is possible to raise productivity against the odds in the public sector. What seems to have worked, as I discussed in the earlier chapter on public sector productivity, is a judicious combination of autonomy and accountability, getting the 'tight–loose' balance right. Head teachers are given high levels of freedom to experiment and innovate, but because their results are public, there is no hiding place for failure.

Other parts of the public sector have taken note. Inspired by the improvements happening in state schools, I introduced similar reforms to the NHS. In my first few months as Health Secretary, I had to deal with the Mid Staffs scandal, where numerous patients died because of degrading and cruel treatment. I asked officials at the Department of Health how many other hospitals were at risk; to my astonishment, they didn't know. So I introduced a similar system to Ofsted, to make sure there was no hiding place for failure. The NHS then became the first health system in the world to grade every hospital as 'outstanding', 'good', 'requires improvement' or 'inadequate'. Soon there was a much greater sense of urgency around improving poorly performing hospitals – not because of new targets, but because of the spotlight it put on them. By the end of my time in the job, nearly three million more patients were being treated in 'good' or 'outstanding' hospitals.[31]

Ofsted-style inspections in the NHS have helped improve key patient safety outcomes in England

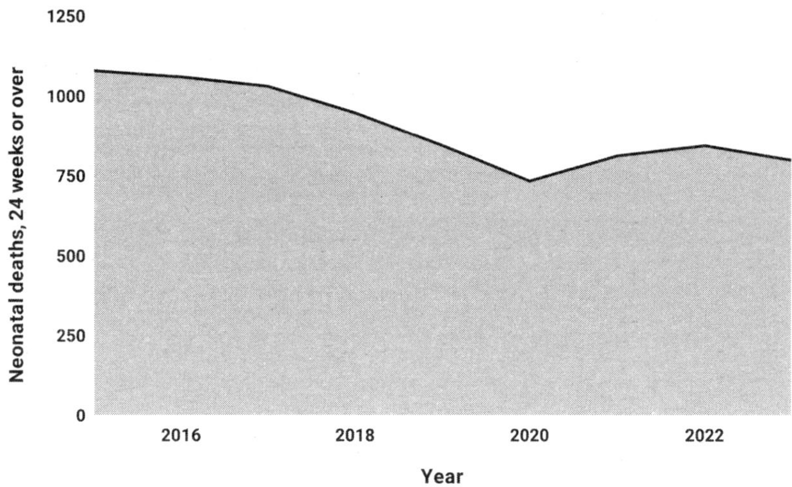

Source: ONS[32]

Improving standards in schools is good social policy, but also good for economic growth. That is because a better-educated person has more productive potential. More educated people then lead to increased output, higher GDP and higher GDP per head. Just how much higher is hard to quantify, because so many other things matter – and you can find plenty of exceptions, including well-educated countries with low growth rates (Japan and Estonia) and others racing ahead despite poor attainment (India, Vietnam and Nigeria). But no one doubts there is a connection.

And the connection between educational attainment and economic growth is backed up by multiple academic studies. A study by Robert Barro, who we came across in the tax chapter, found that each additional year of schooling increases annual GDP per head growth by around 0.4%.[33] The effect is particularly pronounced in developing countries, but even in advanced economies, the increase is 0.2% a year. Stanford economist Eric A. Hanushek has tried to quantify the connection more precisely with research suggesting that the quality of education matters more than the total time spent in school,[34] with countries that improve their PISA test scores tending to grow faster. A report he did for the OECD said the UK could add 0.5% to its annual growth if its PISA scores matched those of Finland, one of the highest-performing countries at the time. Now the top performers tend to be in East Asia so it might be more realistic to aim to close half of the gap between us and them.[35] Doing so would probably take a generation. But it is surely of vital strategic importance to make the effort when AI has already started to disrupt traditional employment patterns. When people have to retrain for multiple careers during their lifetime, it helps to be able to keep learning.

Perhaps the most obvious reason to focus on further improvement in education outcomes is the simplest, namely that a better-educated workforce avoids wasted talent. The economist Daniel Susskind has described it as the 'inefficiency of inequality' – the loss to the whole of society if a country fails to tap into the ideas and talent of people from the poorest backgrounds.[36] That is particularly true in a knowledge economy, where economic growth is as likely to come from innovations in thinking as from investment in machinery. Low educational achievement in large chunks of a population has other disadvantages too, not least that it is socially divisive and drives demand for migration. Societies that do a better job of educating their home-grown workforce are far more likely to be relaxed about filling skills gaps with talent from overseas.

*

Despite its successes, the UK still has a major weakness in its education system: though it generally does a good job for the half of school leavers who go to university, it often fails those who don't. Many still complete eleven years of compulsory schooling with little to show for it. Around two hundred thousand children – over a third of the total – finish schooling every year without passing GCSE English and maths. And even British universities, though good by international standards, are far from perfect: around a third of leavers still do not end up with a graduate-level job fifteen months after graduation.[37]

These should be solvable problems. When it comes to vocational qualifications for those who are not academically driven, we simply need to follow the same journey that has successfully raised standards for A levels and university entry. More rigour in vocational qualifications would make school-leavers more attractive to employers and more likely to earn higher salaries. The easiest way to do that is to learn from countries that do it well, such as Germany, Switzerland and Singapore. They all take great trouble to ensure that every school leaver has the qualifications necessary to earn a good salary. In Germany, half of school leavers enter something called *Ausbildung*, which combines classroom instruction with apprenticeships. Switzerland has a similar system for an even higher proportion of school leavers than Germany, and in Singapore, the institutes for technical education are recognised for their close links to employers. Australia, too, is much better than we are at aligning vocational training with the needs of business.

Countries with better vocational education are more likely to get young people into work

Source: OECD[38]

In the UK, the median wage is £39,000. Our objective should be to ensure that everyone leaving school is equipped with the basic skills necessary to earn it. If they leave without such skills, we should be honest about the fact that the system has failed – and taxpayers' money has not done its job. The social consequences of such wasted talent are severe: there is a strong link between people who do not progress beyond GCSE and future job prospects. Many become 'NEETs' (someone under twenty-five not in education, employment or training), of which there are now a million.[39] The key to progress in this area is a little-known reform called T levels, which now exist as a technical, non-academic alternative to A levels. They have been introduced relatively recently and are promising. But if they are to have the same status as A levels, they will need to be just as rigorously taught and examined.

Getting there will be hard work, but the prize is huge: the positive correlation between PISA scores and economic growth suggests that if half of our school leavers were educated to German or Singaporean levels productivity would increase and youth unemployment would fall. One reading of the data suggests that if we were to close half the gap in maths and science scores to East Asian countries, it could add up to 0.25% to annual GDP growth. We don't know how long that effect would last and it would take a generation to get there. But in the age of AI, it is still worth going for because of the additional flexibility it would give our workers to learn new skills.

> **Improve education standards by closing half the gap with East Asian tigers**
> Potential impact on annual GDP growth: 0.25%

The transformation at Michaela and many English state schools shows what is possible when radical reforms are sustained by successive governments. Indeed, the similarity in approach between Ken Clarke, David Blunkett, Michael Gove and Nick Gibb is far more striking than any differences. In most areas discussed in this book, real change has been held back by caution or incrementalism, but in education the risk is different: the radical reforms of the last three decades are now being reversed by a government that does not understand the philosophy behind them. A properly rigorous Ofsted system with one-word inspection results should be reinstated. Freedoms for academy schools should be restored.

Courses offered by universities need reviewing for rigour and employability outcomes. Vocational courses need the same rigour as academic ones. But even acknowledging the mistakes currently being made, the UK education system still gets far more right than wrong. That is a big advantage for our long-term competitiveness.

Measures to boost educational attainment sit alongside other reforms considered so far including boosting employment levels, making it easier to build things, improving the efficiency of public services, embracing AI, cutting energy costs and tackling regional disparities. But there is one final set of reforms which could make a major difference to our economic competitiveness. They are harder to quantify, because they involve changing how we think about growth – our mindset – rather than simply new laws or policies. But they are all the more important for it.

CONCLUSIONS

- Every school leaver should have the vocational skills necessary to earn the UK median salary of £39,000.

- Introduce greater rigour to vocational education so that qualifications match the quality and status of those in Germany, Switzerland or Singapore.

- Restore clear inspections (with 'outstanding', 'good', 'requires improvement' or 'inadequate' results) to schools so that poor schools are turned around quickly.

- Restore freedoms to academy chains to nurture the next generation of Katharine Birbalsinghs.

10

Risk

'I'm going to make a million before I'm thirty and then become a cabinet minister.'

That was my rather precocious ambition when I left university in 1988. It was a heady time for the Conservatives. Margaret Thatcher was at the height of her powers, and she inspired me to become an entrepreneur as well as an MP. But among my friends I was still the only person to set up a business within a year or two of graduation. Most headed for safer options: law, management consultancy or the City. In this chapter I look at why entrepreneurs take the plunge. What tips the balance, making people give up the prospect of a steady career and a stable income? Equally importantly, what stops them? I start with my own experience, because it illustrates the combination of opportunism and determination that characterises the life of an entrepreneur. Like many, I found that big dreams were soon replaced with the daily grind of keeping the business afloat.

I also wavered. I was offered a well-paid job with a small management consultancy and could not resist. They were lovely people, but working for someone else confirmed to me that I wanted to run my own show. After a year, I quit, heading off to Japan to fulfil an ambition to learn Japanese. But before I left the UK, I registered my first company with my best friend Mike. Even though we didn't have the foggiest idea what we were going to do, that decision ended up defining both our lives. While living in Japan, I mulled over different ideas. I noticed a fascination with all things British. My student room at Oxford was a few doors down the high street from what used to be the Frank Cooper's Oxford Marmalade shop, but their iconic product wasn't on sale in Japan. Could this be our break?

We tracked down the manufacturer (it turned out to be made in Birmingham, not Oxford). Mike and I felt faintly ridiculous as two 25-year-olds bigging up our non-existent business experience to try and get a deal. But being young was also an advantage: with no kids and no mortgage we had nothing to lose. Somehow we managed to secure an exclusive licence for the Japanese market and found ourselves slogging across Japan with pots of marmalade in our backpacks. We got a few orders, but it soon became clear the marmalade boom in Japan had passed (or in truth had never existed). The Japanese, it turned out, loved English preserves but not for breakfast. I should have waited for the release of *Paddington*.

We then tried a series of other ventures. We tried exporting Belgian chocolates to Japan. We had no success with that either, although our tiny office did fill up with delicious samples. Then we tried giving free maps of London to Japanese tourists arriving at Heathrow, a project which worked for about a year until the airport decided to charge us a hefty fee for the privilege. We were forced to close down the operation, migrating many of the advertisers into a school and college guide which we modelled on the Lonely Planet guidebooks, which I had used extensively as a backpacker. We did versions in Japanese, Chinese, Korean and Spanish, and finally – I have no idea why it took us so long – in English. That involved taking on the market leader, a course directory called *Floodlight,* owned at the time by the mayor of London.

We even had a brush with the law. In order to get up-to-date information for our directory, we copied what we thought was public information from *Floodlight* about courses available in London into a database, and then sent it round to colleges to confirm it was still current. At 5 p.m. on the last working day before Easter, we received a fourteen-page fax from *Floodlight*'s solicitors threatening to send us both to prison for theft of intellectual property. It was an aggressive tactic designed to terrify a fledgling competitor – and it succeeded. We spent hours over the weekend talking to a lawyer friend on our Nokia brick phones. We were in the wrong and had to delete the offending database. But we were not going to prison. We had learnt the importance of making sure the risks we took were calibrated rather than foolhardy.

We were also stung into fighting back. We decided to rewrite the whole magazine from scratch – legally – and make sure it came out at least a month earlier than the rival who had tried to destroy us. With our sole employee, a brilliant assistant called Phoebe, we worked all hours. We also quadrupled our advertising budget. The quality of the publication was pretty iffy, but advertisers were impressed with our ballsiness and the venture took off. For publicity, we purchased an old double-decker bus, repainted it in our livery and hired a retired bus driver called Dennis to drive it around London. On one occasion, he knocked out all the upper-deck windows after driving too close to overhanging trees on Birdcage Walk, which was not a bus route. Initially, *Floodlight* outsold us twenty to one. Within a couple of years, though, our sales had drawn level and a decade later we ended up buying the magazine from Ken Livingstone, then London's mayor. We learnt about patiently building market share until you are unstoppable.

But it was an analogue business as the world turned digital. If we wanted to move online, perhaps becoming a kind of Google for courses, we would need investment. It was the middle of the dot-com boom, with small companies like Lastminute.com getting crazy valuations, so our hopes were high. But we were turned down by every venture capitalist in London – frustratingly because they wanted to invest in start-ups rather than existing businesses like us. Our hockey-stick projections of future revenue had failed to convince – probably rightly. In the end we found some private investors who put in a much smaller amount than we had hoped for. They were led by Peter Chadlington, now a great friend, and included the late Sir David Frost. Thanks to an introduction from David, we had the unforgettable experience of hosting comedian Ronnie Corbett as a guest speaker at our Christmas party. He was absolutely delightful.

We called the website Hotcourses, because Hotmail was the rage at the time. In order to get publicity, we invited someone called Ginie Sayles over from Texas, who gave a free one-day course on 'How to Marry a Millionaire'. Her rather politically incorrect books are still available on Amazon. I will never forget seeing queues of young women arriving for the course, some in dark glasses to conceal their identity. 'Marriage will make you cry, ladies, but if you are going to cry it might as well be into a silk pillow,' she told them, as she dispensed wisdom on how to find a rich husband.

Hotcourses became the world's largest database of university and college courses. If you were a Chinese student wanting to do an

MBA in Canada, it told you your options. If you were a Londoner wanting to learn lambada-dancing, all the information was there (that was me, by the way). The laborious job of typing up prospectuses was done at an office we set up in Chennai, in India. The brilliant team there also did most of our IT development. We ended up with seventy employees in London and over two hundred in India. I didn't become a millionaire before I was thirty, but did very well when the company was sold in 2018. More importantly, both Mike and I met our wives through the company.

Lots of things made it easier to take the risks we took. Being young meant we had nothing to lose. We had a fantastic team, many of whom stayed with us for decades. When we hit a brick wall, we remorselessly followed the motto, attributed to Churchill, that 'success is the ability to go from failure to failure without losing your enthusiasm'. But it wasn't just us: the business climate also helped. It was a golden period for start-ups, with governments of both parties trying to make things easier for entrepreneurs. We were – after a struggle – able to raise capital when we needed it. We operated in a market where consumers and businesses were quick to embrace new technology. Advertisers were willing to try out a new company with little pedigree.

All those things matter today as well. And the UK still has plenty to offer entrepreneurs. A big financial services sector makes it easier to raise capital. Innovation from our universities nurtures exciting spin-outs in the industries of the future. A respected legal system means people are confident that wealth created will be secure. Independent data generally supports this. Until 2020, the World Bank did an annual comparison of all economies for *Ease of Doing Business*. In its final ranking, the UK came eighth out of 190 economies.[1] A more recent attempt at the same thing, the 2024 Global Startup Ecosystem Index, ranks Britain second after the US, ahead even of entrepreneurial hotspots like Israel, Hong Kong and Singapore.[2] Similarly, in a 2025 cross-country comparison of entrepreneurial ecosystems, the UK consistently ranked as one of the top performers.[3] Perhaps as a result, just under one in three UK adults either run their own business or plan to start one – with immigrants being by far the most entrepreneurial.[4]

The UK regularly ranks highly in global rankings for ease of setting up a business

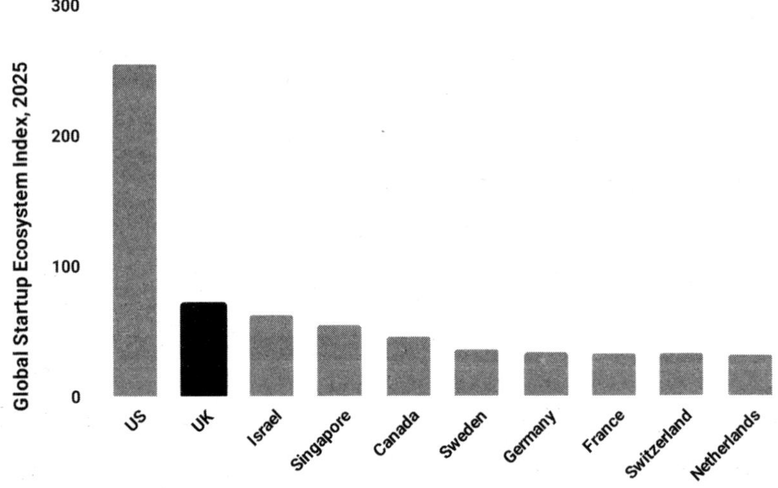

Source: Startup Genome[5]

One reason is that there are fewer bureaucratic hoops to jump through to incorporate a business than in other countries. Companies House manages incorporations through an online process which can be completed in a matter of hours. In Germany, incorporation involves nine procedures which take more than a week. In France you need a notary and then have to cope with restrictive employment regulations. In Denmark you need 40,000 kroner (just under £5,000) to get going. Swiss entrepreneurs have to find even more, as well as deal with fragmented cantonal rules. As a result the number of businesses registered in the UK has risen by 2.4 million over the last fifteen years. It has eighteen new businesses per 1,000 people of working age each year, two and a half times the number in Denmark or France.[6] Our innovation industries, as discussed earlier, attract more capital than those in France and Germany combined. There may be much we can learn from France when it comes to planning, from Scandinavia on employment and from Switzerland on devolution – but when it comes to the base ingredient for a modern capitalist economy, the appetite and ability to set up a business from scratch is somewhere where the UK does pretty well.

More recently, there have been some worrying signs that our attractiveness for entrepreneurs is waning. New employment rights legislation has significantly increased the risk that comes with hiring new people by undermining the UK's traditionally flexible labour market. Costs for start-ups have gone up, partly because of inflation but also because of increases in employers' national insurance and business rates. All of which has come after a global financial crisis, new Brexit border bureaucracy and a spike in energy costs. Lending to small businesses has stagnated and is lower, in real terms, than before 2008. As more people have started to worry about the risk of failure, the number of new business starts has declined.

A fear of failure holds back new business creation in the UK

Source: Global Entrepreneurship Monitor,[7] ONS[8]
Note: The 'fear of failure rate' is defined by GEM as the '[p]ercentage of 18–64 population (individuals involved in any stage of entrepreneurial activity excluded) who indicate that fear of failure would prevent them from setting up a business' (source: https://www.gemconsortium.org/wiki/1154).

On top of which we seem to be less good than we need to be at growing companies after they have been set up. That has important implications for the overall level of competition – and therefore growth in productivity – in the economy. The Resolution Foundation and LSE have measured this by looking at the rate at which capital is being reallocated from lower-productivity older businesses to higher-productivity start-ups. They find that despite the UK's army of small businesses, fewer firms are entering and leaving markets than elsewhere and incumbents are better at maintaining their grip.[9] Modern economies need what Joseph Schumpeter called 'creative destruction', which happens when innovative challengers elbow aside obsolete giants. For that, the UK needs to be better at allowing its fledgling companies to scale up to a level where they can shake up established markets.

For me personally, going from running a small business to becoming Chancellor was less of a leap than might be expected. As an entrepreneur, you don't generally learn how to give a speech or do a media interview. But you do learn about taking structured risks, of which there are plenty in politics. You get a feel for wealth creation which matters for numerous decisions in any budget. As a result, I tried to implement a number of the ideas I've discussed in the earlier chapters, sometimes with success and sometimes without.

The bottom line is that if we want to nurture more entrepreneurs, we need to reduce the risks they are forced to take. Planning reforms, for example, would make it quicker to get approval for new factories, warehouses and offices (also helping small housebuilders like Ben the Builder to grow). A public sector properly focused on improving efficiency would give more contracts to smaller challenger companies offering cheaper and quicker ways to deliver services. Welfare reform would make it easier for start-ups to find the employees they need. Easier access to UK pension fund capital would make it easier for them to scale up and grow in the UK and less likely to move abroad. Lower energy costs would boost the profits of every small business, with particular impact on those involved in manufacturing. Better skills would make it easier to find more productive employees. Faster growth in all UK regions would increase opportunities for smaller companies outside the south-east. Most of all, lower tax and lower debt mean less risk from the killer taxes – business rates, VAT and national insurance. Those taxes have to be paid even before a business has made a penny of profit.

Other things, too, would encourage more entrepreneurs to take the plunge. Inside or outside the EU, Britain has always been a champion of free trade, because it gives innovative businesses access to much larger markets. Inspired by Adam Smith and David Ricardo, Parliament scrapped the Corn Laws and nearly all other protectionist tariffs, the first time any country had done so unilaterally. By the end of the nineteenth century trade had tripled and Britain was the richest country on the planet. Margaret Thatcher followed the same path when she abolished exchange controls in 1979, welcomed Japanese car factories to the UK and removed barriers to foreign firms wanting to buy British ones. In the period from 1990 to 2008, when her reforms had bedded down, Britain grew faster than nearly any G7 country and nearly as fast as the US. At the heart of that success was the insight that openness to new products and ideas from around the globe makes a country more competitive and more productive. For that reason, it makes sense to continue to reduce trade barriers with the EU where an unreasonable price is not being asked in return. Even outside the customs union and single market, it should be possible to reduce border bureaucracy to minimal levels. As the heat of the Brexit divorce battle fades, pragmatic agreements that reduce bureaucracy in both directions should become easier.

Making it easier to borrow would also help reduce the fear of failure that stops businesses being set up and holds them back from growing. We should free banks from over-cautious regulations that restrict their ability to lend to smaller companies. After the global financial crisis, many new rules were introduced that should now be revised: one requires banks to hold capital worth three times the value of any equity stakes they take in small businesses; another stops them selling ancillary services that could make lending to small business clients more profitable; yet another prevents them from taking an active role in managing distressed businesses back to health, even though the last thing they want is for their customers to go bust. All such requirements make lending more expensive and push banks to concentrate on lower-risk property loans, which are far less beneficial for the economy.

Perhaps the biggest change the government could make to help smaller companies would be to overhaul procurement rules. Government contracts account for about 10% of our economy but are often impossible for fledgling companies to win. Departments put in place long procurement processes which many smaller companies simply do not have the time or manpower to engage with. For an incumbent supplier, naturally, the more complex the process the better: they can use a small part of their profits from an existing contract to jump through the hoops, comfortable in the knowledge that most outsiders simply won't bother. The result is that taxpayers end up paying more for more expensive and less innovative results. Far better to require a minimum proportion of government procurement spend to go to smaller, more ground-breaking companies. We should copy the highly successful US Small Business Innovation Research (SBIR) programme which does just that. It requires eleven federal agencies, including the Department of Defense and NASA, to set aside around 3% of their R & D budgets for small innovators.

Finally, if we really want our smaller companies to grow more quickly, we should avoid obvious bear traps when it comes to taxation. Inheritance tax exemptions for farms and family businesses should be restored in full, because entrepreneurs are more likely to invest in growing their businesses if they know they can pass it on to their children. The tax rates on income tax and capital gains should not be equalised, at least when it comes to people setting up businesses: the lower rate charged for the latter fairly reflects the much higher risks they take. Why risk your savings and your home if the state takes as much tax from you as if you were doing a regular job?

Increasing entrepreneurship

A 1% increase in total early-stage entrepreneurial activity is associated with an increase in annual GDP growth of 0.2%

All this matters because making life easier for entrepreneurs leads to more innovation, more displacement of obsolete companies, more competition and higher productivity. That has a big impact on growth. Analysis of data from the Global Entrepreneurship Monitor and the IMF suggests that a 1% increase in total early stage entrepreneurial activity is associated with an increase in annual GDP growth of 0.2%.[10] How much of that we would be able to secure in the UK is harder to judge. But in some ways, with our long tradition of entrepreneurship and high volume of start-ups, we have done the hard bit. We just need to make it easier for new businesses to grow into larger companies that are better able to disrupt established markets. Richard Branson famously wrote a book called *Screw It, Let's Do It* – we need more people to think the same.

CONCLUSIONS

- ► Focus on making it more attractive for entrepreneurs to have a go by reducing the risk and increasing the rewards for people who start businesses.

- ► Relax banking regulations that reduce lending to small and medium-sized businesses.

- ► Require 10% of government procurement contracts to go to insurgent or smaller companies.

- ► Require a fixed proportion of government R & D budgets to go to smaller innovators, as in the US SBIR programme.

- ► Recognise the risks entrepreneurs take in the way they are taxed.

- ► Avoid regulators and civil servants being nobbled by large companies trying to stop new entrants into their market.

CONCLUSION

The best moment of my day as Chancellor was first thing in the morning. Most days, I would go for a run in Hyde Park with my Labrador Poppy. It was often pitch-black but I was completely alone, apart from a couple of protection officers discreetly following. I never listened to music or podcasts but just collected my thoughts for the day ahead. The peace and quiet was magical, as was the sound of birdsong when the mornings got lighter. The rest of the day, by contrast, was a relentless combination of firefighting, media appearances and internal battles. That relentlessness was compounded by staying in the Chancellor's flat in Downing Street. It was a privilege, but also meant literally living above the office. At least my kids could pop their heads around the door of my study during late nights.

The main reason I liked running was because it was a moment to step back and take stock. I sometimes came up with lines for a speech or had policy brainwaves, but mainly it was a chance to think strategically. The same was true on long-haul plane trips and sitting at the table during interminable G20 finance ministers' meetings listening to one scripted speech after another. As your mind wanders, you have time to reflect whether what you are doing will actually make a difference. You also realise that anodyne decisions about numbers on a spreadsheet reflect your values as a human being. Get them wrong and it is a stain on your character as well as your record.

At the same time, you have to get the tactical stuff right. In politics, slip-ups, however trivial, can dominate media time and damage your reputation. Over time, you learn the ropes and things get easier. You get better at answering questions about your brief, whether in Parliament, in interviews or at a never-ending circuit of conferences. But that confidence, which comes to most government ministers over time, can be dangerous. Fluency in batting away difficult questions is not omniscience. Competence matters – but does not mean you are making lasting change. When you write a book that distinction becomes clearer.

And it is lasting change that the economy needs. My analysis shows that delivering it may not be easy but is not impossible either. All the solutions have been tried in other countries with similar democratic constraints to ourselves. In key areas making progress should actually be easier for the UK: for example, our long-standing strengths in innovation, science and technology are a huge advantage in the age of AI. That is why, despite our recent woes, the UK's economic challenges are solvable.

Some policy areas are more ideologically charged, and tax is one of those. It cannot be ignored, because its impact is so far-reaching. Tax policy is the core responsibility of a Chancellor and far more than just the mechanism by which we pay for public services – it defines the social contract between state and citizen. For those on the left, it is a tool of social justice which rebalances wealth and opportunity between rich and poor. For the right, it shapes our attitude towards effort and work. As a result, it has a more direct impact on economic performance than nearly anything else. Tax work, and there will be less of it. Tax profits and there will be less investment. Tax savings, and people will put aside less. Tax consumption and spending goes down. Tax wealth, and you drive entrepreneurs abroad. A dynamic, energetic economy needs to send positive signals about risk and reward, but the more the state takes away in tax, the weaker those signals are. That's why OECD data suggests that countries in the lowest quartile in terms of the tax burden grow on average 2% faster every year than those in the highest quartile.

But it is equally true that taxes pay for infrastructure and public services. They not only matter in their own right but play a key role in economic growth. Invest in nuclear power and energy bills should come down. Keep people healthy and they can go to work. Educate them and we will have more productive workers. For years, people have argued that if we want Scandinavian-quality public services, we will need Scandinavian levels of tax. But when you look at where tax is lower, it becomes clear that there is no simple trade-off between the level of tax and the quality of public services. Many countries – Australia, Canada, Japan, South Korea and Singapore for example – have lower taxes *and* better public services. Norway has better-quality healthcare than the UK despite spending a lower proportion of its GDP on health. The reason is that such countries make sure funding for public services comes as a dividend of economic success and not ahead of it, ensuring it is both affordable and sustainable. And the numbers back that up: every 1% of extra growth generates around £10 billion of additional tax revenue that can be spent on public services without increasing tax.

Nor can debt be ignored. It also crystallises the social contract – this time between generations rather than between social classes. Funding our national debt now costs more than £110 billion every year, nearly £4,000 in tax for every British household. How fair is that on young people starting their first job and hoping to save for a mortgage? How motivated will they be to work hard, take risks and innovate if huge chunks of their earnings will be taken away to service debts generated by their parents and grandparents? Growth is the long-term answer but we need a plan for the short and medium term as well. That's why the debt chapter proposes a new commitment that public spending will never – outside emergencies – grow faster than the rate at which the economy expands. Only then will we honour the spirit of Edmund Burke's famous saying that 'society is indeed a contract… between those who are living, those who are dead, and those who are to be born'.

Having established the importance of reducing both tax and debt, I consider reforms that make it easier to get there. An obvious place to start is measures that increase the number of people in work. As the population ages, the cost of health and pensions will only go up, making it all the more urgent to increase the number of younger adults in employment rather than on welfare. It is also infinitely better for the health of the individuals involved. Why are we signing one thousand people up for sickness benefits every day instead of treating their illness at a fraction of the cost? If we raised employment levels in the UK to Scandinavian levels, an additional 4% of the adult population would be in work. Poverty would be lower and public finances less stretched. Getting there over ten years would add a hefty 0.4% a year to annual economic growth.

Another promising area is planning reform. As the differing experiences of Ben the Builder and Claude le Constructeur show, we should look across the Channel for inspiration. Despite higher taxes and an inflexible labour market, France has kept up with Britain's GDP partly by making it easier to build things. That includes nuclear power stations, which have kept energy prices much lower than in the UK. A simpler, fairer planning system that aligns incentives between local communities and national government means France now has a quarter more dwellings than we have, despite a similar population. A cautious estimate of the impact of bolder planning reform in the UK suggests annual growth could rise by at least 0.2% a year.

An equally important tool that governments have at their disposal is productivity in the public sector. Because the state accounts for one fifth of our output (around half of which is the NHS), ministers have under their direct control the ability to tackle a big chunk of our low productivity issue. Doing so is the first essential step to higher living standards – as well as giving us better and more responsive public services. That doesn't mean it's easy: Labour governments hate taking on the unions and Conservatives often end up with strikes. But if the annual growth in public sector productivity was increased by just 0.7% a year, public spending would stabilise as a proportion of GDP rather than continue its relentless upwards march. An extra 0.1% could be added to annual GDP growth.

Then there is AI. Even though the tech revolution is sometimes over-hyped, it is important for the UK in two ways. The first is through the productivity benefits that all advanced economies are likely to enjoy as a result of faster innovation. The second is more UK-specific: as the world's third largest tech ecosystem, we have an opportunity to become a net exporter of AI solutions. Experts say that could conservatively add around 1% to annual GDP growth.

In a period of instability in the Middle East, energy policy takes on particular importance. It is worth looking at closely, because alongside welfare reform it is probably the area which would have the most immediate impact on economic growth. Our energy prices have doubled in a decade, but some relatively straightforward changes could bring them back down without compromising on our climate change responsibilities. A 20% reduction in energy costs could add 0.2% to annual GDP growth for several years.

I also consider some slower-burn policy areas. They take longer to bear fruit, but are worth pursuing because they have profoundly positive social implications on top of the economic growth they make possible. The first is to reduce regional disparities, which are far worse in the UK than other similar countries. We never used to be an outlier – in the Industrial Revolution, regions outside London were the engine of British growth. But in the late twentieth century London took off as a financial centre while the UK's manufacturing heartlands suffered. Local government was emasculated in order to rein in 'loony left' local councils. It is time to move on with a model we know works in other countries: proper, funded devolution of power to locally elected mayors. Giving local governments the powers their equivalents have enjoyed for years in France, Switzerland or the US would mean they could solve their own problems rather than having to get in the Whitehall queue. Reducing regional imbalances by half over a decade could add 3–4% to GDP or around 0.3% to annual GDP growth.

Then there is education, where there have been a number of recent successes. Reforms spanning several decades have given us world-leading universities and high-quality state schools (at least in England). But there is a big gap when it comes to the skills we give to those who do not go to university. Here, countries like Germany, Switzerland, Singapore and Japan do better at ensuring that every school leaver has at least the basic skills and technical qualifications that allow them to earn a decent salary. According to one set of data, closing half the gap in our PISA scores with East Asian tigers could potentially add 0.25% to annual GDP growth. That would take a generation to achieve and may be optimistic. But given that AI is changing employment patterns in ways we do not fully understand, it is surely worth doing anyway because of the immensely beneficial social impact.

The final slow-burn area is the attitude we adopt towards risk and the role of entrepreneurs. As I say, most of my Oxford classmates chose the law, the civil service or the City, but their counterparts from Stanford, Harvard and Yale think less cautiously about their own futures. We need the same hunger here. We have lots of entrepreneurs, but we still don't make it easy enough for them to turn their fledgling companies into global giants. We also need more widespread recognition of the economic value of risk. Analysis indicates that a 1% increase in total early-stage entrepreneurial activity is associated with an increase in annual GDP growth of up to 0.2%. Setting up a business is ultimately about backing people who have the right mindset. In some ways, every reform in this book is designed to do just that, whether it's getting people into work, reforming planning, reducing the cost of energy or making it easier to raise capital.

Let's return to the table we considered in the introduction and sum up the possible reforms:

Growth impact of reforms

Objective	Potential annual GDP growth impact	Potential 10-year GDP impact	Explanation
Unlocking pension fund investment	0.1%	0.7%	Developing the Mansion House and Solvency II reforms to unlock pension fund investment into the UK economy along Australian lines, including with more mandated pension saving, could unlock billions of pounds in investment. According to analysis by Oxford Economics, this could lead to £220 billion of investment into the UK.
Increasing numbers in work	0.4%	4%	Based on the assumption that the average output per worker remains relatively consistent, if the UK could increase employment levels to 79% (average of Denmark, Finland, Norway, Sweden, Iceland, Switzerland and Netherlands), then this could unlock between 4% and 5%.
Making it easier to build things	0.2%	2%	Analysis indicates that if the UK could match French new dwelling start rates, new dwelling GFCF could increase by £56bn. Similarly, if the UK could match French construction-related GFCF, one would expect an increase of £60–£90bn. Using an ICOR rate of 10 (the UK's average between 2010 and 2019), this would suggest an increase of 0.2% to 0.3% of additional GDP each year.
Making the public sector more efficient	0.1%	1%	Analysis suggests an increase in public sector annual productivity of 0.7% per annum could unlock up to 0.15% of additional GDP growth. This is based on the fact that the public sector accounts for around 20% of national output.
Artificial Intelligence	1%	10%	Analysis by Philippe Aghion and Simon Bunel suggests that AI could improve productivity by anywhere between 0.7% and 1.3%. I have therefore gone with the mid-point of 1%.
Reducing energy bills	0.2%	2%	Based on existing research in the relationship between energy prices, it is suggested here that a 20% reduction in energy prices could add 0.2% to annual GDP growth for a period of years.
Reducing regional imbalances	0.3%	3%	Based on analysis by PwC, if poorer areas in the UK with productivity below the UK average could close half the gap, then this could lead to an increase between 3% and 4% of GDP.
Raising educational standards	0.25%	Minimal but longer-term effect	Based on research by Hanushek and Woessmann, if the UK could add 15 points to the country's average PISA score, this would close half the gap with the tail end of top-performing countries and add up to 0.25% extra annual GDP growth in the long term.
Increasing entrepreneur-ship	0.2%	2%	Analysis suggests that a 1% increase in total early-stage entrepreneurial activity could lead to an annual GDP increase of approximately 0.2%. To take full advantage of this, the UK would also need to provide more support to scale up.

The numbers in the table have been largely independently sourced. They cannot simply be totted up, because the data has been generated using different and sometimes overlapping methodologies. Some reforms will increase growth for a few years while others may create a more permanent uplift. Some will have a cross-cutting impact on others: a new education policy, for example, could have a big impact on AI adoption. Higher productivity generally leads to higher wages, which is good for living standards but could also mean the state pension has to go up. More housebuilding could lead to a greater demand for labour and therefore higher wages for builders. Productivity and interest rates tend to rise together, so policies that increase productivity could make debt servicing more expensive.

But even if overlaps in methodology and watering down halved the combined impact of these solutions, it would still nearly double our current growth rate. Within a decade, GDP per head would rise by £4,000 a year in real terms for the average family – and therefore living standards would rise too. It would also make a big difference for chancellors preparing budgets: if the UK's tax-to-GDP ratio and government spending remained at current levels in real terms, net debt would fall to just 78% of GDP, massively reducing debt interest payments. The Chancellor would also have £160 billion more available to spend on public services or cutting tax. There would be fierce debates as to which – but compared to now, it would be a nice problem to have.[1]

Let me briefly return to the familiar critique: 'If those are the solutions, why didn't you do them when you had the chance?' In order to try to answer that question, each chapter considers previous attempts at reform. Rarely has nothing been attempted, but overall the results have been mixed. Sometimes there have been mistakes (high energy costs, for example), sometimes successes (raising standards in state schools). Sometimes there has been too much timidity (on planning reform), sometimes there have been road-blocks (the pandemic).

Nor – although I cannot be wholly objective – has the issue generally been a lack of political will. In nearly every area, ser-ious efforts at reform have been made by politicians from both sides. Alan Milburn made a big effort to introduce competition into the NHS and cut NHS waiting times. George Osborne took unpopular decisions to reduce a totally unsustainable deficit. Iain Duncan Smith became a hate figure for poverty campaigners when he merged five benefits into the much simpler UC, a reform now accepted as sensible across the political spectrum. Michael Gove's education reforms left us with some of the best state schools in western Europe. Francis Maude had considerable success in slim-ming down central government. The current government has intro-duced some important planning reforms to limit judicial review. And strong support for our burgeoning technology sector has con-tinued over successive administrations, including the current one, giving the UK the largest tech ecosystem in Europe.

Alongside those efforts were plenty of failures. Rishi Sunak and I started to reduce the tax burden, but were succeeded by a government that has increased it again. Under Conservative administrations, corporation tax went down, then up, then down because of full expensing. Greg Clark's planning reforms simplified a very complex system but we are still not building enough. Boris Johnson's levelling-up reforms were pursued with great energy but little success. Our national debt has continued its relentless rise under all parties. Nearly two decades on from the global financial crisis we are still in a low-growth trap.

Learning from previous attempts at reform is vital if we are to get things right this time. Three lessons stand out in particular: firstly, radicalism is more likely to work than incrementalism. I appreciate that might sound strange from someone often considered a safe pair of hands, but if I was advising a new cabinet minister, I would strongly urge them to choose one big thing to change rather than multiple smaller ones. It is not that incrementalism always fails or that being radical always works (ask Liz Truss). But the problem with more marginal improvements is that you need a lot of them to make a difference. Unless a minister is there for a decent period of time, reforms tend to sink without trace – and in British politics ministers rarely stick around. The average tenure for a cabinet minister is just two years. Since 2019, it has been just eight months. Junior ministers have an even shorter shelf life. Better, then, to focus on a few big changes – and be politically savvy enough to push them through. But that is difficult, in a system that rewards caution at every stage. As a cabinet minister, your career – and your survival in a reshuffle – generally depends on keeping things calm rather than stirring the pot. No 10 wants things to be quiet so they can pick a limited number of battles for the prime minister to fight. But reducing noise and keeping countless 'stakeholders' happy leads to less radicalism, more incrementalism and often no change at all.

That is true for chancellors as well. For all of my political life-time, centre-right chancellors have been able to cut taxes and protect public services, sometimes with a little borrowing to help the numbers add up. Centre-left chancellors have been able to increase funding for public services, again oiled by borrowing to avoid hefty tax rises. Now things have changed because the markets have effectively taken additional borrowing off the table. That means spending rises have to be funded by tax rises at the same time and of equivalent size. Tax cuts, too, have to be paid for with spending cuts, again at the same time and of equivalent size. That makes choices much starker and much noisier. It can turn the job into a straitjacket in which all but the smallest decisions are paralysed. Only radical policies will get you out of the straitjacket – but that needs support from your Downing Street neighbour, which is not always forthcoming.

A second lesson from previous reforms is the need to make implementing them easier and quicker. Why does it take a decade or more to get a shovel in the ground for a new nuclear power station or airport runway? We need big reforms to the plumbing of government, including to the structures of the civil service. That starts with the Treasury, much as I admire the formidable officials I worked with when I was there. Its beating heart revolves around its accountancy function – necessary for budgets – rather than its responsibility for economic growth. Large and capable tax and spending teams make the calculations necessary to meet fiscal rules, with only much smaller teams focused on growth. Some countries try to address this by giving responsibility for growth to a different government department, perhaps an economics ministry, as in Germany. But if growth is so vital, it would be a mistake to move it out of our most powerful ministry. When the Treasury wants something, it usually gets it, because power sits where the money is. But does it want growth enough? Ultimately ministers need to take the lead, but Treasury officials need to make sure there is a proper focus on long-term growth.

Likewise with the OBR. Journalists base their verdict on a budget on its forecasts and what it says about meeting a Chancellor's fiscal rules. Those matter, of course, but the focus of their budget reports needs to shift to how much is being done to promote longer-term growth. The OBR's institutional scepticism about 'scoring' new growth policies from the Chancellor is understandable but ultimately negative: if you make it too hard to make long-term decisions in budgets, politicians will ultimately give up. Far better to give a Chancellor the benefit of the doubt – and come down hard in later budgets if they don't deliver what they promise.

But reform needs to range much wider than the Treasury and the OBR. New laws massively slow down the speed at which governments can effect change, particularly when it comes to building vital infrastructure. Micromanagement from Whitehall has defenestrated our largest public service, the NHS, and made it much harder for local leaders to innovate and find solutions on the front line. That in turn means it takes too long to get even small problems sorted out, something that contributes to widespread voter disaffection. In my next book, I will explore in more detail the broader reforms necessary to improve the functioning of our democracy.

The final lesson is a more personal one for the prime minister. Too often our leaders are obsessed with 'the narrative'. Of course you need to be able to tell voters a story. You need to explain your policies and often also the need for short-term pain. If you can, it helps to come across as a human being in the process, although that can be easier said than done. But the reputation of a government ultimately depends on just one thing: what it changes for the better.

That means leaving ministers in post long enough to deliver big reforms. It means backing them when things get difficult. It means making sure delivery teams – and not just media teams – work 24/7 in Whitehall. It means making sure your own diary is focused on the big changes you want posterity to remember rather than the weekly grind of Prime Minister's Questions or international summits.

The most important long-term change we need is faster growth. Even if the solutions are in plain sight, that doesn't make them easy in a democratic system. Jean-Claude Juncker, former president of the European Commission, famously said, 'We all know what to do, but we don't know how to get re-elected once we have done it.'[2] But in the UK, governments with a clear economic plan often do get re-elected, most recently in 2015 but also in 1983 and 1987. To do that, leaders need to be able to explain why ducking difficult choices is ultimately more painful than embracing them, not least in a period of international instability and energy price fluctuation. Leaning into problems is better for politicians as well as voters: if governments don't do what it takes to secure prosperity, taxes go up, public services get worse – and they get thrown out.

One final point: in an unpredictable and unstable world, economic growth is about more than the prosperity of citizens. Since the Second World War, rising living standards have underpinned the rise of liberal democracy. Higher levels of prosperity allowed the West to bankrupt the Soviet Union in the Cold War. But as growth has stagnated across advanced economies so too have voting rights, free elections and civil liberties in the rest of the world. That is because when growth falters in liberal democracies, they become a less compelling example for others to follow. Countries like China show there are other ways to develop.

Liberal democracy has declined globally as growth has fallen in the countries where it started

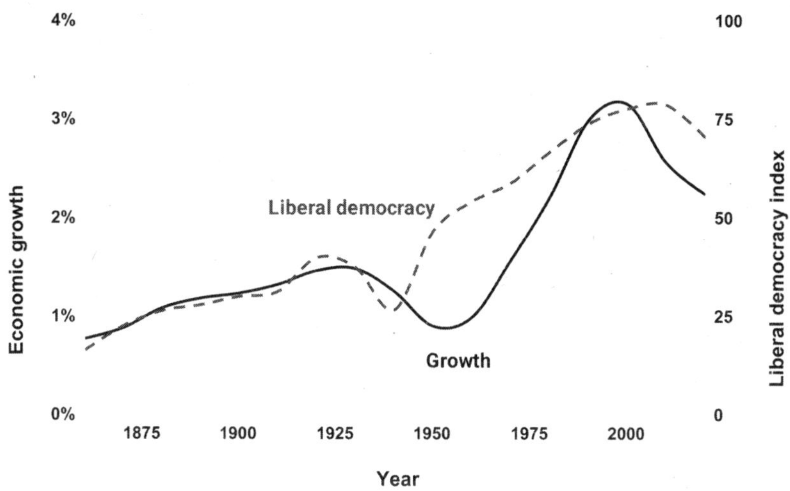

Credit: John Burn-Murdoch / *Financial Times*[3]
Sources: Maddison Project database,[4] V-Dem (2025) – processed by Our World in Data[5]
Note: Growth rate was calculated as compound annual growth rate over 21 years. Both metrics are weighted by population of constituent countries (1990 OECD members).

The power of example is particularly important when it comes to the UK, because, alongside the US, it was one of the architects of the post-1945 international order. Because of the English language, our universities and cultural influence, the rest of the world notices whether we are prospering or in decline. Perhaps more than anything else, they notice whether we are able to defend ourselves – but strong armed forces can only be paid for with economic growth.

Much, therefore, hangs on us turning things around. But we are not starting from scratch. With a good education system, a large technology sector and a long-standing tradition of entrepreneurialism, the UK is already predicted to rise from the sixth largest economy in the world to the fifth largest by the end of the decade. We face profound and unsettling challenges. But few would swap out the cards Britain holds. With a bit of leadership and our famously pragmatic approach to solving problems, there is all to play for.

POSTSCRIPT

Putting this book together has been a team effort, and I would like to thank the numerous people who have helped me. Many friends showed enormous patience reading through versions and pointing out multiple errors and omissions. I am particularly grateful to Nick Macpherson for his waspish wisdom, Charlie Bean for his calm good sense and Ruth Curtice, one of the best civil servants I worked with at the Treasury, who now runs the Resolution Foundation. Rupert Harrison, who gave me excellent advice in my early days as Chancellor, made good suggestions, as did my fellow entrepreneur Simon Philips, who inspired me to write the chapter on risk.

The two most difficult chapters to write were on tax and debt, so I was lucky to get help from the eminent Martin Wolf and the ever-thoughtful Emma Duncan as well as experts from the Bank of England such as Andrew Bailey and Clare Lombardelli (the sage), both of whom I much enjoyed working with when in office. Jon Moynihan patiently challenged me to get to the bottom of the link between economic growth and levels of taxation. Norman Lamont was particularly perceptive about supply-side reforms and Philip Hammond identified important areas needing improvement.

The public sector productivity chapter was greatly enhanced by advice from Paul Johnson, whom I (mostly) enjoyed sparring with during my time as Chancellor. I was also aided by people who have much longer experience than I do of the challenges involved in public sector reform, including Francis Maude and John Manzoni. Cat Little is one of the most outstanding civil servants I worked with and made useful suggestions following her experience in the Treasury, the Cabinet Office and the private sector.

On the work chapter, David Miles of the much-feared OBR gave me good advice on labour market reform, particularly when it comes to misunderstandings about migration. Quite properly we did not talk about the current government's relationship with the OBR.

The chapter on building things was originally inspired by appearing on a panel with Ben Southwood, who then gave me much help with the chapter. Oliver Letwin and Greg Clark generously shared their experience of trying to push through reform in office. Torsten Bell's book *Great Britain?* got me thinking hard about the ways we should and should not copy smaller European countries.

The education chapter was helped by many discussions with Nick Gibb and Michael Gove, both colleagues for whom I have immense respect. Their education reforms inspired many of my NHS reforms and remain a shining example of what can be achieved. But in writing this book I had the additional bonus of meeting the remarkable Katharine Birbalsingh at the Michaela Community School. Thank you to students Ifra and Summer for an unforgettable tour.

Energy policy is not an area I have ever really dealt with in detail, so I am most grateful to Greg Jackson for endless cups of tea at the Octopus HQ as he proselytised on zonal pricing and the evils of constraint payments. I also got great advice from Simone Rossi of EDF and John Pettigrew of National Grid.

The chapter on the regions was inspired by numerous exchanges in and out of office with Andy Street, who is one of the most impressive leaders I have ever met. But I also need to thank Jim O'Neill and Andy Haldane for their superb insights and encouragement – they have been devolvers for much longer than me. Tony Travers kindly introduced me to the brilliant Andrés Rodríguez-Pose, who helped me understand the concept of funded autonomy.

Ministers writing books are subject to regulations called the Radcliffe Rules. They unfortunately required me to remove the names of many of the talented civil servants I worked with. But I do want to thank my Treasury private office. Delivering budgets and Autumn Statements requires extraordinary determination, patience and humour, and I was proud to work alongside a hard-working, loyal and fun team. Thank you to Matt Cornford, Ellie Tack, Delia Leonte, Jenny Chaplin, Josh Platt, JK Kangur, Alex Craig and Sophie Welch for coming along for the ride – I miss you all. Alongside them in the trenches were the best special advisers I could ever have hoped for: Adam Smith, my extraordinarily talented chief of staff, Simon Finkelstein, Peter Lineen, Adam Memon, Cameron Brown and Kristen McLeod were all brilliant in different ways, as was Tim Pitt in No 10 and Christina Robinson on the phone.

I need to thank Anthony Jarvis, now on his second book with me (what endurance!), who has done an incredibly diligent job as my researcher, helping me with numerous challenging facts and figures. Thank you also to the brilliant Gesche Ipsen, whose eagle eyes never cease to amaze, and the whole team at Swift – Mark, Ruth and Diana – for helping me to produce the book so quickly. Thank you too to Elspeth McPherson and her team at Strathmore for their wonderful patience as we did the audiobook. As ever, I am in debt to the wisest man on the London publishing scene, my agent Jonny Geller, who has stuck by me through thick and thin.

My last thank you is to my wife Lucia and my kids Jack, Anna and Ellie. Politics is a nightmare for families – and being Chancellor even more so. Yes, we had adventures, but you also had a very busy dad whose focus was not always on home life (to say the least). Thank you for making it all possible and, in a strange way, for making none of it matter. I am so lucky to have the love of my wonderful wife Lucia. When you are in office you think you are doing the most important thing you will ever do. Only when you leave it do you realise that the most important thing in your life – your family – is still with you.

IMAGE CREDITS

A tale of two politicians called Reeves: 'Tate Reeves' by Gage Skidmore, distributed under a CC BY-SA 4.0 license (cropped and converted to greyscale by the author); 'The Chancellor of the Exchequer leaves Downing Street to deliver the Budget' by Simon Walker/HM Treasury, distributed under a CC BY-NC-ND 4.0 license (cropped and converted to greyscale by the author) (p. 17)

Denis Healey was notorious for the IMF bailout but walked a political tightrope with great skill: Keystone Pictures USA/ZUMAPRESS (p. 41)

The Olympic Park before and after 2012 – built on time and to budget: Sergio Dionisio / Associated Press ('before' photo); PAL News ('after' photo) (p. 101)

Inspirational leaders like Abi Tierney at the Passport Office show that radical improvements can be made to public sector productivity: Jordan Pettitt / PA Images (p. 124)

Sir Tim Berners-Lee, the inventor of the World Wide Web: CERN (p. 146)

Scotsman James Blyth built one of the world's first wind turbines: Pictorial Press (p. 160)

A tale of two cities: Mayor Street and Mayor Adler: 'West Midlands Mayor Andy Street, Minister for Skills and Apprenticeships Anne Milton MP, Dr. Neil Bentley – CEO of WorldSkills UK LIVE' by WorldSkills UK, CC BY 2.0 (cropped and converted to greyscale by the author); 'Austin

Mayor Steve Adler delivers closing remarks on Tuesday, April 26, 2016, at the end of the first day's panel discussions held during the LBJ Presidential Library's three-day Vietnam War Summit', LBJ Library photo (DIG13870dhk_002) by David Hume Kennerly, Public Domain Mark (cropped and converted to greyscale by the author) (p. 179)

The Transjurane: Switzerland skilfully uses referenda to secure support for infrastructure projects: 'Portail sud tunnel de choindez' by Dråfølin, distributed under a CC BY-SA 4.0 license (converted to greyscale by the author) (p. 186)

Katharine Birbalsingh: unlikely hero of a revolution in English schools: Author (p. 198)

NOTES

Introduction

1   Productivity growth in this instance was measured as output per hour worked. Elliott Christensen and Gregory Thwaites, *Trend Setters* (Resolution Foundation, 2025), https://www.resolutionfoundation.org/app/uploads/2025/10/Trend-setters.pdf.

2   For house pricing and SME lending data, see the following sources: HM Land Registry, 'UK House Price Index', GOV.UK, 17 December 2025, https://www.gov.uk/government/statistical-data-sets/uk-house-price-index-data-downloads-october-2025; 'Monthly Amounts Outstanding of Monetary Financial Institutions' Sterling and All Foreign Currency Loans to Small and Medium Sized Enterprises (in Sterling Millions) Not Seasonally Adjusted', [RPMZ8YH], Bank of England, January 2026.

3   *World Economic Outlook Update* (IMF, 2026), https://www.imf.org/-/media/files/publications/weo/2026/january/english/text.pdf.

4   Alistair MacDonald, *Global Perceptions 2025: How 18–34 Year Olds See the UK and the World* (British Council, 2025), application/pdf, https://doi.org/10.57884/V8XY-N723.

5   'How London Can Rise Again', *The Economist*, 28 January 2026, https://www.economist.com/britain/2026/01/28/how-london-can-rise-again.

6   *UK Innovation 2025 Review* (dealroom.co, HSBC Innovation Banking, 2026), https://dealroom.co/reports/uk-innovation-2025-review.

7   'World Economic Outlook Database: April 2025', IMF, 2025, https://www.imf.org/en/publications/weo/weo-database/2025/april.

8   *Economic and Fiscal Outlook – March 2024* (OBR, 2024), https://obr.uk/docs/dlm_uploads/E03057758_OBR_EFO-March-2024_Web-AccessibleFinal.pdf.

1. Tax

1   Author's comparison of Mississippi's GDP per capita adjusted for regional price parity with the UK's GDP per head adjusted for USD PPP. It should also be noted that whilst annual data for 2025 was not available at the time of writing, current price quarterly GDP figures suggest that the UK may have caught back up with Mississippi – but it remains a very tight race. See adjacent notes for Mississippi GDP data and UK GDP data. Mississippi's regional price parity data can be found here: 'Regional Price Parities by State', [SARPP], US Bureau of Economic Analysis, 19 February 2026, https://apps.bea.gov/.

2   Author's calculation using real GDP growth data from 'World Economic Outlook Database: April 2025' and 'Real GDP by State', [SQGDP9], US Bureau of Economic Analysis, 23 January 2026, https://apps.bea.gov/.

3   'State Annual Summary Statistics: Personal Income, GDP, Consumer Spending, Price Indexes, and Employment', [SASUMMARY], US Bureau of Economic Analysis, 2025, https://www.bea.gov/.

4   'Resident Population in Mississippi [MSPOP]', US Census Bureau, retrieved from FRED, Federal Reserve Bank of St. Louis, 23 December 2024, https://fred.stlouisfed.org/series/MSPOP.

5   'World Economic Outlook Database: April 2025', IMF, 2025, https://www.imf.org/en/publications/weo/weo-database/2025/april.

6   The Associated Press, 'Bryant Signs Largest Tax Cut in Mississippi History', *Clarion-Ledger*, 13 May 2016, https://www.clarionledger.com/story/news/politics/2016/05/13/bryant-signs-bill-cut-415-million-business-income-taxes/84353830/.

7   Emily Wagster Pettus, 'Mississippi Lawmakers Pass Largest-Ever State Income Tax Cut', AP News, 27 March 2022, https://apnews.com/article/business-mississippi-tate-reeves-legislature-15134876a4f232f0d7860974772d1c7f.

8   David A. Lieb, 'No State Has Ended Personal Income Taxes since 1980, but Mississippi and Kentucky May Change That', *The Independent*, 6 April 2025, https://www.independent.co.uk/news/mississippi-tennessee-new-hampshire-alaska-donald-trump-b2728186.html.

9   Aaron Robinson, *Annual Report – Fiscal Year 2024*, Mississippi Department of Revenue, https://www.dor.ms.gov/sites/default/files/statistics/annual-reports/

MSDOR%20Annual%20Report%20FY%202024%20full%2012302024%20%281%29.pdf.

10 Tate Reeves, 'Reeves: Hearings Look to Build on Budget Successes', *Clarion-Ledger*, 27 September 2014, https://www.clarionledger.com/story/opinion/columnists/2014/09/27/reeves-hearings-look-build-budget-successes/16357389/.

11 Geoff Pender, 'MS Tax Cuts: What Do We Really Know about Them?', *Clarion-Ledger*, 2 July 2016, https://www.clarionledger.com/story/news/politics/2016/07/02/tax-cuts-list/86606928/.

12 *Annual Report – Fiscal Years 2015 to 2024* (Mississippi Department of Revenue, n.d.), https://www.dor.ms.gov/taxonomy/term/63.

13 'Mississippi Again Sets Historic New Records for Employment', Office of Governor Tate Reeves, 20 May 2025, https://governorreeves.ms.gov/mississippi-again-sets-historic-new-records-for-employment-2/.

14 'AWS Plans to Invest $10 Billion in Mississippi, the Largest Capital Investment in the State's History', Amazon News, 25 January 2024, https://www.aboutamazon.com/news/aws/aws-10-billion-investment-mississippi; 'Compass Project Generates $10B Investment in Lauderdale County', *Compass Datacenters*, 9 January 2025, https://www.compassdatacenters.com/news/compass-10b-investment-lauderdale-county-mississippi/.

15 'State Annual Summary Statistics'.

16 'Quarterly Summary of State & Local Taxes', US Census Bureau, 15 January 2026, https://www.census.gov/econ/currentdata/?programCode=QTAX.

17 'MSDH Declares Public Health Emergency on Infant Mortality', Mississippi State Department of Health, 21 August 2025, https://msdh.ms.gov/page/23,30305,341.html.

18 'Infant Mortality Quarterly Provisional Estimates', CDC – National Center for Health Statistics, 20 August 2025, https://www.cdc.gov/nchs/nvss/vsrr/infant-mortality-dashboard.htm; 'Child and Infant Mortality in England and Wales: 2023', ONS, 22 April 2025, https://www.ons.gov.uk/peoplepopulationandcommunity/birthsdeathsandmarriages/deaths/bulletins/childhoodinfantandperinatalmortalityinenglandandwales/2023.

19 'Obesity, Physical Activity and Nutrition', Fingertips – Department of Health & Social Care, accessed 9 December 2025, https://fingertips.phe.org.uk/.

20 'Adult Obesity Prevalence Maps', CDC, 3 December 2025, https://www.cdc.gov/obesity/data-and-statistics/adult-obesity-prevalence-maps.html.

21 'Adults' Gender Distribution, by Educational Attainment Level and Age Group', OECD Data Explorer, 9 October 2025, https://data-explorer.oecd.org/.

22 'Educational Attainment – American Community Survey, ACS 1-Year Estimates Subject Tables, Table S1501', US Census Bureau, 2024, https://data.census.gov/table/ACSST1Y2024.S1501?g=040XX00US28.

23 'National Life Tables: UK', ONS, 10 December 2025, https://www.ons.gov.uk/peoplepopulationandcommunity/birthsdeathsandmarriages/lifeexpectancies/datasets/nationallifetablesunitedkingdomreferencetables.

24 Elizabeth Arias et al., 'U.S. State Life Tables, 2022', *National Vital Statistics Reports* 74, no. 12 (2025), https://dx.doi.org/10.15620/cdc/174620.

25 Health Survey for England, 2024 (NHS England, 2026), https://digital.nhs.uk/data-and-information/publications/statistical/health-survey-for-england/2024.

26 'BRFSS Prevalence & Trends Data [Online] – Weight Classification by Body Mass Index', Centers for Disease Control and Prevention, National Center for Chronic Disease Prevention and Health Promotion, Division of Population Health, n.d., accessed 7 February 2026, https://www.cdc.gov/brfss/brfssprevalence/.

27 'Income Distribution Database', OECD Data Explorer, 16 June 2025, https://data-explorer.oecd.org/.

28 Craig Benson, *Poverty in States and Metropolitan Areas: 2023*, ACSBR-022 (2024), https://www2.census.gov/library/publications/2024/demo/acsbr-022.pdf.

29 *Mississippi's 2024 National Assessment of Educational Progress* (Mississippi Department of Education, 2025).

30 Frank Corder, 'Mississippi Graduation Rate Continues to Exceed National Average', *Magnolia Tribune*, 21 February 2025, https://magnoliatribune.com/2025/02/21/mississippi-graduation-rate-continues-to-exceed-national-average/.

31 It should be noted that poverty is measured differently in the US, so the important factor to focus on is the magnitude of change. 'Estimated Percent of People of All Ages in Poverty for Mississippi', [PPAAMS28000A156NCEN], US Census Bureau, retrieved from FRED, Federal Reserve Bank of St. Louis, 17 December 2025, https://fred.stlouisfed.org/series/PPAAMS28000A156NCEN.

32 'Real Median Household Income in Mississippi', [MEHOINUSMSA672N], US Census Bureau, retrieved from FRED, Federal Reserve Bank of St. Louis, 17 December 2025, https://fred.stlouisfed.org/series/MEHOINUSMSA672N.

33   *The Sit Down with Russ Latino – 10/23/2024 – Governor Tate Reeves*, produced by Mississippi Public Broadcasting, 2024, 54:51, https://www.youtube.com/watch?v=3zAL4VNK6JE.

34   'Gross Domestic Product – Regions', OECD Data Explorer, 2 October 2025, http://oe.cd/geostats.

35   Torsten Bell, *Great Britain? How We Get Our Future Back* (The Bodley Head, 2024).

36   Resolution Foundation & Centre for Economic Performance, LSE, *Ending Stagnation: A New Economic Strategy for Britain* (Resolution Foundation, 2023).

37   'Tax Revenue', OECD, accessed 17 December 2025, https://www.oecd.org/en/data/indicators/tax-revenue.html; 'Average Annual Wages', OECD, accessed 17 December 2025, https://www.oecd.org/en/data/indicators/average-annual-wages.html.

38   'World Economic Outlook Database: April 2025'.

39   Ed Cornforth, 'Which Taxes Are Best and Worst for Growth?', *Economics Observatory*, 20 May 2024, https://www.economicsobservatory.com/which-taxes-are-best-and-worst-for-growth.

40   Quentin Peel, 'Merkel Warns on Cost of Welfare', *Financial Times*, 16 December 2012, https://www.ft.com/content/8cc0f584-45fa-11e2-b7ba-00144feabdc0.

41   This is an illustrative point highlighting the reliance of public sector wages on taxes generated by private sector workers. In the US, there are approximately 135 million non-farm private sector employees, compared with 23 million government employees, which is approximately a ratio of 6 to 1. In the UK, there are around 28 million private sector workers, compared with 6 million public sector workers, which equates to a ratio of around 5 to 1. See: *The Employment Situation – January 2026* (Bureau of Labor Statistics, 2026), https://www.dol.gov/newsroom/economicdata/empsit_02112026.pdf; 'EMP02: Public and Private Sector Employment', ONS, 16 December 2025, https://www.ons.gov.uk/employmentandlabourmarket/peopleinwork/employmentandemployeetypes/datasets/publicandprivatesectoremploymentemp02.

42   In accordance with the attribution requirements set out by the researchers at the University of Groningen, in addition to the Maddison Project Database, the original papers the project used were: Jutta Bolt and Jan Luiten van Zanden, 'Maddison-style Estimates of the Evolution of the World Economy: A New

2023 Update', *Journal of Economic Surveys* 39, no. 2 (2025): 631–71, https://doi.org/10.1111/joes.12618; Christian Stohr, *Trading Gains: New Estimates of Swiss GDP, 1851 to 2008*, Economic History Working Papers 245/2016 (2016), https://researchonline.lse.ac.uk/id/eprint/67032/; Lennart Schön and Olle Krantz, *New Swedish Historical National Accounts since the 16th Century in Constant and Current Prices*, Lund Papers in Economic History 140 (2015); Søren Larsen, *Reviderede Tidsserier for Produktionsvaerdi Og Bruttofaktorindkomst for Perioden 1947–65* (CBS, 1992); C.A. van Bochove and T.A. Huitker, *Main National Accounting Series, 1900–1986*, CBS Occasional Paper 17 (The Hague, 1987); Walter G. Hoffmann et al., *Das Wachstum der deutschen Wirtschaft seit der Mitte des 19. Jahrhunderts* (Springer, 1965); *Central Bureau of Statistics Norway* (1970); Angus Maddison, *Monitoring the World Economy: 1820–1992*, Reprinted (OECD, 2000); Riitta Hjerppe, *The Finnish Economy 1860–1985: Growth and Structural Change* (Bank of Finland, 1989); C. H. Feinstein, *National Income, Expenditure and Output of the United Kingdom, 1855–1965*, Studies in the National Income and Expenditure of the United Kingdom (Cambridge University Press, 1972).

43 'Public Finances in Modern History', IMF, 2026, https://www.imf.org/external/datamapper/datasets/FPP.

44 *Economic and Fiscal Outlook – October 2024* (OBR, 2024), https://obr.uk/docs/dlm_uploads/OBR_Economic_and_fiscal_outlook_Oct_2024.pdf.

45 'Average Annual Hours Actually Worked per Worker', OECD Data Explorer, 27 June 2025, https://data-explorer.oecd.org/.

46 'Global Revenue Statistics – Comparative Tax Revenues', OECD Data Explorer, 9 January 2026, https://data-explorer.oecd.org/; 'Average Annual Hours Actually Worked per Worker'.

47 Author's calculations using data from 'World Economic Outlook Database: April 2025'.

48 Jon Moynihan, *Return to Growth: How to Fix the Economy. Volume Two* (Biteback Publishing, 2025).

49 'Global Revenue Statistics – Comparative Tax Revenues'.

50 'World Economic Outlook Database: April 2025'.

51 'NAAG Chapter 3: Expenditure', OECD, 10 October 2025, https://data-explorer.oecd.org/.

52 Calculations by the author assuming an economy-wide effective tax rate of between 35 and 40%.

53 Due to the way the OECD calculates tax revenues, the tax-to-GDP ratio is lower than the one published by the ONS – which can be more than 1% of GDP higher. However, in order to better make cross-country comparisons, it is better to use the figures published by the OECD. OECD data can be found here: 'Global Revenue Statistics – Comparative Tax Revenues', https://data-explorer.oecd.org/.

54 'The Burden of Health Insurance Premiums on Small Business', JPMorganChase, June 2024, https://www.jpmorganchase.com/institute/all-topics/business-growth-and-entrepreneurship/small-business-health-insurance-burdens.

55 *Corporate Tax Statistics 2025* (OECD, 2025), https://www.oecd.org/en/publications/corporate-tax-statistics-2025_6a915941-en.html; *Consumption Tax Trends 2024* (OECD, 2024), https://www.oecd.org/en/publications/consumption-tax-trends-2024_dcd4dd36-en.html.

56 'GOV.UK – Direct Effects of Illustrative Tax Changes Bulletin (June 2022)', National Archives, 16 June 2022, https://webarchive.nationalarchives.gov.uk/ukgwa/20221003174938/https://www.gov.uk/government/statistics/direct-effects-of-illustrative-tax-changes/direct-effects-of-illustrative-tax-changes-bulletin-june-2022.

57 Based on internal Treasury analysis.

58 According to the government's summary of the 2024 Budget, the OBR expected the reductions to 'lead to the equivalent of around 200,000 extra full-time workers by 2028/29'. See *Economic and Fiscal Outlook – March 2024* (OBR, 2024), https://obr.uk/docs/dlm_uploads/E03057758_OBR_EFO-March 2024_Web AccessibleFinal.pdf; 'Vacancies and Jobs in the UK', ONS, 12 March 2024, https://www.ons.gov.uk/employmentandlabourmarket/peopleinwork/employmentandemployeetypes/bulletins/jobsandvacancies intheuk/march2024.

59 'Autumn Statement 2023 Speech', GOV.UK, 22 November 2023, https://www.gov.uk/government/speeches/autumn-statement-2023-speech.

60 'Autumn Statement 2023 Speech'.

61 'CBI Responds to Autumn Statement', CBI, 22 November 2023, https://www.cbi.org.uk/media-centre/articles/cbi-responds-to-autumn-statement/.

62 See 'Chart 5 – Machinery investment intensiveness over time' in Investment Monitor 2025 (Make UK/RSM, 2025), https://www.makeuk.org/insights/reports/investment-monitor-2025.

63 'Universal Credit – How Your Wages Affect Your Payments', GOV.UK,

accessed 30 January 2026, https://www.gov.uk/universal-credit/how-your-wages-affect-your-payments.

64 Universal Credit is tapered post-tax income, so for every pound earned above the threshold, only 72p of it is used in the taper calculation. The marginal tax rate is therefore calculated by taking income tax (20%), national insurance (8%) and adding a 39.6% UC taper (0.72 x 55%).

2. Debt

1 Ian Aitken, 'Bulldozer Healey Tramples on Left', *The Guardian*, 1 October 1976, https://www.theguardian.com/politics/1976/oct/01/labour.uk. For footage from the speech, see 'Healey's Finance Speech at Labour Party Conference', AP Archive, 2015, 01:43, https://www.youtube.com/watch?v=RpKz54bxXuU.

2 Richard Roberts, *When Britain Went Bust: The 1976 IMF Crisis* (OMFIF, 2016).

3 Information on the events beforehand, during and afterwards are detailed in Kathleen Burk, *Goodbye, Great Britain: The 1976 IMF Crisis* (Yale University Press, 1992).

4 Denis Healey, *Time of My Life* (Penguin Group, 2015).

5 For the financial year 2022/23, total payments reached £111 billion, including interest paid out via the BoE's Asset Purchase Facility. This was double the previous year. See full public sector finance data here: 'Public Sector Finances Time Series', ONS, 20 February 2026, https://www.ons.gov.uk/economy/governmentpublicsectorandtaxes/publicsectorfinance/datasets/publicsectorfinances.

6 In 2024/25, the UK paid £106 billion in interest. Dividing by 28.6 million households results in around £3,700 per household. 'Public Sector Finances Time Series'; 'Families and Households', ONS, 23 July 2025, https://www.ons.gov.uk/peoplepopulationandcommunity/birthsdeathsandmarriages/families/datasets/familiesandhouseholdsfamiliesandhouseholds.

7 Converted to USD, UK interest per household comes to around $4,700, and Germany's to $1,200. Sources for Germany's interest per household calculation: 'Government Interest Expenditure, Germany, Annual', 23 October 2025, https://data.ecb.europa.eu/data/datasets/GFS/GFS.A.N.DE.W0.S13.S1.C.D.D41._Z._Z._T.XDC._Z.S.V.N._T; 'Private Households

by Household Composition, Number of Children and Labour Status within Households', Eurostat, 8 January 2026, https://doi.org/10.2908/ LFST_HHNHWHTC.

8 US Census Bureau, 'Total Households', [TTLHH], retrieved from FRED, Federal Reserve Bank of St. Louis, 4 December 2025, https://fred.stlouisfed. org/series/TTLHH; 'Interest Expense on the Public Debt Outstanding', US Treasury, 5 February 2026, https://fiscaldata.treasury.gov/datasets/interest-expense-debt-outstanding/interest-expense-on-the-public-debt-outstanding.

9 'Public Sector Finances Time Series'; 'Families and Households'.

10 'Total Households'.

11 'Interest Expense on the Public Debt Outstanding'.

12 'Public Sector Finances Time Series'; 'Families and Households'.

13 'Government Interest Expenditure, Italy, Quarterly', ECB, 26 January 2026, https://data.ecb.europa.eu/data/datasets/GFS/GFS.Q.N.IT.W0.S13. S1.C.D.D41._Z._Z._T.XDC._Z.S.V.N._T; 'Government Interest Expenditure, France, Annual', ECB, 23 October 2025, https://data.ecb.europa.eu/data/ datasets/GFS/GFS.A.N.FR.W0.S13.S1.C.D.D41._Z._Z._T.XDC._Z.S.V.N._T; 'Government Interest Expenditure, Germany, Annual'.

14 'Private Households by Household Composition, Number of Children and Labour Status within Households'.

15 *Canada Strong – Budget 2025* (Government of Canada, 2025), https://budget. canada.ca/2025/report-rapport/pdf/budget-2025.pdf.

16 'Table 17-10-0159-01 Estimates of the Number of Private Households by Size on July 1st', Statistics Canada, 7 November 2025.

17 'Family Income and Expenditure Survey 2024 – Table 1-1. Yearly Average of Monthly Disbursements per Household (Total Households)', e-Stat, 8 August 2025, https://www.e-stat.go.jp/en/stat-search/files?tclass=000000330013&c ycle=7&year=20240.

18 *Japanese Public Finance Fact Sheet* (Ministry of Finance of Japan, 2024), https://www.mof.go.jp/english/policy/budget/budget/fy2024/02.pdf.

19 'NAAG Chapter 9: Reference Series', OECD Data Explorer, 19 February 2026, https://data-explorer.oecd.org/.

20 'World Economic Outlook Database: April 2025', IMF, 2025, https://www. imf.org/en/publications/weo/weo-database/2025/april.

21 'World Economic Outlook Database: April 2025'.

22 'Families and Households'.

23 In the financial year ending 31 March 2024, the UK government spent £53.7 billion on unfunded pensions, which equated to £1,877 per household. Public sector pension calculation based on the following sources: *Whole of Government Accounts – Year Ended 31 March 2024* (UK Government, 2025), https://assets.publishing.service.gov.uk/media/68776746352c290d20dcaef9/WGA_2023-24_accounts.pdf; 'Families and Households'.

24 Debt interest plus unfunded public sector pension payments equates to over £160 billion a year, which is the equivalent of increasing both the basic and higher tax rates by 19p. For more about illustrative changes to tax bands, see: 'Direct Effects of Illustrative Tax Changes Bulletin (June 2025)', GOV.UK, 24 June 2025, https://www.gov.uk/government/statistics/direct-effects-of-illustrative-tax-changes/direct-effects-of-illustrative-tax-changes-bulletin-january-2025.

25 Warren Buffett, 'Warren Buffett: Here's How I Would Solve the Trade Problem', *Fortune*, 29 April 2016, https://fortune.com/article/warren-buffett-foreign-trade/.

26 DWP, 'Benefit Expenditure and Caseload Tables 2025', GOV.UK, 5 January 2026, https://www.gov.uk/government/publications/benefit-expenditure-and-caseload-tables-2025.

27 In 2025/26 prices, the working-age benefit bill is forecast to increase to £141 billion in 2030/31, compared with around £85 billion in 2019/20. Therefore, by returning to 2019 levels, the government would save £56 billion in real terms. For a full breakdown see: DWP, 'Benefit Expenditure and Caseload Tables 2025'.

28 Oxford Economics, *A Blueprint for Growth* (L&G, 2025), https://group.legalandgeneral.com/media/5vvabnne/a-blueprint-for-growth.pdf.

3. Work

1 I am grateful to Camilla Tominey for alerting me to this in one of her articles. See: Camilla Tominey, 'Work-Shy Britain Only Cares about "Me, Me, Me"', *The Telegraph*, 10 December 2021, https://www.telegraph.co.uk/news/2021/12/10/work-shy-britain-cares/.

2 'LFS: Econ. Inactivity Reasons: Long Term Sick: UK: 16-64:000s:SA', ONS, 16 December 2025, https://www.ons.gov.uk/employmentandlabourmarket/peoplenotinwork/economicinactivity/timeseries/lf69/lms.

3 Natasha Plaister, 'A Closer Look at Pupils Who Did Not Achieve the Basics at GCSE', *FFT Education Datalab*, 18 September 2024, https://ffteducationdatalab. org.uk/2024/09/a-closer-look-at-pupils-who-did-not-achieve-the-basics-at-gcse/.

4 'PISA 2022 Results (Volume I and II) – Country Notes: United Kingdom', OECD, OECD Publishing, 4 December 2023, https://www.oecd.org/en/publications/pisa-2022-results-volume-i-and-ii-country-notes_ed6fbcc5-en/united-kingdom_9c15db47-en.html.

5 Between Q4 2019 and Q4 2025, the total number of non-UK-born people in employment increased from 5.8 to 7.4 million. At the same time, the number of UK-born people in employment decreased from 27.3 to 26.9 million. See full data here: 'EMP06: Employment by Country of Birth and Nationality', ONS, 17 February 2026, https://www.ons.gov.uk/employmentandlabourmarket/peopleinwork/employmentandemployeetypes/datasets/employmentbycountryofbirthandnationalityemp06.

6 'OECD Family Database – PF3.4. Childcare Support', OECD, January 2026, https://webfs.oecd.org/Els-com/Family_Database/PF3-4-Childcare-support.pdf.

7 'OECD Family Database – LMF1.2. Maternal Employment Rates', OECD, January 2026, https://webfs.oecd.org/els-com/Family_Database/LMF1_2_Maternal_Employment.pdf.mater.

8 Calculation by the author using OECD working-age population data.

9 Calculations based on data published by Eurostat and the ONS. Denmark's disability employment rate was calculated by subtracting the published disability employment gap from the employment rate of that year. It should be noted that the Eurostat figures look at ages 20 to 64, whereas the ONS data looks at ages 16 to 64, thus affecting the precision of the comparison. Nevertheless, for the purposes of illustrating the point that more can be done to support disabled people into work, this discrepancy is not a major issue. The raw data can be accessed here: 'Employment and Activity by Sex and Age – Annual Data', lfsi_emp_a, Eurostat, 21 January 2026, https://doi.org/10.2908/LFSI_EMP_A; 'Disability Employment Gap by Level of Activity Limitation and Sex', tepsr_sp200, Eurostat, 30 January 2026, https://doi.org/10.2908/TEPSR_SP200; 'Data Tables: The Employment of Disabled People 2025', ONS, 18 November 2025, https://www.gov.uk/government/statistics/the-employment-of-disabled-people-2025.

10 Calculation by the author using OECD infra-annual labour statistics. In 2024, the UK's working age population was 42 million, therefore 5% of this would be just over 2 million.

11 'Income Distribution Database', OECD Data Explorer, 16 June 2025, https://data-explorer.oecd.org/.

12 'Annual GDP and Consumption per Capita, US $, Current Prices, Current PPPs', OECD Data Explorer, 5 February 2026, https://data-explorer.oecd.org/; 'Employment and Unemployment by Five-Year Age Group and Sex – Indicators', OECD Data Explorer, 30 October 2025, https://data-explorer.oecd.org/.

13 'Infra-Annual Labour Statistics', OECD Data Explorer, 19 February 2026, https://data-explorer.oecd.org/; 'Average Annual Wages', OECD Data Explorer, 2 February 2026, https://data-explorer.oecd.org/.

14 'Personal Independence Payment (PIP)', GOV.UK, accessed 8 January 2026, https://www.gov.uk/pip/how-much-youll-get.

15 Department for Work and Pensions, 'Universal Credit Local Housing Allowance Rates: 2025 to 2026', GOV.UK, 3 February 2025, https://www.gov.uk/government/publications/universal-credit-local-housing-allowance-rates-2025-to-2026.

16 When annualised, £892 a week equates to £46,400 a year. After accounting for the tax-free threshold, basic rate of tax and national insurance contributions, this would result in a weekly take-home pay of £710. Benefits equivalent does not include any council tax reductions which may also be granted.

17 When annualised, £588 a week equates to around £30,600 a year. After accounting for the tax-free threshold, basic rate of tax and national insurance contributions, this would result in a weekly take-home pay of £491. Benefits equivalent does not include any council tax reductions which may also be granted.

18 Calculations by the author.

19 This figure is based on decision outcomes, not the net increase of LCWRA caseload. It also does not include people transitioning from employment and support allowance (ESA). 'Universal Credit Work Capability Assessment Statistics, April 2019 to September 2025', GOV.UK, 11 December 2025, https://www.gov.uk/government/statistics/universal-credit-work-capability-assessment-statistics-april-2019-to-september-2025.

20 'Spring Statement 2025 Health and Disability Benefit Reforms – Equality Analysis', GOV.UK, 30 October 2025, https://www.gov.uk/government/

consultations/pathways-to-work-reforming-benefits-and-support-to-get-britain-working-green-paper/spring-statement-2025-health-and-disability-benefit-reforms-equality-analysis.

21 *The Benefits Budget* (The Centre for Social Justice, 2025), https://www.centreforsocialjustice.org.uk/wp-content/uploads/2025/11/CSJ-Benefits_Budget.pdf.

22 Michael Simmons, 'Labour Is Now the Party of Welfare, Not Work', *The Spectator*, 6 December 2025, https://spectator.com/article/labour-is-now-the-party-of-welfare-not-work/.

23 Charlie McCurdy and Louise Murphy, *We've Only Just Begun Action to Improve Young People's Mental Health, Education and Employment* (Resolution Foundation, 2024), https://www.resolutionfoundation.org/app/uploads/2024/02/Weve-only-just-begun.pdf.

24 'Universal Credit Work Capability Assessment Statistics, April 2019 to September 2025'.

25 'Universal Credit Work Capability Assessment Statistics, April 2019 to September 2025'.

26 In 2024, nearly 400,000 people were granted LCWRA. This figure is currently much higher if you include those transitioning from ESA. Available data indicates that 2025 will have a similar decision rate. See the WCA Decisions tab of 'Universal Credit Work Capability Assessment Statistics, April 2019 to September 2025'.

27 On page 4 of the following report, it was noted that when median income fell during the pandemic, the UK's poverty rate fell, and when wages returned to previous levels, the poverty rate increased again. More information here: Sam Ray-Chaudhuri et al., *Poverty*, IFS Report R264 (IFS, 2023), https://ifs.org.uk/sites/default/files/2023-07/Poverty-R264-IFS-Report.pdf.

28 'Spring Statement Social Security Changes – Updated Impact on Poverty Levels in Great Britain', GOV.UK, 30 June 2025, https://www.gov.uk/government/publications/spring-statement-social-security-changes-updated-impact-on-poverty-levels-in-great-britain/spring-statement-social-security-changes-updated-impact-on-poverty-levels-in-great-britain.

29 'Autumn Statement 2023 Speech', GOV.UK, 22 November 2023, https://www.gov.uk/government/speeches/autumn-statement-2023-speech.

30 *Economic and Fiscal Outlook – March 2024* (OBR, 2024), https://obr.uk/docs/dlm_uploads/E03057758_OBR_EFO-March-2024_Web-AccessibleFinal.pdf.

31 *R (on the Application of ELLEN CLIFFORD) v the Secretary of State for Work and Pensions*, AC-2023-LON-003619 (Royal Courts of Justice 16 January 2025), https://publiclawproject.org.uk/content/uploads/2025/01/Clifford-v-SSWP-Judgment-16-January-2025-1.pdf.

32 Author's calculations based on HMT public spending and DWP benefit expenditure statistics. See: HM Treasury, 'Public Spending Statistics Release: July 2025', GOV.UK, 17 July 2025, https://www.gov.uk/government/statistics/public-spending-statistics-release-july-2025; DWP, 'Benefit Expenditure and Caseload Tables 2025', GOV.UK, 5 January 2026, https://www.gov.uk/government/publications/benefit-expenditure-and-caseload-tables-2025.

33 DWP, 'Benefit Expenditure and Caseload Tables 2025'.

34 David Miles 'B. Population Ponzi scheme – Migration, public services and the fiscal outlook' in Robin Hodgson, *Don't Stop Thinking about Tomorrow* (The Common Good Foundation, 2025), https://www.dontstopthinkingabouttomorrow.co.uk/dont-stop-thinking-about-tomorrow.pdf.

35 Technically, this could result in up to a 5.35% increase in GDP, but I have left it at 4%, given that other variables mentioned may pull it down.

36 'Infra-Annual Labour Statistics'; 'Average Annual Wages', OECD Data Explorer, 2 February 2026, https://data-explorer.oecd.org/.

4. Building Things

1 'Population Density (People per Sq. Km of Land Area)', World Bank Group, n.d., https://data.worldbank.org/indicator/EN.POP.DNST.

2 'Full Set of Local Data – France Entière', Insee, 5 February 2026, https://www.insee.fr/en/statistiques/6457611?geo=FE-1; 'Dwellings by Tenure in the UK by Country – UK Housing Review 2025 Compendium of Tables', with Gillian Young and Andrew Watson, UK Housing Review, March 2025, https://www.ukhousingreview.org.uk/ukhr25/compendium.html; 'Population Estimates Time Series Dataset', 27 November 2025, https://www.ons.gov.uk/peoplepopulationandcommunity/populationandmigration/populationestimates/datasets/populationestimatestimeseriesdataset.

3 Author's calculations using the following sources: 'Full Set of Local Data – France Entière'; 'Dwellings by Tenure in the UK by Country – UK Housing

Review 2025 Compendium of Tables'; 'Population Estimates Time Series Dataset'; 'Dwelling Stock by Years', Destatis, 17 September 2025, https://www.destatis.de/EN/Themes/Society-Environment/Housing/Tables/liste-dwellings.html.

4   Adam Corlett and Lindsay Judge, *Housing Outlook Q1 2024* (Resolution Foundation, 2024), https://www.resolutionfoundation.org/publications/housing-outlook-q1-2024/.

5   Richard Donnell, 'Research: The Viability of Homebuilding – Zoopla for Business', Zoopla, 26 September 2025, https://business.zoopla.co.uk/research-the-viability-of-homebuilding.

6   'Real Residential Property Prices for United Kingdom', (QGBR628BIS), retrieved from FRED, Federal Reserve Bank of St. Louis, 30 December 2025, https://fred.stlouisfed.org/series/QGBR628BIS; 'Real Residential Property Prices for France', (QFRR628BIS), retrieved from FRED, Federal Reserve Bank of St. Louis, 30 October 2025, https://fred.stlouisfed.org/series/QFRR628BIS.

7   'Earnings Time Series of Median Gross Weekly Earnings from 1968 to 2025', ONS, 23 October 2025, https://www.ons.gov.uk/employmentandlabourmarket/peopleinwork/earningsandworkinghours/datasets/earningstimeseriesofmediangrossweeklyearningsfrom1968to2022; HM Land Registry, 'UK House Price Index', GOV.UK, 17 December 2025, https://www.gov.uk/government/statistical-data-sets/uk-house-price-index-data-downloads-october-2025.

8   Pascale Bourquin et al., 'Trends in Income and Wealth Inequalities', *Oxford Open Economics* 3, no. Supplement_1 (2024): i103–46, https://doi.org/10.1093/ooec/odad100.

9   Gill Plimmer et al., 'Cost of Sizewell C Nuclear Project Expected to Reach Close to £40bn', *Financial Times*, 14 January 2025, https://www.ft.com/content/0b483728-de5b-4f2e-8d00-c49885c572c9.

10   Ben Hopkinson, 'Infrastructure Costs: Nuclear Edition', Notes on Growth, 25 August 2023, https://www.samdumitriu.com/p/infrastructure-costs-nuclear-edition.

11   Simon Jack, 'Hinkley C: UK Nuclear Plant Price Tag Could Rocket by a Third', BBC News, 23 January 2024, https://www.bbc.co.uk/news/business-68073279; Hinkley Point C media team, 'Hinkley Point C Project Cost', EDF, 12 May 2016, https://www.edfenergy.com/energy/nuclear-new-build-projects/hinkley-point-c/news-views/cost-clarification.

12 'Hinkley Point C', GOV.UK, 17 July 2018, https://www.gov.uk/government/collections/hinkley-point-c; 'Hinkley Point C Construction Creates 3,000 New Somerset Jobs', BBC News, 10 February 2025, https://www.bbc.co.uk/news/articles/crm7rk9ly82o.

13 Committee of Public Accounts, *Prison Estate Capacity*, Fifteenth Report of Session 2024–25 (UK Parliament, 2025), https://committees.parliament.uk/publications/46985/documents/242927/default/.

14 UK Foundations, 20 September 2024, https://ukfoundations.co/.

15 *The Cost Incurred So Far: Lower Thames Crossing*, FOI release case reference EIR2025/00604 (National Highways, 2025), https://nationalhighways.disclosurelog.co.uk/disclosures/e820a241-c4cd-4fed-a6fa-e990d8c02415.

16 'Liberté, Égalité, Radioactivité', *Works in Progress*, 4 September 2025, https://worksinprogress.co/issue/liberte-egalite-radioactivite/.

17 Ben Hopkinson, 'Britain's Infrastructure Is Too Expensive', Notes on Growth, 17 December 2025, https://www.samdumitriu.com/p/britains-infrastructure-is-too-expensive.

18 'NAAG Chapter 3: Expenditure', OECD Data Explorer, 10 October 2025, https://data-explorer.oecd.org/.

19 Calculations by the author using GDP data published by the ONS.

20 'NAAG Chapter 3: Expenditure'.

21 'Business Investment Time Series', ONS, 22 December 2025, https://www.ons.gov.uk/economy/grossdomesticproductgdp/datasets/businessinvestment; 'Dwelling Stock by Tenure, UK', ONS, 19 May 2025, https://www.ons.gov.uk/peoplepopulationandcommunity/housing/datasets/dwellingstockbytenureuk; 'Indicators of House Building, UK: Permanent Dwellings Started and Completed by Country', ONS, 21 November 2025.

22 'Number of Started Dwellings – Total – France Excluding Mayotte – Estimates Calculated at the Time of Event', Insee, 30 January 2026, https://www.insee.fr/en/statistiques/serie/001718154; 'Annual Estimate of Housing Stock – Total Number of Dwellings – France Excluding Mayotte', Insee, 2 October 2025.

23 'Minister: Planning Changes "Sorely Needed"', BBC, 27 March 2012, http://news.bbc.co.uk/democracylive/hi/house_of_commons/newsid_9709000/9709323.stm; 'National Planning Policy Framework', GOV.UK, 27 March 2012, https://www.gov.uk/guidance/national-planning-policy-framework.

24 'Planning Applications in England: October to December 2024 – Statistical Release', GOV.UK, 20 March 2025, https://www.gov.uk/government/statistics/

planning-applications-in-england-october-to-december-2024/planning-applications-in-england-october-to-december-2024-statistical-release.

25 Rt Hon. Sir Oliver Letwin MP, *Independent Review of Build Out – Final Report* (Ministry of Housing, Communities and Local Government, 2018), https://assets.publishing.service.gov.uk/media/5bd6eb3940f0b6051e77b6a6/Letwin_review_web_version.pdf.

26 Kumail Jaffer, 'House-Building in London Fall by 84% in a Decade, Study Finds', BBC News, 25 January 2026, https://www.bbc.co.uk/news/articles/cy099qv9qjlo.

27 Michael Dnes, *Making Britain Build Again* (Stonehaven Global, 2025), https://www.stonehavenglobal.com/making_britain_build_again.

28 Olympic Delivery Authority, *London 2012 Venues Guide* (GOV.UK, 2012), https://assets.publishing.service.gov.uk/media/5a7a478e40f0b66a2fc01323/ODA_Venues_Guide.pdf.

29 Matt Georges, *Environmental Costs and Benefits at the Site of the London 2012 Olympics* (Environment Agency, 2018), https://assets.publishing.service.gov.uk/media/5aaa4cb1ed915d4f563b75e6/London_Olympics_environmental_costs_and_benefits_-_report.pdf.

30 *Plans for the Legacy from the 2012 Olympic and Paralympic Games* (DCMS, 2010), https://assets.publishing.service.gov.uk/media/5a74f325e5274a3cb28687cc/201210_Legacy_Publication.pdf.

31 'London 2012: Olympics and Paralympics £528m under Budget', BBC, 23 October 2012, https://www.bbc.co.uk/sport/olympics/20041426.

32 Kathryn Dobinson, 'Lessons from London 2012 Olympics: A Cribsheet for Major Projects', *The Guardian*, 22 January 2013, https://www.theguardian.com/public-leaders-network/2013/jan/22/lessons-london-2012-government-projects.

33 'East Bank', Mayor of London, accessed 11 January 2026, https://www.london.gov.uk/programmes-strategies/arts-and-culture/culture-and-good-growth/east-bank.

34 Chris Smyth, 'Revealed: How Tunnel through the Woods Cost £300,000 per Bat', *The Times*, 24 January 2025, https://www.thetimes.com/uk/environment/article/revealed-the-tunnel-through-the-woods-which-cost-300000-per-bat-kz7pm2s8m.

35 'Britain to Have New National High-Speed Rail Network', GOV.UK, 10 January 2012, https://www.gov.uk/government/news/britain-to-have-new-national-high-speed-rail-network; Gwyn Topham, 'Cost of HS2 Could Pass £80bn as

Estimated Bill Jumps 15% in a Year', *The Guardian*, 17 December 2024, https://www.theguardian.com/uk-news/2024/dec/17/cost-of-hs2-estimate-euston.

36 Carol Yang, 'China's High-Speed Rail Nears 50,000km Milestone – but Is It Sustainable?', *South China Morning Post*, 5 August 2025, https://www.scmp.com/economy/china-economy/article/3320817/chinas-high-speed-rail-nears-50000km-milestone-debt-and-profit-concerns-mount.

37 'NAAG Chapter 3: Expenditure'.

38 This figure was reached using two different methods: the first was to compare UK and French new dwelling start rates and estimate the corresponding increase in new dwellings gross fixed capital formation using data from the ONS and Insee; the second was to compare rates of construction-related GFCF as a percent of GDP using OECD data. The former suggested a £56-billion increase in new dwelling investment, and the latter between £60–£90 billion. Using an Incremental Capital Output Ratio (ICOR) rate of 10 (the UK's average between 2010 and 2019), this would suggest an increase of 0.2% to 0.3% of additional GDP each year.

5. Public Sector Productivity

1 'UK National Accounts, The Blue Book: 2025', ONS, 31 October 2025, https://www.ons.gov.uk/economy/grossdomesticproductgdp/compendium/unitedkingdomnationalaccountsthebluebook/2025.

2 Will Dahlgreen, 'Reputation: Jeremy Hunt Faring Worse than Andrew Lansley', YouGov, 14 February 2016, https://yougov.co.uk/politics/articles/14670-jeremy-hunt-faring-worse-andrew-lansley.

3 Nicholas Watt, 'Blair Berates Old Labour "Snobs"', *The Guardian*, 7 July 1999, https://www.theguardian.com/politics/1999/jul/07/uk.politicalnews2.

4 Olly Harvey-Rich and Max Warner, *The Outlook for Public Sector Productivity* (2025), https://ifs.org.uk/sites/default/files/2025-09/IFS_Report_The_Outlook_for_Public_Sector_Productivity_0.pdf.

5 Author's calculations based on ONS productivity data for the years of 2010 to 2014 (inclusive). The long-term average was calculated using growth rates from 1997 to 2007. 'Multi-Factor Productivity, Annual, UK', ONS, 23 May 2025, https://www.ons.gov.uk/economy/economicoutputandproductivity/productivitymeasures/datasets/growthaccountingannualuk.

6   'Multi-Factor Productivity, Annual, UK'; 'Public Service Productivity, Quarterly, UK', ONS, 3 November 2025, https://www.ons.gov.uk/economy/economic outputandproductivity/publicservicesproductivity/bulletins/publicservicep roductivityquarterlyuk/apriltojune2025.

7   *Fiscal Risks and Sustainability* (OBR, 2023), https://obr.uk/docs/dlm_uploads/ Fiscal_risks_and_sustainability_report_July_2023.pdf.

8   Treasury officials had originally told me 0.5%, as mentioned in the below speech. This figure was later revised to 0.7%. See the full speech here: 'Chancellor Jeremy Hunt's Speech at the Centre for Policy Studies', GOV.UK, 12 June 2023, https://www.gov.uk/government/speeches/chancellor-jeremy-hunts-speech-at-the-centre-for-policy-studies.

9   George Stoye, *UK Health Spending*, IFS Briefing Note no. BN201 (IFS, 2017), https://ifs.org.uk/publications/uk-health-spending.

10 *Fiscal Risks and Sustainability – September 2024* (OBR, 2024), https://obr.uk/ docs/dlm_uploads/Fiscal-risks-and-sustainability-report-September-2024-1. pdf.

11 *Efficiency and Reform in the Next Parliament* (UK Government, 2014), https:// www.gov.uk/government/publications/efficiency-and-reform-in-the-next-parliament.

12 Jack Worlidge et al., 'Civil Service Staff Numbers', Institute for Government, 15 December 2017, https://www.instituteforgovernment.org.uk/explainer/ civil-service-staff-numbers.

13 *Annual Report and Accounts 2024/25* (Crown Commercial Service, 2025), https://assets.publishing.service.gov.uk/media/6878b417a52cca025ef5bd81/ HC1091_CCS_AR_A_24_25_Certified.pdf.

14 'Whitehall Palaces: A Thing of the Past', GOV.UK, 3 October 2014, https:// www.gov.uk/government/news/whitehall-palaces-a-thing-of-the-past.

15 *Efficiency and Reform in the Next Parliament.*

16 *Savings Delivered in Financial Year 2014 to 2015 in Government Departments: Technical Note* (GOV.UK, 2015), https://www.gov.uk/government/ publications/government-savings-in-2014-to-2015.

17 '2023 OECD Digital Government Index', OECD, 30 January 2024, https://www. oecd.org/en/publications/2023-oecd-digital-government-index_1a89ed5e-en.html.

18 '2025/26 NHS Priorities and Operational Planning Guidance: What You Need to Know', NHS Confederation, 30 January 2025, https://www.nhsconfed.org/

publications/202526-nhs-priorities-and-operational-planning-guidance-what-you-need-know; *Quality and Outcomes Framework Guidance for 2025/26* (NHS England, 2025), https://www.england.nhs.uk/wp-content/uploads/2025/03/quality-outcomes-framework-guidance-for-2025-26.pdf.

19 Between the 2009/10 and 2023/24 academic years, the percentage of schools inspected by Ofsted each year that were rated good or outstanding increased from 56% to 83%. While the inspection framework has changed several times over this period, and inspection results do vary each year, the proportion of good or outstanding schools has been over 70% since the 2021/22 academic year. This shows a marked improvement in standards since 2010. Sources: Ofsted, 'State-Funded Schools Inspections and Outcomes as at 31 August 2022', GOV.UK, 15 December 2022, https://www.gov.uk/government/statistics/state-funded-schools-inspections-and-outcomes-as-at-31-august-2022.; Ofsted, 'State-Funded Schools Inspections and Outcomes as at 31 August 2025', GOV.UK, 25 November 2025, https://www.gov.uk/government/statistics/state-funded-schools-inspections-and-outcomes-as-at-31-august-2025.

20 The public sector accounts for nearly 20% of GDP, so improving productivity by 0.7% would equate to nearly 0.15% higher GDP growth – or a 1.5% higher GDP after ten years. The number has been rounded down.

21 ONS, 'Public Service Productivity, Quarterly, UK'.

22 Nick Kituno, 'Revealed: The Targets the NHS No Longer Has to Meet', *Health Service Journal*, 4 January 2023, https://www.hsj.co.uk/policy-and-regulation/revealed-the-targets-the-nhs-no-longer-has-to-meet/7033976.article.

23 'Spring Budget 2024', GOV.UK, 6 March 2024, https://www.gov.uk/government/publications/spring-budget-2024/spring-budget-2024-html.

24 'Record Numbers Using NHS App to Manage Health', NHS England, 24 December 2025, https://www.england.nhs.uk/2025/12/record-numbers-using-nhs-app-to-manage-health/.

25 'The NHS Genomic Medicine Service: Achievements in 2024', NHS England, 6 February 2025, https://www.england.nhs.uk/long-read/the-nhs-genomic-medicine-service-achievements-in-2024/.

26 Maia Davies, 'NHS Plans to DNA Test All Babies in England to Assess Disease Risk', BBC News, 21 June 2025, https://www.bbc.co.uk/news/articles/c1ljg7v0vmpo.

27 NHS England, *NHS England: Annual Report and Accounts 2024 to 2025* (GOV. UK, 2025), https://www.gov.uk/government/publications/nhs-england-annual-report-and-accounts-2024-to-2025.

28 Katie Fozzard et al., 'Can the NHS Meet Its 2% Productivity Challenge? Here's What Experts Think', The Health Foundation, 21 October 2025, https://www.health.org.uk/features-and-opinion/blogs/can-the-nhs-meet-its-2-productivity-challenge-here-s-what-experts-think.

6. Innovation

1 *Major Balance Sheet Interventions* (OBR, 2023), https://obr.uk/docs/dlm_uploads/March-2023-Major-balance-sheet-interventions.pdf.

2 Stuart White, 'Tokamak Energy Raises $125m to Commercialise Transformative Fusion and Magnet Technologies', Tokamak Energy, 20 November 2024, https://tokamakenergy.com/2024/11/20/tokamak-energy-raises-125m-to-commercialise-transformative-fusion-and-magnet-technologies/.

3 Gerard Taylor, 'Scientist Thinks the World's First 200-Year-Old Person Has Already Been Born', *Norway Today*, 23 March 2017, https://norwaytoday.info/everyday/scientist-thinks-worlds-first-200-year-old-person-already-born/.

4 Rohan Silva, 'When AI Steals Our Jobs We Create New Ones', *The Times*, 1 July 2025, https://www.thetimes.com/comment/columnists/article/artificial-intelligence-jobs-ai-careers-w5vn3vd0g.

5 Andrew Ellson, 'Graduate Jobs Crisis "Similar to Blue-Collar Recession of 1980s"', *The Times*, 16 September 2025, https://www.thetimes.com/uk/education/article/graduate-jobs-crisis-recession-reed-cg0nr3xw2.

6 Zoë Schiffer, 'Here's What Mark Zuckerberg Is Offering Top AI Talent', *Wired*, 1 July 2025, https://www.wired.com/story/mark-zuckerberg-meta-offer-top-ai-talent-300-million/.

7 'Generative AI Could Raise Global GDP by 7%', Goldman Sachs, 5 April 2023, https://www.goldmansachs.com/insights/articles/generative-ai-could-raise-global-gdp-by-7-percent.

8 Kristalina Georgieva, 'AI Will Transform the Global Economy. Let's Make Sure It Benefits Humanity'., IMF, 14 January 2024, https://www.imf.org/en/blogs/articles/2024/01/14/ai-will-transform-the-global-economy-lets-make-sure-it-benefits-humanity.

9   For more information about the life of Tim Berners-Lee, see: Tim Berners-Lee, *This Is for Everyone*, with Stephen Witt (Macmillan, 2025).

10   Jane Martinson, 'The Man Who Made the Web', *The Guardian*, 24 November 1999, https://www.theguardian.com/technology/1999/nov/24/internet.guardianweekly.

11   Tim Berners-Lee, 'Lessons from the Past and Present for the Future of the Web', Knight Foundation, 29 October 2021, https://knightfoundation.org/sir-tim-berners-lee/.

12   Tim Berners-Lee, 'Information Management: A Proposal', CERN, March 1989, https://repository.cern/records/6kxvc-v6203/preview/dd-89-001.pdf.

13   'Longer Biography', W3.Org, accessed 13 January 2026, https://www.w3.org/People/Berners-Lee/Longer.html.

14   Julian Ring, '30 Years Ago, One Decision Altered the Course of Our Connected World', NPR, 30 April 2023, https://www.npr.org/2023/04/30/1172276538/world-wide-web-internet-anniversary.

15   'About Us', W3C, accessed 14 January 2026, https://www.w3.org/about/.

16   *UK Innovation 2025 Review* (dealroom.co, HSBC Innovation Banking, 2026), https://dealroom.co/reports/uk-innovation-2025-review.

17   *Venture Capital as 21st Century Growth Catalyst* (The Purposeful Company, 2025), https://thepurposefulcompany.org/wp-content/uploads/2025/05/The-Growth-Trilogy-Paper-Two.pdf.

18   'How London Became the Rest of the World's Startup Capital', *The Economist*, 26 January 2026, https://www.economist.com/britain/2026/01/26/how-london-became-the-rest-of-the-worlds-startup-capital.

19   'The Complete List of Unicorn Companies', CB Insights, accessed 8 February 2026, https://instapage.cbinsights.com/research-unicorn-companies.

20   'Europe', dealroom.co, accessed 8 February 2026, https://dealroom.co/guides/europe/.

21   'About Our Data', UK Biobank, 20 November 2025, https://www.ukbiobank.ac.uk/about-our-data/.

22   *UK Innovation 2025 Review*.

23   'Largest Tech Companies by Market Cap', CompaniesMarketCap.Com, accessed 2 February 2026, https://companiesmarketcap.com/gbp/tech/largest-tech-companies-by-market-cap/.

24   According to the following report, in 2024 there were 25,190 DC schemes, 4,610 DB schemes, 280 hybrid (mixed benefit) and 480 hybrid (dual-section),

totalling around 30,500. 'Occupational Defined Contribution Landscape in the UK 2024', 4 March 2025, https://www.thepensionsregulator.gov.uk/en/document-library/research-and-analysis/occupational-defined-contribution-landscape-2024.

25 William Wright, *Unlocking the Capital in Capital Markets* (New Financial, 2023), https://www.newfinancial.org/reports/unlocking-the-capital-in-capital-markets.

26 William Wright and James Thornhill, *Comparing the Asset Allocation of Global Pension Systems* (New Financial, September 2024), https://www.newfinancial.org/reports/comparing-the-asset-allocation-of-global-pension-systems.

27 *Venture Capital as 21st Century Growth Catalyst.*

28 William Wright, *How to Boost Investment in UK Equities by UK Pensions* (New Financial, 2025), https://www.newfinancial.org/reports/how-to-boost-investment-in-uk-equities-by-uk-pensions; Marek Kacer and Nicholas Wilson, 'Supporting Innovative Start-Up and Growing Businesses: Equity Finance Provision through the Pandemic: Interim Report', *Leeds University Business School Working Paper*, ahead of print, 23 March 2023, https://doi.org/10.2139/ssrn.4456252.

29 Eamonn Ives and Derin Kocer, *Job Creators 2024* (The Entrepreneurs Network, 2024), https://www.tenentrepreneurs.org/research/job-creators-2024.

30 IMF European Dept., *United Kingdom* (IMF, 2024), 1, https://doi.org/10.5089/9798400279379.002.

31 Public First, *Unlocking the UK's AI Potential: Harnessing AI for Economic Growth* (Microsoft, 2024), https://microsoftuk.publicfirst.co.uk/uploads/Unlocking_the_UKs_AI_Potential.pdf.

32 *Generating Growth: How Generative AI Can Power the UK's Reinvention* (Accenture, 2024), https://www.accenture.com/content/dam/accenture/final/accenture-com/document-3/Accenture-Accelerating-The-UKs-Generative-AI-Reinvention.pdf.

33 Ryan Hawk et al., *The Leader's Guide to Value in Motion* (PwC, 2025), https://www.pwc.com/gx/en/issues/value-in-motion.html.

34 In an article published in 2024, Philippe Aghion and Simon Bunel applied two different methods to gauge the potential impact of AI on productivity growth. One approach estimated that aggregate productivity growth could increase by between 0.8 and 1.3% over the following decade. The other estimated an additional 0.68% of annual total factor productivity growth over the same

period. I have therefore gone with the mid-point of 1%. Philippe Aghion and Simon Bunel, *AI and Growth: Where Do We Stand?* (Federal Reserve Bank of San Francisco, 2024), https://www.frbsf.org/wp-content/uploads/AI-and-Growth-Aghion-Bunel.pdf.

35 Calculations by the author using data from the UK ONS, US BEA and World Bank. This figure was reached by comparing select elements of UK and Californian tech sectors, including the manufacture and wholesale of computers and electronics, software publishing and programming, and other information services. Using this method, it was estimated that a similarly sized UK tech sector would quadruple its current economic output. Assuming the UK's tax-to-GDP ratio is around 39%, this would result in approximately £120bn more in public sector taxes and social contributions.

7. Energy

1 Kevin Keane, 'James Blyth: The Scots Engineer Who Pioneered the Wind Turbine', BBC News, 8 May 2024, https://www.bbc.co.uk/news/articles/cw4r2v4j7mwo.

2 Royal Philosophical Society of Glasgow, *Proceedings of the Royal Philosophical Society of Glasgow, Volume 19* (The Society, 1888).

3 Trevor J. Price, 'James Blyth – Britain's First Modern Wind Power Pioneer', *Wind Engineering* 29, no. 3 (2005): 191–200.

4 Royal Scottish Society of Arts, *Transactions of the Royal Scottish Society of Arts, Volume 13* (Neill & Company, 1891).

5 Erik Möllerström et al., 'Wind Power Development: A Historical Review', *Wind Engineering* 49, no. 2 (2025): 499–512, https://doi.org/10.1177/0309524X241260061.

6 Paul Simons, 'Wind Power Has Billowed over Three Decades', *The Times*, 21 December 2021, https://www.thetimes.com/uk/article/wind-power-has-billowed-over-three-decades-fh3mth63w.

7 Alok Jha, 'UK Overtakes Denmark as World's Biggest Offshore Wind Generator', *The Guardian*, 21 October 2008, https://www.theguardian.com/environment/2008/oct/21/windpower-renewableenergy1.

8 'Dogger Bank Offshore Wind Farm', accessed 15 January 2026, https://www.sserenewables.com/offshore-wind/projects/dogger-bank/.

9 'Our History', Dogger Bank Wind Farm, n.d., accessed 15 January 2026, https://doggerbank.com/our-history/.

10 *UK Offshore Energy Strategic Environmental Assessment – Non-Technical Summary* (Department of Energy and Climate Change, 2009).

11 Royal HaskoningDHV, *Dogger Bank Teesside A & B: Environmental Statement Non-Technical Summary* (Forewind, 2014), https://doggerbank.com/wp-content/uploads/2021/11/Non-Technical-Summary.pdf.

12 Rachel Lawrence, 'World's Largest Offshore Wind Farm Produces Power for the First Time', Dogger Bank Wind Farm, 10 October 2023, https://doggerbank.com/construction/worlds-largest-offshore-wind-farm-produces-power-for-the-first-time/.

13 'Dogger Bank D – Project', Dogger Bank D Wind Farm, accessed 15 January 2026, https://doggerbankd.com/about/.

14 Department for Energy Security and Net Zero, 'Energy Trends December 2025: Fuel Used in Electricity Generation and Electricity Supplied (ET 5.1 – Quarterly)', GOV.UK, 18 December 2025, https://www.gov.uk/government/statistics/electricity-section-5-energy-trends.

15 Georgina Rannard, 'Wind Generated a Record Amount of Electricity in 2022', BBC News, 6 January 2023, https://www.bbc.co.uk/news/science-environment-64179918.

16 'UK Wind Energy Database (UKWED)', RenewableUK, accessed 15 January 2026, https://www.renewableuk.com/energypulse/ukwed/.

17 The author acknowledges the Global Carbon Project, which is responsible for the Global Carbon Budget, and thanks the national fossil carbon emissions modelling group for producing and making available their model output. Source: Pierre Friedlingstein et al., 'Global Carbon Budget 2025', ESSD – Anthroposphere/Energy and anthropogenic emissions, 13 November 2025, https://doi.org/10.5194/essd-2025-659 (data file: https://globalcarbonbudget.org/download/2345/?tmstv=1762815968).

18 Jan Burck et al., *Climate Change Performance Index 2026* (Germanwatch, NewClimate Institute & Climate Action Network, 2025), https://ccpi.org/download/climate-change-performance-index-2026/.

19 Department for Energy Security and Net Zero (DESNZ), 'Non-Domestic Energy Prices – Industrial Electricity Prices in the IEA (QEP 5.3.1)', GOV.UK, 30 September 2025, https://www.gov.uk/government/statistical-data-sets/international-industrial-energy-prices.

20 DESNZ, 'International Domestic Energy Prices', GOV.UK, 27 November 2025, https://www.gov.uk/government/statistical-data-sets/international-domestic-energy-prices.

21 *Fiscal Risks and Sustainability – July 2022* (OBR, 2022), https://obr.uk/docs/dlm_uploads/Fiscal_risks_and_sustainability_2022-1.pdf.

22 Veronika Samborska, 'Scaling Up: How Increasing Inputs Has Made Artificial Intelligence More Capable', Our World in Data, 20 January 2025, https://ourworldindata.org/scaling-up-ai.

23 Allison Parshall, 'What Do Google's AI Answers Cost the Environment?', *Scientific American*, 11 June 2024, https://www.scientificamerican.com/article/what-do-googles-ai-answers-cost-the-environment/.

24 Josh Saul et al., 'AI's Insatiable Need for Energy Is Straining Global Power Grids', Bloomberg, 21 June 2024, https://www.bloomberg.com/graphics/2024-ai-data-centers-power-grids/.

25 'Non-Domestic Energy Prices'.

26 For more on the cost of constraint payments, see the following articles: Oliver Wright and Adam Vaughan, 'Britons Spend £1 Billion to Switch off Wind Farms This Year', *The Times*, 2 October 2025, https://www.thetimes.com/uk/environment/article/britons-spend-1-billion-to-switch-off-wind-farms-this-year-zq6tsqdst; Emily Gosden and Oliver Wright, 'How Wasted Wind Is Pushing up Electricity Bills in the UK', *The Times*, 9 January 2026, https://www.thetimes.com/uk/environment/article/wasted-wind-electricity-bills-rbtgnfhwr.

27 Emily Gosden, 'Cost of Turning off Wind Farms If Network Cannot Cope Hits £1.5bn', *The Times*, 28 December 2025, https://www.thetimes.com/business/energy/article/cost-of-turning-off-wind-farms-if-network-cannot-cope-hits-15bn-gm5wqrshz.

28 Calculations by the author using UK energy statistics. It should be highlighted that, according to DESNZ, if you 'de-rate' the capacity of wind, small scale hydo and solar PV to account for the intermittency of these sources, the UK's capacity actually decreased over the same time period. But overall, installed capacity has increased. DESNZ, 'Digest of UK Energy Statistics (DUKES): Electricity', GOV.UK, 31 July 2025, https://www.gov.uk/government/statistics/electricity-chapter-5-digest-of-united-kingdom-energy-statistics-dukes.

29 DESNZ, 'Digest of UK Energy Statistics (DUKES): Electricity'.

30 Andrew Sissons, 'To Make Energy Cheaper, We Need to Raise Levies on Gas', Nesta, 30 September 2024, https://www.nesta.org.uk/blog/to-make-energy-cheaper-we-need-to-raise-levies-on-gas/.

31 For research into the effect of this policy, see: Miguel Haro Ruiz et al., *The Effects of the Iberian Exception Mechanism on Wholesale Electricity Prices and Consumer Inflation: A Synthetic-Controls Approach*, IWH Discussion Papers No. 5/2024 (Halle Institute for Economic Research (IWH), Halle (Saale), 2024), https://www.econstor.eu/bitstream/10419/283618/1/18812 4461X.pdf; H. K. Lou et al., *The Iberian Exception: What Was the Cost of Distorting Electricity Markets During the 2021–23 European Energy Crisis?*, 31 May 2025, https://doi.org/10.17863/CAM.119666.

32 Wilhelmine Preussen, 'Le Maire: Europe Must Stand Firm Against US Aid to Industry', Politico, 7 November 2022, https://www.politico.eu/article/bruno-le-maire-france-europe-must-stand-against-united-states-subsidies/.

33 'Nuclear Regulatory Review 2025: Summary', GOV.UK, 24 November 2025, https://www.gov.uk/government/publications/nuclear-regulatory-taskforce/nuclear-regulatory-review-2025-summary.

34 *Summary of the GDA Issue Close-out Assessment of the Electricité de France SA and AREVA NP SAS UK EPR™ Nuclear Reactor* (Office for Nuclear Regulation, 2012), https://www.onr.org.uk/media/2a4jmcxw/summary.pdf.

35 Simon Jack, 'Hinkley C: UK Nuclear Plant Price Tag Could Rocket by a Third', BBC News, 23 January 2024, https://www.bbc.co.uk/news/business-68073279.

36 'Clean Energy Projects Prioritised for Grid Connections', GOV.UK, 1 May 2025, https://www.gov.uk/government/news/clean-energy-projects-prioritised-for-grid-connections.

37 *Building Grids Faster: The Backbone of the Energy Transition* (Energy Transitions Commission, 2024), https://www.energy-transitions.org/wp-content/uploads/2024/09/Grids-briefing-note_DIGITAL.pdf.

38 Researchers found that over the long term a 10% increase in energy prices reduces annual GDP growth by 0.15%. See: Hillard Huntington and Brantley Liddle, 'How Energy Prices Shape OECD Economic Growth: Panel Evidence from Multiple Decades', *Energy Economics* 111 (July 2022): 106082, https://doi.org/10.1016/j.eneco.2022.106082.

39 The OBR's 2015 Economic and Fiscal outlook assessed the link between oil prices and economic growth, including both price increases and decreases. Referenced in this assessment were two pieces of research, one by NIESR

and the other by the Bank of England. The NIESR report estimated that a permanent 20% reduction in oil prices could lead to a permanent 0.5% increase in GDP over three years. Similarly, the Bank of England report estimated that a 10% decrease in oil prices would permanently increase GDP by 0.1%. Taken together with the research earlier in this chapter, it would therefore be fair to suggest a 20% reduction in energy prices could add 0.2% to annual GDP growth for a period of years. For more information, see: *Economic and Fiscal Outlook – March 2015* (OBR, 2015), https://obr.uk/docs/dlm_uploads/March2015EFO_18-03-webv1.pdf; Simon Kirby and Jack Meaning, 'Oil Prices and Economic Activity', *National Institute Economic Review* 231 (February 2015): F43–48, https://doi.org/10.1177/002795011523100114; *Inflation Report – February 2015* (Bank of England, 2015), https://www.bankofengland.co.uk/-/media/boe/files/inflation-report/2015/february-2015.pdf.

40 *Civil Nuclear: Roadmap to 2050* (Department for Energy Security and Net Zero, 2024), https://www.gov.uk/government/publications/civil-nuclear-roadmap-to-2050.

8. Regions

1 Toby Helm, 'West Midlands Mayor Distances Himself from Tories, Urging Voters to "Distinguish between Party and Me"', *The Guardian*, 6 April 2024, https://www.theguardian.com/politics/2024/apr/06/west-midlands-mayor-distances-himself-from-tories-urging-voters-to-distinguish-between-party-and-me.

2 'Region's Ambitious Target to Build 215,000 New Homes Remains on Track', West Midlands Combined Authority, accessed 16 January 2026, https://www.wmca.org.uk/news/region-s-ambitious-target-to-build-215-000-new-homes-remains-on-track/.

3 J.R. Duren, 'This Texas City Is the Fastest Growing in the Country for Small Businesses', *The Independent*, 20 January 2026, https://www.independent.co.uk/us/money/austin-fastest-growing-small-business-city-b2904098.html.

4 'Austin Climbs into Top Five North American Tech Market in CBRE's Annual "Scoring Tech Talent" Report', CBRE, 4 September 2024, https://www.cbre.com/press-releases/austin-climbs-into-top-five-north-american-tech-market-in-cbres-annual-scoring-tech-talent-report; Harvey Schwartz says, 'The Top

Tech Cities in the US: Ranking 100 Cities in 2026', Cloudwards, 16 February 2024, https://www.cloudwards.net/top-tech-cities-us/.

5   'Regional Gross Domestic Product: All ITL Regions', ONS, 17 April 2025, https://www.ons.gov.uk/economy/grossdomesticproductgdp/datasets/regio nalgrossdomesticproductallnutslevelregions.

6   'CAGDP1 County Gross Domestic Product (GDP) Summary', US Bureau of Economic Analysis, 5 February 2026, https://apps.bea.gov/.

7   '2020 Mobility Elections Proposition A', City of Austin, accessed 3 February 2026, https://www.austintexas.gov/2020PropA.

8   Josephine Cordero Sapién, 'Austin Voters Give Project Connect the Go-Ahead', *Railway-News*, 13 November 2020, https://railway-news.com/austin-voters-give-project-connect-the-go-ahead/.

9   In 2021–22, West Midlands Combined Authority had a total budget of around £927 million, including both revenue budget and capital expenditure, with 1.1 million households. Around this time, the City of Austin had a total budget of $4.6 billion (£3.7 billion), which includes the budgets of the city's utility enterprises, with a total of 456 thousand households. This equates to approximately £800 and £8,000 per household, respectively. *Statement of Accounts – For the Year Ended 31 March 2022* (West Midlands Combined Authority, 2022), https://www.wmca.org.uk/media/qnhg4hbd/wmca-2021-22-audited-accounts-24.pdf; *2021 Census* (n.d.), https://www.nomisweb.co.uk/sources/census_2021; *FY22 Approved Budget* (City of Austin, 2021), https://www.austintexas.gov/sites/default/files/files/Finance/Financial%20 Transparency/AnnualBudgets/FY22_Approved_Budget.pdf; 'QuickFacts. Austin City, Texas', US Census Bureau, accessed 3 February 2026, https:// www.census.gov/quickfacts/fact/table/austincitytexas/LND110210; 'HMRC Currency Exchange Average Rates – December 2022 Average Exchange Rates', GOV.UK, 31 December 2025, https://www.trade-tariff.service.gov. uk/exchange_rates/average.

10   'For Once, London Is Short-Changed by the Government', *The Economist*, 12 June 2025, https://www.economist.com/britain/2025/06/12/for-once-london-is-short-changed-by-the-government.

11   Austin's homicide rate calculated by the author using US Census and City of Austin data. The West Midlands homicide rate was sourced from a House of Commons Library Research Briefing. See US Census Bureau, 'QuickFacts: Austin City – Texas'; 'Austin Police Department Homicide Unit Achieves

100% Clearance Rate for 2023', City of Austin, 13 May 2025, https://www. austintexas.gov/news/austin-police-department-homicide-unit-achieves-100-clearance-rate-2023; Grahame Allen and Elliot Bridges, *Homicide Statistics* (House of Commons Library, 2025), https://researchbriefings.files.parliament. uk/documents/CBP-8224/CBP-8224.pdf.austin.

12 In 2023, in Travis County, where the City of Austin is based, 85.6% of people aged 18–64 had insurance. Source: 'HDPulse: An Ecosystem of Minority Health and Health Disparities Resources', National Institute on Minority Health and Health Disparities, n.d., accessed 22 February 2026, https:// hdpulse.nimhd.nih.gov/data-portal/healthcare/table.

13 Janelle Fritts et al., *2026 State Tax Competitiveness Index* (Tax Foundation, 2025), https://taxfoundation.org/wp-content/uploads/2025/10/26_STCI_ Book_10-31.pdf.

14 'Subregional Productivity: Labour Productivity Indices by Combined Authorities and Economic Enterprise Regions', ONS, 19 June 2025, https://www. ons.gov.uk/employmentandlabourmarket/peopleinwork/labourproductivity/ datasets/subregionalproductivitylabourproductivityindicesbycombinedauth oritiesandeconomicenterpriseregions.

15 'Earnings and Hours Worked, Place of Residence by Local Authority: ASHE Table 8', ONS, 23 October 2025, https://www.ons.gov.uk/ employmentandlabourmarket/peopleinwork/earningsandworkinghours/ datasets/placeofresidencebylocalauthorityashetable8.

16 Note: median salary data was not available for Lyon and Paris. While not explicit, the source likely used an arithmetic mean of private sector salaries. 'Private Sector Salaries by Gender and Socio-Professional Category (Local Dataset)', Insee, 26 November 2025, https://catalogue-donnees.insee.fr/en/ explorateur/DS_BTS_SAL_EQTP_SEX_PCS.

17 *Minkan Bumon No Jisshitsu Chingin Ni Kansuru Chosa – 2024* [Survey of real wages in the private sector – 2024] (National Tax Agency of Japan, 2025), https://www.nta.go.jp/publication/statistics/kokuzeicho/minkan2024/pdf/ R06_000.pdf.

18 *Analyse Zur Entgeltstatistik 2024* [Analysis of the 2024 Pay Statistics] (Federal Employment Agency of Germany, 2025), https://statistik.arbeitsagentur.de/DE/ Statischer-Content/Statistiken/Fachstatistiken/Beschaeftigung/Generische-Publikationen/Blickpunkt-Arbeitsmarkt-Analyse-zur-Entgeltstatistik.pdf?__ blob=publicationFile&v=9.

19 Philip McCann, 'Perceptions of Regional Inequality and the Geography of Discontent: Insights from the UK', *Regional Studies* 54, no. 2 (2020): 256–67, https://doi.org/10.1080/00343404.2019.1619928.

20 Will Hutton, *This Time No Mistakes: How to Remake Britain* (Head of Zeus, 2024).

21 'Chancellor Announces Tax Cuts to Support Families with Cost of Living', GOV.UK, 23 March 2022, https://www.gov.uk/government/news/chancellor-announces-tax-cuts-to-support-families-with-cost-of-living.

22 Adam Corlett, *It's Personal (Taxation)* (Resolution Foundation, 2025), https://www.resolutionfoundation.org/app/uploads/2025/10/Personal-tax-levels-spotlight.pdf.

23 'Employee Earnings in the UK: 2025', 23 October 2025, ONS, https://www.ons.gov.uk/employmentandlabourmarket/peopleinwork/earningsandworkinghours/bulletins/annualsurveyofhoursandearnings/2025.

24 'Spring Budget 2024 Speech', GOV.UK, 6 March 2024, https://www.gov.uk/government/speeches/spring-budget-2024-speech.

25 'OECD Regions, Cities and Local Areas Database (Economy – FUAs)', OECD Data Explorer, 2 February 2026, http://oe.cd/geostats.

26 'Incidence of Low and High Pay', OECD Data Explorer, 2 February 2026, https://data-explorer.oecd.org/.

27 'L'autoroute Transjurane change le Jura', *Le Temps*, 5 December 2016, https://www.letemps.ch/suisse/jura/lautoroute-transjurane-change-jura.

28 'A16 Transjurane – 85 kilomètres de Boncourt à Bienne', Jura.ch, accessed 3 February 2026, https://www.jura.ch/fr/Autorites/Administration/DEC/SIN/Section-des-constructions-routieres-SCR/Route-nationale-A16/A16-Transjurane-85-kilometres-de-Boncourt-a-Bienne.html.

29 'Gross Domestic Product – Regions', OECD Data Explorer, 2 October 2025, http://oe.cd/geostats.

30 'World Economic Outlook Database: April 2025', IMF, 2025, https://www.imf.org/en/publications/weo/weo-database/2025/april.

31 'Worldwide Governance Indicators', World Bank Group, n.d., accessed 23 February 2026, https://www.worldbank.org/en/publication/worldwide-governance-indicators/interactive-data-access.

32 John F. Helliwell et al., eds, *World Happiness Report 2025* (Sustainable Development Solutions Network, 2024), https://files.worldhappiness.report/WHR25.pdf.

33 Julia Kollewe, 'Swiss Voters Reject Plan to Establish World's Highest Minimum Wage', *The Guardian*, 18 May 2014, https://www.theguardian.com/world/2014/may/18/switzerland-voters-minimum-wage-plan-rejected.

34 Author's calculations using the following sources: 'Full Set of Local Data – France Entière'; 'Dwellings by Tenure in the UK by Country – UK Housing Review 2025 Compendium of Tables'; 'Population Estimates Time Series Dataset'.

35 'Liberté, Égalité, Radioactivité', *Works in Progress*, 4 September 2025, https://worksinprogress.co/issue/liberte-egalite-radioactivite/.

36 'Subregional Productivity'.

37 *UK Economic Outlook* (PwC, 2019), https://www.pwc.co.uk/economic-services/ukeo/ukeo-november-2019-full-report.pdf.

38 *Unleashing Metro Growth – Final Recommendations of the City Growth Commission* (RSA City Growth Commission, 2014), https://ke.org.uk/wp-content/uploads/2024/12/City-Growth-Commission-Final-Report.pdf.

39 Resolution Foundation & Centre for Economic Performance, LSE, *Ending Stagnation: A New Economic Strategy for Britain* (Resolution Foundation, 2023), https://economy2030.resolutionfoundation.org/wp-content/uploads/2023/12/Ending-stagnation-final-report.pdf.

9. Education

1 Simon Collins, 'Britain's Strictest Teacher: "You Have to Have Order and Structure"', *NZ Herald*, 30 May 2018, https://www.nzherald.co.nz/nz/new-zealand-born-woman-dubbed-britains-strictest-teacher-ignores-it-and-teaches-french/3IQF76BPNSV723DIZDETRALA7E/; Peter Wilby, 'Katharine Birbalsingh – Undaunted by Free School Setback', *The Guardian*, 27 February 2012, https://www.theguardian.com/education/2012/feb/27/katharine-birbalsingh-interview.

2 Sian Griffiths, 'Is This the Strictest Teacher in Britain?', *The Times*, 13 November 2016, https://www.thetimes.com/uk/education/article/is-this-the-strictest-teacher-in-britain-7jhclv5wx.

3 Nick Robinson, 'Katharine Birbalsingh: New Social Mobility Chief Challenges Assumptions', BBC News, 17 December 2021, https://www.bbc.co.uk/news/uk-politics-59686359.

4 Rory Sachs, 'Why the UK's Strictest Headteacher Supports Private Schools',

Spear's, 24 November 2022, https://spearswms.com/wealth/why-uks-strictest-headteacher-katharine-birbalsingh-supports-private-schools/.

5 'Appointment of the Chair of the Social Mobility Commission: Katharine Birbalsingh – Appendix D: Preferred Candidate's CV', UK Parliament, 29 October 2021, https://publications.parliament.uk/pa/cm5802/cmselect/cmwomeq/782/78207.htm.

6 'Tory Conference Speech Teacher Leaves School', BBC News, 18 October 2010, https://www.bbc.co.uk/news/education-11567053.

7 Sally Weale, 'Katharine Birbalsingh: I Regret Telling Tories Education System Was Broken', *The Guardian*, 5 September 2014, https://www.theguardian.com/education/2014/sep/05/katharine-birbalsingh-regret-telling-tories-education-system-broken.

8 'What Is a Free School? Everything You Need to Know – The Education Hub', GOV.UK, 10 June 2022, https://educationhub.blog.gov.uk/2022/06/what-is-a-free-school-everything-you-need-to-know/.

9 Rithika Siddhartha, 'Katharine Birbalsingh: "Being Strict Means Keeping Standards High for Students"', *EasternEye*, 18 April 2022, https://www.easterneye.biz/katharine-birbalsingh-being-strict-means-keeping-standards-high-for-students/.

10 Oscar Quine, 'Katharine Birbalsingh: The Anonymous Blogger Turned Free School Head', *The Independent*, 28 August 2014, https://www.independent.co.uk/news/people/profiles/katharine-birbalsingh-the-anonymous-blogger-turned-free-school-head-on-discipline-a-memorable-pupil-and-an-old-teacher-s-love-dots-9695691.html.

11 Helena Horton, 'Britain's Strictest School's First GCSE Results Are Four Times Better than National Average', *The Telegraph*, 22 August 2019, https://www.telegraph.co.uk/news/2019/08/22/britains-strictest-schools-first-gcse-results-four-times-better/.

12 'Overall Performance at End of Key Stage 4 in 2025 – All Pupils', GOV.UK, 2025, https://www.compare-school-performance.service.gov.uk/schools-by-type?step=default&table=schools®ion=all-england&for=secondary.

13 Flora Carr, 'A Day at Britain's Strictest School', *TIME*, 20 April 2018, https://time.com/5232857/michaela-britains-strictest-school/.

14 Richard Adams, '"No Excuses:" Inside Britain's Strictest School', *The Guardian*, 30 December 2016, https://www.theguardian.com/education/2016/dec/30/no-excuses-inside-britains-strictest-school.

15 J. Bradshaw et al., *Programme for International Student Assessment 2009: Achievement of 15-Year-Olds in England* (Dept. for Education, 2010).

16 'England among Highest Performing Western Countries in Education', GOV.UK, accessed 16 January 2026, https://www.gov.uk/government/news/england-among-highest-performing-western-countries-in-education.

17 Ina Mullis et al., *PIRLS 2021 International Results in Reading* (TIMSS & PIRLS International Study Center, 2023), https://doi.org/10.6017/lse.tpisc.tr2103.kb5342.

18 Mattias Von Davier et al., *TIMSS 2023 International Results in Mathematics and Science* (TIMSS & PIRLS International Study Center, Boston College, 2024), https://doi.org/10.6017/lse.tpisc.timss.rs6460.

19 Chris Bryant, 'Education Is a Bright Spot in the Tories' Record', Bloomberg, 6 June 2024, https://www.bloomberg.com/opinion/articles/2024-06-06/uk-election-sunak-was-right-education-is-a-bright-spot-in-the-tories-record.

20 'Programme for International Student Assessment (PISA 2022): Scotland's Results – Highlights', 5 December 2023, https://www.gov.scot/publications/programme-international-student-assessment-pisa-2022-highlights-scotlands-results/.

21 OECD, *PISA 2022 Results (Volume I): The State of Learning and Equity in Education*, PISA (OECD Publishing, 2023), https://doi.org/10.1787/53f23881-en.

22 Luke Sibieta, *Major Challenges for Education in Wales*, ed. Judith Payne (IFS, 2024), https://ifs.org.uk/sites/default/files/2024-03/Major-challenges-for-education-in-Wales-IFS-REPORT_0.pdf.

23 'Scotland to Rejoin International Education League Tables 13 Years after Quitting', *The Herald*, 18 April 2023, https://www.heraldscotland.com/politics/23464675.scotland-rejoin-international-education-league-tables/.

24 OECD, *PISA 2022 Results (Volume I)*.

25 Nicola Woolcock, 'Labour's Education Bill Catastrophic for Children, Birbalsingh Warns', *The Times*, 17 January 2025, https://www.thetimes.com/uk/education/article/labours-education-bill-catastrophic-for-children-birbalsingh-warns-j3wblx6ct.

26 'Country Rank', Scimago, https://www.scimagojr.com/countryrank.php.

27 *World Intellectual Property Indicators 2025* (World Intellectual Property Organization, 2025), https://www.wipo.int/edocs/pubdocs/en/wipo-pub-941-17-2025-en-world-intellectual-property-indicators-2025.pdf.

28 Calculation by the author based on data from https://www.nobelprize.org/.

29 'Total Number of International Students in Tertiary Education (by Destination Country)', UNESCO via the Migration Data Portal, n.d., accessed 23 February 2026, https://www.migrationdataportal.org/.

30 *Global Tech Talent Guidebook 2025* (CBRE, 2025), https://www.cbre.com/insights/books/global-tech-talent-guidebook-2025.

31 'Release of Analysis of Hospital Admission Data', CQC, 16 July 2019, https://www.cqc.org.uk/news/stories/release-analysis-hospital-admission-data.

32 'Child and Infant Mortality (by Year of Death), England and Wales', ONS, 22 April 2025, https://www.ons.gov.uk/peoplepopulationandcommunity/birthsdeathsandmarriages/deaths/datasets/childmortalitystatisticschildhoodinfantandperinatalchildhoodinfantandperinatalmortalityinenglandandwales.

33 Robert Barro, 'Education and Economic Growth', *Annals of Economics and Finance* 14, no. 2 (2013): 301–28.

34 Eric A. Hanushek and Ludger Wößmann, *The Role of Education Quality in Economic Growth* (World Bank, 2007), https://documents1.worldbank.org/curated/en/260461468324885735/pdf/wps4122.pdf.

35 According to Hanushek and Wößmann, an increase of one standard deviation in the average of maths and science PISA scores (which is 100 points) leads to approximately 1.74% additional annual GDP growth. In his example, the UK would need to gain 28.5 points to close the gap with Finland, which would boost annual GDP growth by 0.49%. Currently, the top performing PISA scores are mostly from Asia. If the UK could add 15 points to its average PISA score, this would close half the gap between the UK and the tail end of the top performing group, namely Hong Kong and South Korea, and result in up to 0.25% extra annual GDP growth. See the original research here: OECD, *The High Cost of Low Educational Performance: The Long-Run Economic Impact of Improving PISA Outcomes* (PISA, OECD Publishing, 2010), https://doi.org/10.1787/9789264077485-en.

36 Daniel Susskind, *Growth: A Reckoning* (Allen Lane, 2024).

37 'Crackdown on Rip-off University Degrees', GOV.UK, 17 July 2023, https://www.gov.uk/government/news/crackdown-on-rip-off-university-degrees.

38 'Employment Rates of Adults, by Educational Attainment, Age Group and Gender', OECD Data Explorer, 5 February 2026, https://data-explorer.oecd.org.

39 Kate McGough, 'Almost One Million Young People Still Not in Work or Education, Figures Show', BBC News, 20 November 2025, https://www.bbc.co.uk/news/articles/c62920440m2o.

10. Risk

1   World Bank, *Doing Business 2020: Comparing Business Regulation in 190 Economies* (Washington, DC: World Bank, 2020), https://doi.org/10.1596/978-1-4648-1440-2.

2   *The Global Startup Ecosystem Report 2025* (Startup Genome, 2025), https://startupgenome.com/contents/report/gser-2025_4786.pdf.

3   *Entrepreneurial Ecosystem Diagnostics* (OECD, 2025), https://www.oecd.org/en/publications/entrepreneurial-ecosystem-diagnostics_7096961f-en.html.

4   'Global Entrepreneurship Monitor – UK Entrepreneurship Is on the Rise', NatWest Group, 23 July 2024, https://www.natwestgroup.com/news-and-insights/news-room/press-releases/enterprise/2024/jul/global-entrepreneurship-monitor-uk-entrepreneurship-is-on-the-ri.html.

5   *The Global Startup Ecosystem Report 2025.*

6   'New Business Density (New Registrations per 1,000 People Ages 15–64)', World Bank Group, n.d., https://data.worldbank.org/indicator/IC.BUS.NREG.

7   'Total Early-Stage Entrepreneurial Activity (TEA)', GEM, n.d., accessed 8 February 2026, https://www.gemconsortium.org/data.

8   Business Demography, UK', ONS, 20 November 2025, https://www.ons.gov.uk/businessindustryandtrade/business/activitysizeandlocation/datasets/businessdemographyreferencetable/current.

9   Richard Davies et al., *Ready for Change* (Resolution Foundation & Centre for Economic Performance, LSE, 2023), https://economy2030.resolutionfoundation.org/wp-content/uploads/2023/09/Ready-for-change-report.pdf.

10 'Total Early-Stage Entrepreneurial Activity (TEA)'; 'World Economic Outlook Database', IMF, April 2025, https://www.imf.org/en/publications/weo/weo-database/2025/april.

Conclusion

1   In November 2025, the OBR forecast that over the next few years, real annual GDP growth will be 1.5%. Using this as a baseline and then adding

half of the total of potential annual growth rate from the table (1.25%), you get a new hypothetical growth rate of 2.75%. If the tax-to-GDP ratio and government spending remain unchanged in real terms, by increasing growth from 1.5% to 2.75%, there would be more than £160 billion in additional tax revenue and net debt-to-GDP would fall to 78% by 2036. This is based on the assumption that additional tax revenue from higher growth would lead to the budget being in surplus by 2030, as well as assuming no new debt is taken on for public investment. The result of this would be the value of total debt decreasing progressively as a proportion of GDP.

2   'The Quest for Prosperity', *The Economist*, 17 March 2007, https://www. economist.com/special-report/2007/03/17/the-quest-for-prosperity.

3   See original article here: John Burn-Murdoch, 'Is Liberal Democracy in Terminal Decline?', *Financial Times*, 23 January 2026, https://www.ft.com/ content/b4d2c7a3-587d-440f-a7a9-7e5e85b93a88.

4   Jutta Bolt and Jan Luiten van Zanden, 'Maddison-style Estimates of the Evolution of the World Economy: A New 2023 Update', *Journal of Economic Surveys* 39, no. 2 (2025): 631–71, https://doi.org/10.1111/joes.12618.

5   V-Dem – processed by Our World in Data, 'Liberal Democracy Index – V-Dem', 2025.

INDEX

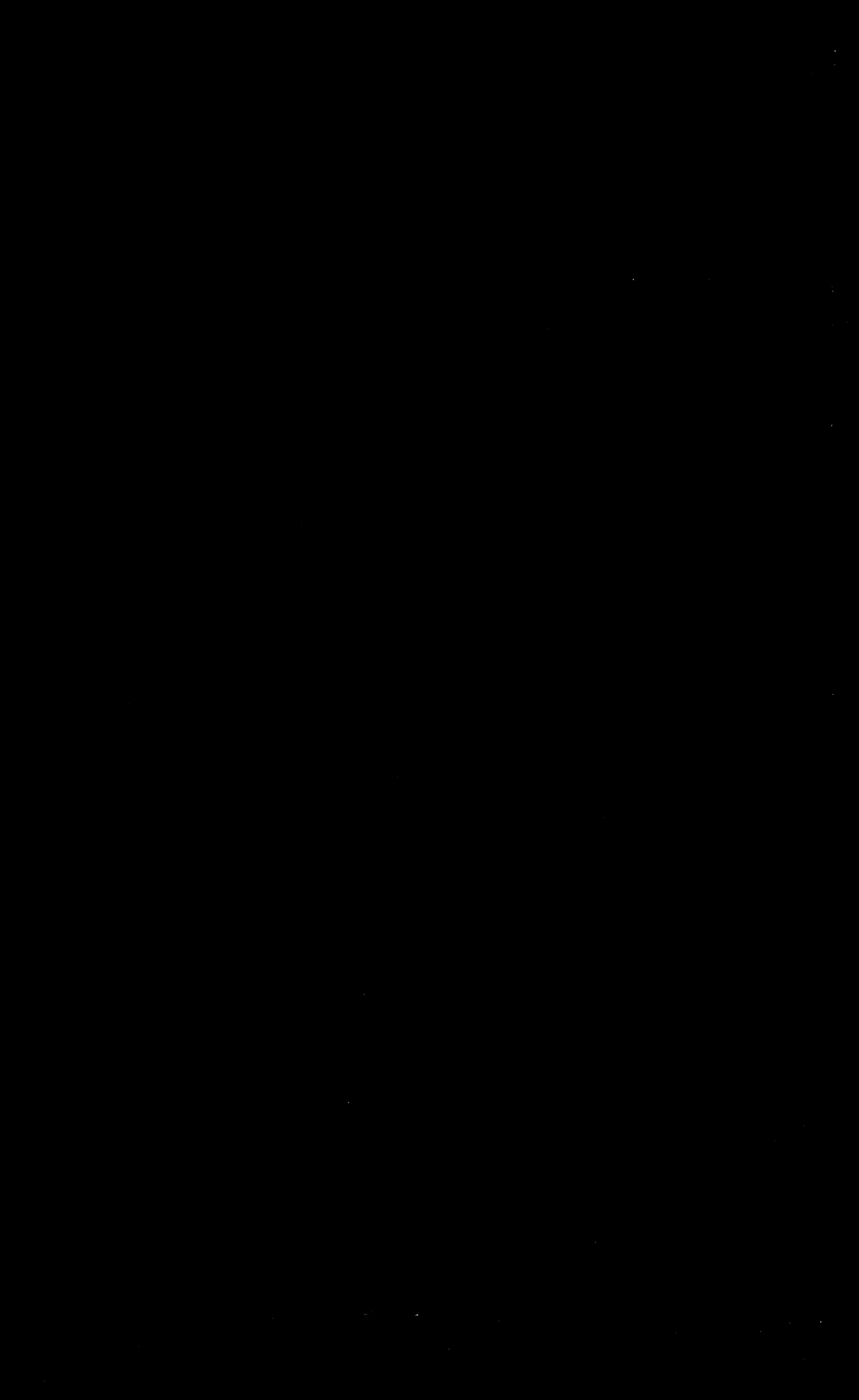